PAUPER LIMERICK

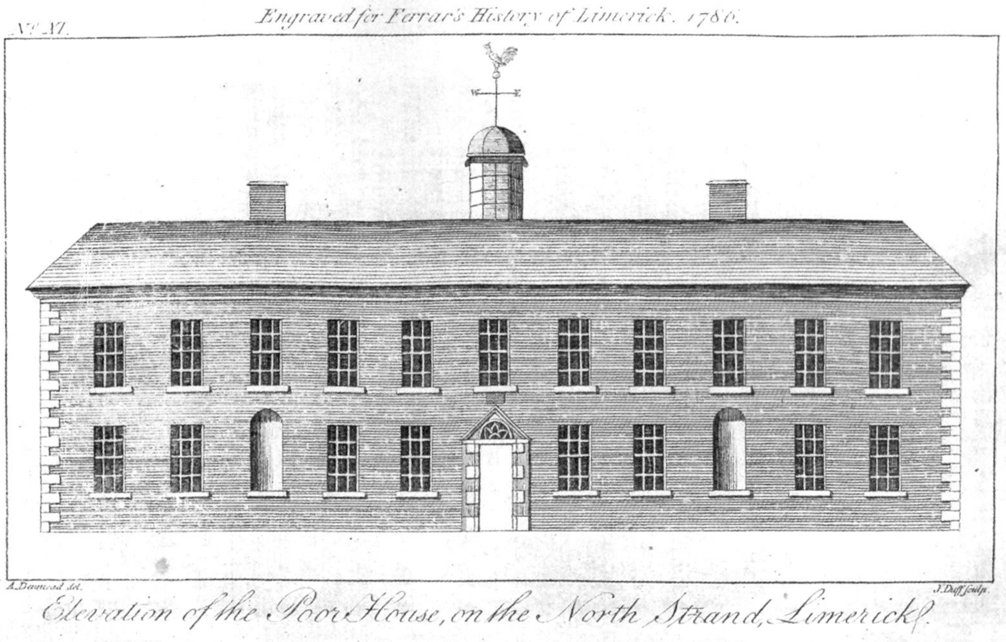

'Elevation of the Poor House, on the North Strand, Limerick' drawn by A. Drummond, engraved by J. Duff, in John Ferrar, *A history of Limerick, ecclesiastical, civil and military from the earliest records to the year 1787* (Limerick, 1787), plate 11.

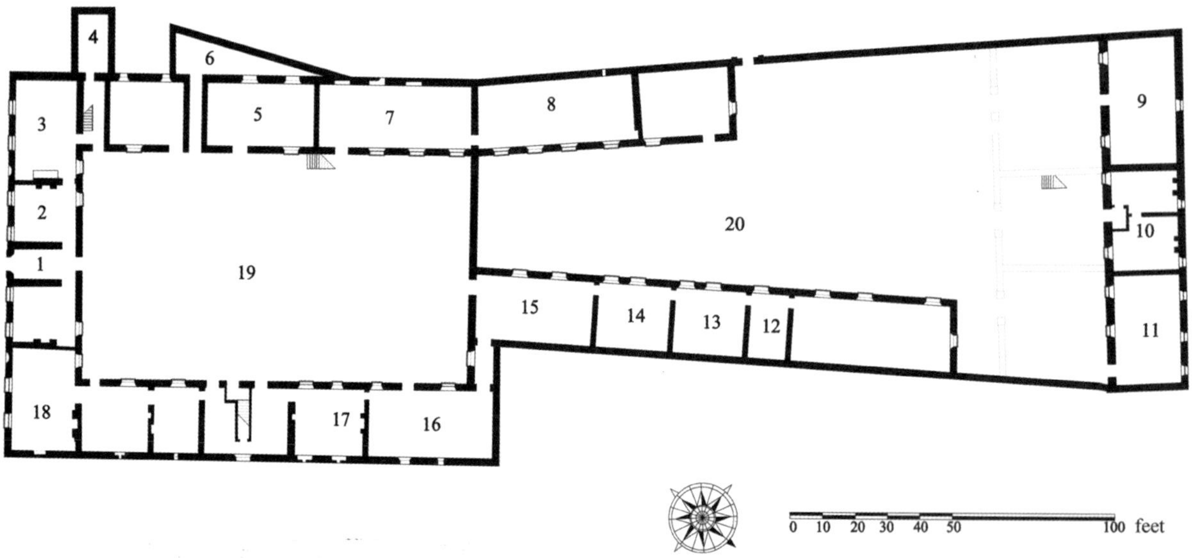

Plan of the House of Industry, *c.* 1837, by Shane Walsh (2010), based on a report by John Spence and James O'Dowd in *Royal commission for inquiring into the condition of the poorer classes in Ireland*, Appendix C, part 1, xxx, (1836), pp 6–7. The elevation above is of the front façade, which on this plan is to the left of the drawing.

Key: 1, Entrance; 2, Refectory; 3, Kitchen; 4, Pantry; 5, Nursery; 6, Necessary house; 7, Boys' schoolroom; 8, Boys' dormitory; 9, Men's cells;10, Superintendent's rooms; 11, Women's cells; 12, Mangling room; 13, Spinning room; 14, Weaving room; 15, Girls' schoolroom; 16, Girls' dormitory; 17, Schoolmistress' room; 18, Steward's rooms; 19, Yard; 20, Garden.

PAUPER LIMERICK

The Register of the Limerick House of Industry
1774–93

edited by

David Fleming and John Logan

Irish Manuscripts Commission
2011

Published by
Irish Manuscripts Commission
45 Merrion Square
Dublin 2
Ireland
www.irishmanuscripts.ie

ISBN 978-1-906865-10-8

Front jacket: Detail from 'View of Baal's Bridge, looking west' by James Henry Brocas, *c.* 1790–1846 (by permission of the National Gallery of Ireland).

Back jacket detail: 'View of Limerick & Newtown Pery from the Watch House on the N: Strand' by Henry Pelham, 1786 (by permission of Jim Kemmy Municipal Museum). The House of Industry is the building numbered '2' on the far left.

Typeset in Adobe Garamond and Times New Roman
Printed by Brunswick Press, Dublin
Index prepared by John Logan and David Fleming

CONTENTS

ACKNOWLEDGMENTS

THE MANUSCRIPT DEALT WITH HERE was presented to the City of Limerick in 1989 by the late Patrick Edmund Pery, 6th earl of Limerick. It is a pleasure to acknowledge his generosity and that of his family and to record their enduring interest in the history of the city that their forebears did much to shape. The historical significance of the manuscript was at once appreciated by the archivist of the then Mid-West Regional Development Organisation, the late Dr Chris O'Mahony, to whom it had been entrusted. He made it available to researchers and it was he who first suggested that it should be published in its entirety. The manuscript is now in the care of Limerick City Archives and we are grateful to the city archivist, Ms Jacqui Hayes, for her enthusiasm and support for this project and for making the manuscript available for study, transcription and publication. Thanks are also due to her former colleague Ms Ellen Murphy. The transcription was facilitated by the Jim Kemmy Municipal Museum and we thank Mr Larry Walsh, former curator, and Mr Brian Hodkinson for their gracious hospitality.

An initial coding and analysis of the manuscript was made possible by the support of the director of the Limerick Civic Trust, the late Dr Denis Leonard, and through the enthusiasm and commitment of two trainees at the Trust, Ms Michelle Kenny and Ms Nicola O'Dwyer. A full transcription was conducted by Mr Gary Gould of the Department of History, University of Limerick, and we would like to note the care that he committed to the task and his deep interest in its subject matter. The data were processed using the Statistical Package for the Social Sciences (SPSS) and for technical support we are indebted to Dr Helen Purtill of the Statistical Consulting Unit, to Mr Brendan Bolger of the Information Technology Division and to Mr Eoin Stephenson in the University of Limerick. Thanks are also due to Mr Ken Bergin and his colleagues Ms Jean Turner and Ms Siobhan Morrissey at Special Collections, Glucksman Library, University of Limerick. Ms Jennifer Moore and Mr George Quane provided additional information. Our thanks are due to Mr Shane Walsh, who drew the plan of the Limerick House of Industry. We are indebted to Professor Paul Finucane for his advice on disease classification and also to Professor Leslie Clarkson for guidance on occupational classification and to Professor Marco van Leeuwen. From start to finish the project received the generous support of the Department of History, University of Limerick and we are very grateful to our colleagues there, Dr Bernadette Whelan and Dr Ruán O'Donnell, for their interest and encouragement.

The transcribed manuscript and reproductions of selected pages are published by permission of Limerick City Archives. The cover illustration is reproduced by permission of the governors and director of the National Gallery of Ireland; that on the back cover is reproduced by permission of the Jim Kemmy Municipal Museum. The elevation of the House of Industry from John Ferrar, *A history of Limerick* (1787), is reproduced by courtesy of the Glucksman Library, University of Limerick.

We are grateful to the chairman and members of the Irish Manuscripts Commission for their interest and for their decision to publish the manuscript and for the encouragement given at key points by Professor David Dickson, Professor James Kelly and Professor Mary O'Dowd. The Commission's administrator, Dr Cathy Hayes, has been most generous with her time and advice, for which we are very grateful.

EDITORIAL NOTE

The register of the Limerick House of Industry for the period 1774 to 1793, formerly in the Limerick family papers at Chiddingly in Sussex, is now part of Limerick City Archives where is has been given the serial number P18/1. The register consists of 198 pages of which 191 contain text. The register is bound in reverse calf and is inscribed on the front 'Work House, Limerick; General Registry. 1774'. A title page carries the text 'General Registry of the Poor Received into the House of INDUSTRY from the Institution thereof 1774.' Each page is ruled vertically and horizontally, the details on each person admitted usually taking up a single line, initially divided into twenty columns, as follows: (1) 'current number'; (2) 'names'; (3) 'age'; (4) 'religion' — 'roman catholic'; (5) 'religion' — 'protestant'; (6) 'occupation'; (7) 'late residence'; (8) date of admission; (9) if 'voluntary' admission; (10) if 'compulsory' admission; (11) 'number of bed'; (12) if 'healthy' when received; (13) if 'sickly' when received; (14) 'disease when received'; (15) date on which 'discharged'; (16) date on which 'died'; (17) date on which 'eloped'; (18) if 'healthy' when discharged; (19) if 'sickly' when discharged; (20) 'observations'. Shortly after the commencement of the register the recording of information on 'number of bed' was discontinued. Occasionally the column headings for religion (4, 5) and medical condition on entry (12, 13) were reversed. The transcript standardises column headings throughout. The register finishes in 1793 when there is no further space for additional entries. The location of later registers, if they existed, is unknown.[1]

The aim here has been to provide a faithful transcription of the register. Consequently the temptation to expand a date from its simplest and most common form — the day in the month — to the full form of 'day, month, year' by reference to adjacent dates, has been resisted, except where the 'Admitted' column breaks onto a new page; here the date is repeated for ease of reference. Similarly the spelling of personal names, place names, occupations and ailments are given as in the register. No attempt was made to expand an abbreviated word or to replace the frequently used abbreviations 'd', 'do', or 'ditto' with the word to which they referred. The inconsistent and irregular use of colons, dashes and dots to indicate an abbreviation has been removed except where the meaning might be unclear. On rare occasions the clerk repeats a word or numeral unnecessarily; such instances are noted in the transcription by the use of *sic*. Finally, superscripted letters have not been reproduced here and are rendered as normal text.

1 The one-time existence of other books belonging to the House is highlighted in two observations (459 and 463) in the register where a 'Remark Book' is mentioned.

LIST OF ILLUSTRATIONS, FIGURES, AND TABLES

Illustrations

Figures

Tables

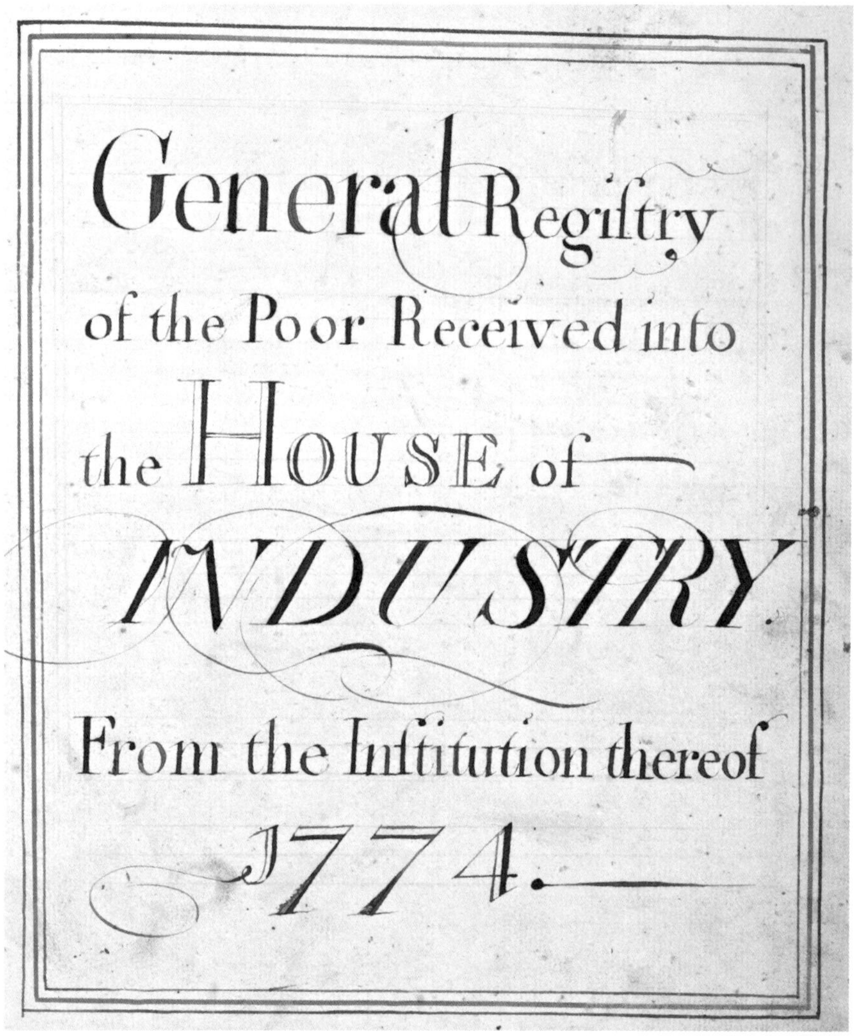
General Regiſtry
of the Poor Received into
the HOUSE of
INDUSTRY
From the Inſtitution thereof
1774.

Title page of the Register of the Limerick House of Industry
(by permission of Limerick City Archives).

INTRODUCTION

THE POOR LAW IN EARLY MODERN IRELAND

From the late medieval period European states increasingly grappled with perceived problems associated with poverty. Distinctions were made between the old and impotent poor who deserved relief and those who were able-bodied but unemployed and deserving of punishment rather than help, if found begging or troublesome. English initiatives provided an example from which the Irish drew. From 1542, Irish legislation copied from a 1532 English law, provided for the registration of the impotent poor and allowed them to beg within their parish and punished those who wandered from it. The able-bodied were to be confined to the stocks.[2] Yet the most significant English legislative measure, adopted in the sixteenth century and recast in 1598 and 1601, which provided for a national system of parochial relief, was never adopted in Ireland, partly because of fears that it would lead to increased taxation.[3] For the most part, relief for the poor in Ireland was *ad hoc* and left to private initiatives and to parishes.[4]

Vagrancy received far more attention. In 1576 and again in 1610 the English parliament agreed to establish 'houses of correction' for the able-bodied poor who refused to work and for other miscreants.[5] In 1635 the Irish parliament adopted a similar measure, stipulating that houses of correction should be built in every county.[6] Only a handful of places including Downpatrick, Kilkenny, Limerick and Mullingar, implemented the legislation.[7] In the eighteenth century there was renewed interest in poverty and its consequences, while a regular-sitting Irish parliament provided greater opportunities for tackling it.[8] In 1703 and 1735, parliament established workhouses in Dublin and Cork respectively in response to local initiatives.[9] Individuals planned and sometimes established institutions for poor relief. In 1749, Dean Charles Massy advocated the building of a Limerick workhouse, but nothing was done. Ten years later, the idea was adopted by the new bishop of the diocese, James Leslie, who subscribed fifty guineas to establish a workhouse, but his enthusiasm was not matched by others and the scheme failed.[10] A poorhouse operated by the Belfast Charitable Society was instituted in 1771.

2 33 Hen. VIII, c. 15: *Act directing how aged poor and impotent persons compelled to live by alms shall be ordered, and how vagabonds and beggars shall be punished* (1542).

3 P. Slack, *The English poor law, 1531–1782* (Cambridge, 1995), pp 3–26; D. Dickson, 'In search of the old Irish poor law' in R. Mitchinson and P. Roebuck (eds), *Economy and society in Scotland and Ireland* (Edinburgh, 1988), pp 149–70.

4 17 & 18 Chas. II, c. 7 (1665); R. Dudley, 'The Dublin parish, 1660–1730' in E. FitzPatrick and R. Gillespie (eds), *The parish in medieval and early modern Ireland* (Dublin, 2006), pp 289–94; T. Barnard, 'The eighteenth-century parish' in ibid., pp 314–17; R. Lavelle and P. Huggard, 'The parish poor of St. Mark's' in D. Dickson (ed.), *The gorgeous mask: Dublin, 1700–1850* (Dublin, 1987), pp 86–97.

5 Slack, *The English poor law*, pp 9–13.

6 10 & 11 Chas. I, c. 4 (1634–5).

7 R. H. Buchanan and A. Wilson, *Irish Historic Towns Atlas: Downpatrick* (Dublin, 1997), p. 10; J. H. Andrews and K. Davies, *Irish Historic Towns Atlas: Mullingar* (Dublin, 1992), p. 10; E. O'Flaherty, *Irish Historic Towns Atlas: Limerick* (Dublin, 2010), p. 28; 'Power O'Shee papers', *Analecta Hibernica*, No. 20 (1958), pp 256–7.

8 *Some few letters selected, from an account of work-houses and charity-schools for employment of the poor in England, with a preface to excite some such application of our charity in Ireland* (Dublin, 1728), p. ii.

9 2 Anne c. 19: *Act for erecting a workhouse in the city of Dublin for imploying and maintaining the poor thereof* (1703); 9 Geo. II, c. 25: *Act … for erecting a work-house in the city of Cork for employing and maintaining the poor, punishing of vagabonds and providing for and educating foundling children* (1735); 11 & 12 Geo. III, c. 11: *Act for better regulating the Foundling Hospital and Workhouse in the city of Dublin and increasing the fund for the support thereof* (1771–2).

10 *A collection of resolutions, queries, &c. wrote on occasion of the present dispute in the city of Limerick* (Limerick, 1749), p. 13; *Public Gazetteer*, 17 Apr. 1759.

A NEW POOR LAW, 1772

A proposal for a national system of county workhouses funded by subscription and local taxation was first proposed in 1729 by Arthur Dobbs.[11] In the decades that followed a number of similar schemes, based on the English and Dutch poor laws, were promoted, but with little affect.[12] It was not until 1766 that any serious attention was given to the subject again. In that year Richard Woodward, dean of Clogher, proposed a network of county poorhouses, supported through taxation and donations, to maintain the aged and infirm and ensure that vagrants were put to work.[13]

The 1771–2 parliamentary session initiated two uncoordinated measures to reform the existing arrangements of poor relief. The first regulated the Dublin workhouse and foundling hospital.[14] The second, more substantial measure repealed the earlier Tudor and Stuart laws, and permitted a system of licensed begging for the 'helpless poor' who had been resident within a specific city, town, barony or parish for at least one year. Those licensed were to display badges giving their name, place of birth, character, and cause of poverty. Licensed beggars were permitted to have one child with them; any other child would be sent to the nearest charity school or be apprenticed. Unlicensed beggars would be placed in the stocks for a specified number of hours. Significantly, the act provided for the establishment of houses of industry, divided into four departments to cater for poor helpless men, poor helpless women, 'vagabonds and sturdy beggars', and 'idle, strolling and disorderly women'. Where houses were established all unlicensed beggars should be admitted and set to work.[15]

Each county and the counties of cities and towns were to establish a poor-law corporation to grant licenses to beggars and build, maintain and regulate houses of industry. These corporations were to be presided over by the archbishop or bishop in whose diocese the corporation operated, and were to have the county's members of parliament, justices of the peace, mayor and sheriffs as *ex-officio* members, together with all those who subscribed a single payment of £20 or £3 annually for its support. Bishops were permitted to provide land from their sees for houses, while the grand juries were to raise not less than £100 and not more than £4,000 annually to support them. Moreover, the legislation provided for an annual church collection and charity sermons.[16] In the years that followed, further legislation refined the requirements, but the system broadly remained until reforms in the 1830s established a 'new' poor law.[17]

The 1772 legislation was largely unsuccessful. Besides the earlier foundations at Dublin,[18] Cork, Belfast, Lisburn and Coleraine, on which the system was largely based, only seven new houses were built: in Limerick (1774), Ennis (1775), Maryborough (1775), Waterford (1779), Clonmel (1811), Kilkenny (1814), and Wexford (1816). As there was no compulsion on grand juries to fund a house of industry and as the scheme would have increased local taxes, most opted not to establish one.

11 A. Dobbs, *An essay on the trade and improvement of Ireland* (Dublin, 1729), pp 49–54.

12 'Publicola', *A dissertation on the inlargement of tillage, the erecting of public granaries, and the regulating, employing, and supporting the poor* (Dublin, 1741), pp 54–67.

13 Richard Woodward, *A scheme for establishing county poor-houses in the kingdom of Ireland* (Dublin, 1766); Woodward, *An argument in support of the right of the poor in the Kingdom of Ireland* (Dublin, 1768, reprinted 1772, 1775).

14 11 & 12 Geo. III, c. 11: *Act for better regulating the Foundling hospital and work-house in the city of Dublin* (1771–2).

15 11 & 12 Geo. III, c. 30: *Act for badging such poor as shall be found unable to support themselves by labour and otherwise providing for them; and for restraining such as shall be found able to support themselves by labour or industry from begging* (1771–2).

16 Ibid.

17 21 & 22 Geo III, c. 45; 23 & 24 Geo III c. 58; 27 Geo. III, c. 44; 27 Geo. III, c. 52; 27 Geo. III, c. 57; 46 Geo. III., c. 95; 58 Geo. III., c. 47.

18 For the Dublin House of Industry see J. H. Widdess, 'The Dublin House of Industry' in W. Doolin and O. Fitzgerald (eds), *What's past is prologue* (Dublin, 1952); Eoin O'Broin *et al.*, *The house of industry hospitals, 1772–1987* (Dublin, 1988). The minutes of the Dublin House of Industry are deposited in the National Archives of Ireland.

The Limerick House of Industry, 1774–1841

Limerick city was the first to establish a poor-law corporation and build a house of industry. Bishop William Gore provided a site on the North Strand across the river Shannon from the city. In 1773 the county and city grand juries granted £500 towards the cost of building the House, the first stone of which was laid on 10 March 1774 and completed sometime in late 1774 or early 1775.[19] As stipulated by the act, it was managed by a corporation of *ex-officio* officers and magistrates, as well as perpetual and annual subscribers. By April 1774 there were twenty annual subscribers and four life governors, of whom Bishop Gore subscribed the largest amount of £500.[20] He along with the Rev. Deane Hoare and Captain Lancelot Hill were its main promoters. Designed by Hoare, it had sixteen rooms and a separate building (completed in 1777) at the foot of its garden with cells for lunatics and an infirmary.[21] The House joined the city's other institutions for the relief of the poor, namely Hall's almshouses, the corporation's almshouses, Craven's almshouses, the Blue School, and a county infirmary.[22]

Between April and September 1774, while the House was under construction, the governors began to implement the 1772 legislation by badging the poor, removing vagrants from the streets and by accommodating the helpless poor in a disused military infirmary in the city's Irishtown.[23] On 19 September the first eight paupers were admitted to the temporary House.[24] By October the newspapers reported that the city's streets were entirely cleared of beggars.[25] If such was the case, the numbers were small. The register records twenty admissions between 19 September and 27 October; all, except two, had been compelled. While the governors were eager to implement this aspect of the legislation, they chose to ignore other parts of it. For example, although the law stipulated that the able-bodied poor should be subject to a work regime within the house, there is little to indicate that one existed in the early years, though some inmates were occasionally assigned duties in kitchen and garden. It was only in 1799 that the governors sought to employ a person to oversee unspecified work then underway in the House.[26]

A corporation was also established for county Limerick, but the anticipated costs and the success of the city's venture prompted an amalgamation in 1775–6.[27] In neighbouring Clare, a corporation had been formed in September 1775, and had built its house in Ennis by 1779.[28] Nevertheless, between 1774 and 1793 the Limerick House admitted 258 individuals from Clare, amounting to 9.4 percent of all admissions.

While Church of Ireland clergymen were at the forefront in having the Limerick House established, Roman Catholic clergy were also consulted on how best to relieve the poor. In 1783, catholic priests met the governors on at least two occasions to arrange for distribution of food rations and, in what must have been an attempt to prevent the spread of disease, to discuss the best means of 'bathing' the poor of the city.[29] In 1792 the governors asked both the Church of Ireland and Roman Catholic bishops and their clergy to

19 *Limerick Chronicle*, hereafter *LC*, 10 Mar. 1774; J. Ferrar, *The history of Limerick* (Limerick, 1787), p. 223.

20 *LC*, 18 Apr. 1774.

21 Ferrar, *Limerick*, p. 223; *Report from the select committee on the lunatic poor in Ireland … 1817*, p. 14, H.C. 1817 (430), xviii, 46.

22 Ferrar, *Limerick*, pp 211–23.

23 *LC*, 18 Apr., 1, 12 Sept. 1774, *Freeman's Journal*, 17 Jun. 1773.

24 See register. *LC*, 19 Sept. 1774.

25 *LC*, 24 Oct. 1774.

26 Ibid., 22 May 1794.

27 15 & 16 Geo. III, c. 35 (1775–6).

28 Minutes of the first meeting of the corporation of Co. Clare, 15 September 1775 (Limerick City Museum, LM 0000.5117); *LC*, 1 Mar. 1779.

29 *LC*, 14 Apr., 21 July 1783.

seek contributions. Charity sermons for the benefit of the House were preached in both catholic and protestant churches into the nineteenth century.[30]

The most significant crisis that the House faced during the period covered by the register was the food shortages caused by poor weather and harvest failure in the mid 1780s.[31] As in other cities, Limerick experienced an influx of individuals seeking relief. The governors adopted two strategies, one of which was to feed the poor outside the House, the other to admit as many as the institution could reasonably take. Between November 1781 and December 1782, 74,219 meals were provided at a cost of £593 11*s.* 1¾*d.*[32] Again between March 1784 and February 1785, 25,189 were provided at a cost of £257 16*s.* 5*d.*[33] In 1781, 247 were admitted, the largest annual total since opening, while 258 entered the following year. By December 1782, the House was accommodating 190 people, the largest number it had ever held. Concerned at the growing number of foundlings being admitted, the governors met the city's parish officers to see if additional relief could be provided.[34] Although the dearth continued into 1783, the House had exhausted much of its limited funds in feeding the poor, and, as a result, the number admitted fell from 121 in 1783 to twenty-six in 1784.[35] In September 1783, despite their financial worries the governors gave instructions to clear the streets. Beggars who wished to be admitted to the House were to approach a bellman hired by the governors to walk through the city.[36] Yet, only fifteen individuals were admitted that September, nine in October, four in November and one in December, suggesting that few availed of the offer.

Street clearances of the miscreant continued.[37] In May 1805, several prostitutes had their heads forcibly shaved before being admitted into the House, together with a number of pick-pockets.[38] Four months later, the mayor intended to force vagrants either to leave the city or enter the House.[39] Again in 1809, prostitutes were targeted.[40] However, for the period covered by the register, nearly half (48.3 per cent) of the sixty women described variously as harlot, strumpet, whore or bad woman, entered the House voluntarily.

The failure of most counties to implement the 1772 legislation meant that poor relief was patchy across the country. Moreover, the original scheme which accommodated the aged, infirm, sick, lunatic and mendicant together in one establishment was increasingly viewed as unsatisfactory. By the 1820s district lunatic asylums had been built to accommodate the insane and remove the responsibility from the houses of industry, prisons and other institutions where they had been confined. Additionally, the expanding population and increasing poverty meant that by the beginning of the nineteenth century existing houses were incapable of catering for the vast numbers in need of relief. In 1820 tenders were sought for adding a wing to the Limerick House to accommodate a greater number of lunatics, which, when completed

30 *LC*, 28 Jan., 28 Mar. 1792, 28 Nov. 1804, 24, 28 June 1809, 8 Jan., 2 March, 25 June 1814.

31 J. Kelly, 'Scarcity and poor relief in eighteenth-century Ireland: the subsistence crisis of 1782–4', *IHS*, xxviii, 109 (1992), pp 38–62; D. Dickson, 'The gap in famines: a useful myth?' in E. M. Crawford (ed.), *Famine: the Irish experience, 900–1900* (Edinburgh, 1989), pp 96–111; L. Kennedy and P. M. Solar, *Irish agriculture: a price history from the nineteenth century to the eve of the First World War* (Dublin, 2007), pp 56–62.

32 *LC*, 16 Jan. 1783.

33 *LC*, 28 Feb. 1785.

34 *LC*, 19 May, 21 July 1783.

35 *LC*, 14 Apr. 1783. Compare the admissions to Dublin's House of Industry given in Kelly, 'The subsistence crisis of 1782–4', p. 42.

36 *LC*, *c*.Sept. 1783.

37 *LC*, 21 May, 27 Aug., 8 Oct. 1814, 25 Jan. 1817.

38 *LC*, 4 May 1805.

39 *LC*, 7 Sept. 1805.

40 *LC*, 13 Sept. 1809.

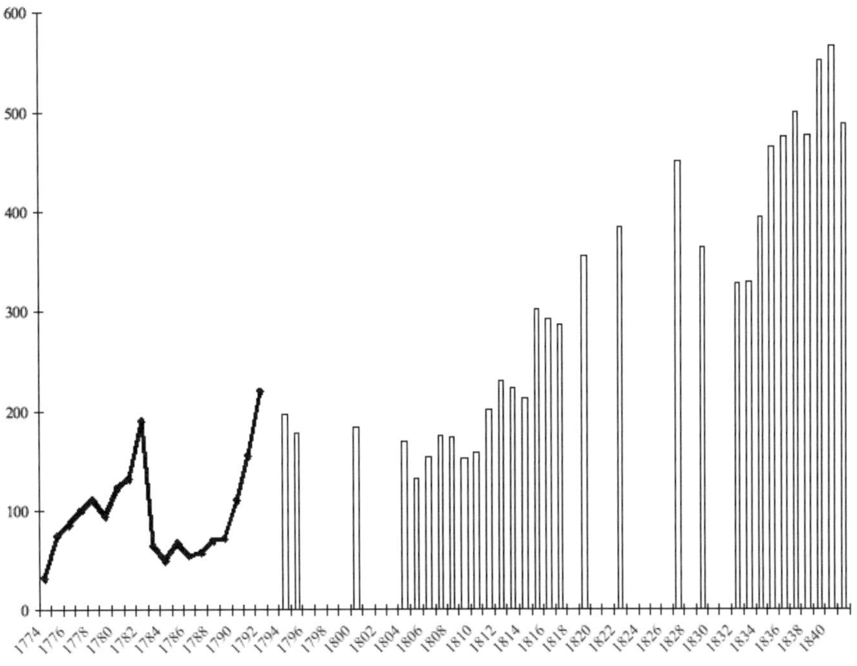

Fig. 1. Number of inmates in the House of Industry, 1774–1841

Sources: 1774–92: the register; 1794–5, 1800, 1832–40: *Limerick Chronicle*; 1819: *Limerick Evening Post*; 1822: *Limerick News*; 1804–17: British parliamentary papers; 1827: P. Fitzgerald and J. J. McGregor, *The history, topography and antiquities of the county and city of Limerick* (2 vols, Dublin, 1827), ii, 596; 1829: J. E. Bicheno, *Ireland and its economy* (London, 1830); 1841: W. P. Mulligan, 'The closure of the Limerick House of Industry', *North Munster Antiquarian Journal*, (2006), pp 51–82.

Note: The number in the House for the period 1774–92, indicated by the continuous line, has been calculated for 31 December each year from the Register. The enumeration point for the following years varies with the source.

later that decade, increased its accommodation two-fold.[41] The opening of a district lunatic asylum in Limerick in January 1827 reduced the number of inmates so categorised, though the House continued to admit lunatics thought to be 'incurable'.[42] Despite the provision of additional space, the House was often crowded. In January 1840 it contained 567 inmates, nearly twice the number it could ordinarily cater for, which may have been the highest number it had accommodated since it opened (see fig. 1).[43]

A new poor law, enacted in 1838, modelled on that of 1834 for England, provided for the creation of 130 unions of parishes, each with its own workhouse. The Limerick Poor Law Union was formed on 20 December 1838, the first in Ireland. Forty guardians were elected and thirteen appointed *ex-officio*. When the new poor law commissioners carried out an audit of existing facilities in Limerick, they reported that to accommodate the 1,600 estimated as needing relief the building would require extensive refurbishment and the erection of additional accommodation on adjacent land. Their architect found that the costs would be prohibitive: '… the advantages being considered on the whole much in favour of a new house'.[44] As a result a new building was erected about a half mile west of the House of Industry and it was to there, in 1841, that its last 489 inmates were transferred.[45]

41 *Limerick Advertiser*, 24 Oct. 1820.

42 *Correspondence and communications … 1827 … on public lunatic asylums in Ireland*, p. 16, H.C. 1828 (234) xxii, 238; *LC*, 13 Apr. 1833.

43 *LC*, 18 Jan. 1840.

44 Ibid.

45 The list of those transferred can be found in W. P. Mulligan, 'The closure of the Limerick House of Industry', *North Munster Antiquarian Journal*, (2006), pp 51–82.

The Inmates, 1774–93

The register records 2,747 admissions between 9 September 1774 and 9 May 1793. Fifty-one per cent of admissions were male, forty-nine per cent female. Though it did not assign each inmate a unique number or note any previous admission, a comparison and linking of entries facilitates the identification of at least 1,838 individuals who were admitted just once and 373 admitted on at least one other occasion, in all a total of 2,257 different individuals. Of the recidivist inmates a total of 278 were admitted twice, sixty-five were admitted three times, fifteen were admitted four times, eight were admitted five times, five were admitted six times, one was admitted eight times, and two were admitted ten times.

Each admission was numbered consecutively. Occasionally, having made a mistake, the clerk corrected it to maintain the sequence. However, overlooked mistakes remain and upset the sequence: at 634 (number repeated), at 720 (skips to 729), at 747 (missing), at 748 (number repeated), at 856 (number repeated), at 1,226 (number repeated), at 1,236 (number repeated), at 1,282 (an inmate not assigned a number), after 1,300 (skips to 1,302), at 1,362 (number repeated), after 1,441 (skips to 1,452, and then to 1,453, and sequence resumed at 1,444), at 1,444 (number repeated), at 1,466 (number repeated), at 1,769 (skips to 1,833), at 2,058 (skips to 2,060), at 2,059 (skips to 2,600), at 2,610 (skips to 2,612), at 2,619 (skips to 2,629), at 2,670 (additional digit added to make 20,671, continuing to 20,705 after which the mistake was corrected), at 2,760 (number repeated), at 2,796 (number repeated), and at 2,808 (skips to 2,899 and then to 2,890 from where the sequence resumed).

The registration process served mainly to emphasise an individual's personal characteristics but occasionally it noted family ties or a relationship ruptured by admission to the House. For example the register records the admission of seventeen women, each described as a soldier's wife though in no case is the soldier's identity noted. When Jane Loughlin (1528) was admitted she was stated to be the wife of a Mr Bouchier, while Mary Dea (1466) was noted to be the wife of a Joe Phair, though neither man was then an inmate. When John Sullivan (1917) died in November 1787 the register recorded that his coffin was paid for by his wife, and when Honor Brian (679) was discharged in March 1779 it was on condition that she would go back to her husband. But there were eleven occasions, all between November 1780 and May 1782, when the clerk explicitly recorded a family relationship between inmates, specifically nine instances of a mother and her children, one instance of a man and his grandson, and one married couple.

These cases prompt the question of the extent to which other family or kin groups were present in the House. Without a formal recording of family status, such information appears elusive, though it is tempting to assume that there were many related individuals among those of the same surname, admitted consecutively on the same day. There are a total of 211 such 'surname groups' in the register. Having the same surname – whether patronymic or matronymic – will not establish a relationship, however. Of the eleven cases of co-resident kin that were explicitly noted, only eight shared the same surname. Neither can admission alongside someone of the same surname be the basis of determining a relationship: when Judy Hennessy (1204) was admitted on 21 January 1782 the clerk noted that she was the daughter of a Nell Hennessy (1200) who had been admitted eleven days before. A comparison and matching amongst the 211 surname groups reveals a total of twenty-two groups admitted more than once, consisting in whole or in part of individuals whose details match and it is among these groups, perhaps, that ties of family or kin might be posited. An example is that of the six Devitt groups admitted between February 1783 and June 1792. While only two of the six groups consisted exclusively of the same four matching individuals, all six groups are connected by the presence therein of Mary Devitt (1485, 1972, 1993, 2005, 2606, 2668), while Margaret or Peg (1487, 1994, 2006), Eleanor (1973, 1995, 2007), and James (1974, 1996, 2008) are present in four intersecting groups, Mary (2607, 2669) in two and Henry (1486) in one. Less

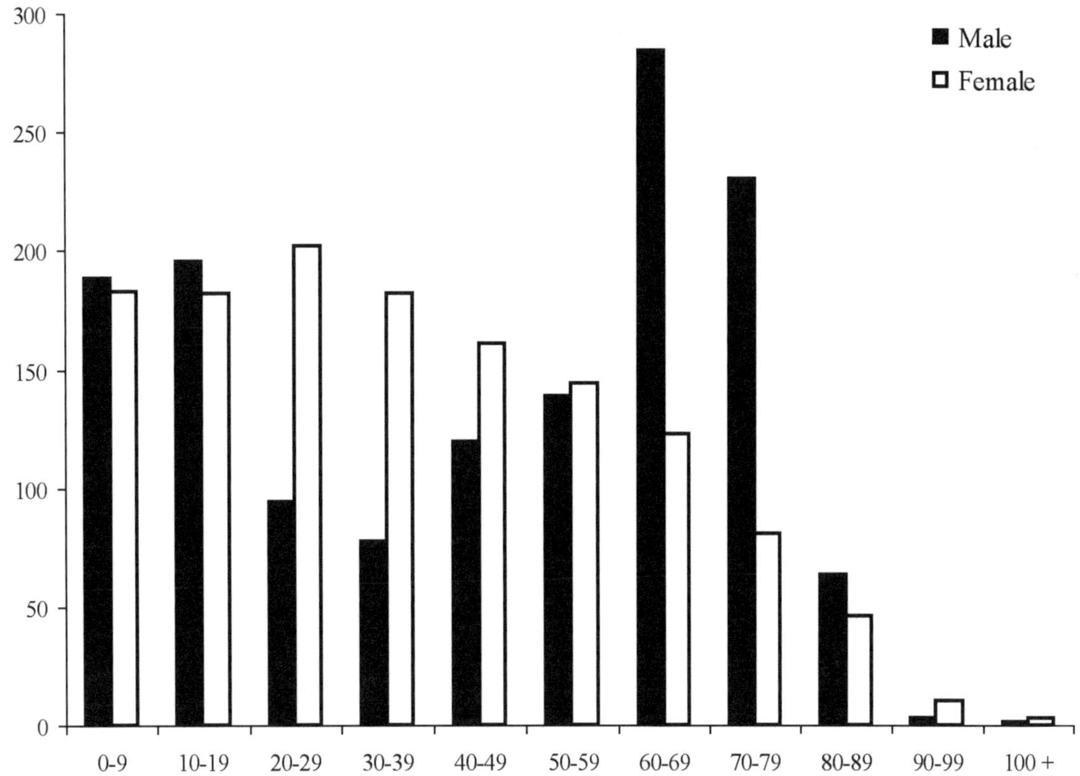

Fig. 2. Number of male and female inmates by age cohort, 1774–93
Source: The register

complex is the case of thirty-year-old servant Catherine Cloghesy (321) and two-year-old John Cloghesy (322), both of county Clare, admitted on 4 February 1777 and discharged on 29 June 1777, and the two people (415 and 416) of the same name, age, religion and county admitted on 22 September and discharged on 9 October 1777. As was the case with the Devitts, there is no record of a family tie between the Cloghesys, but if the register does not note a web of blood or kin relationships it hints at a set of interdependencies that could be just as durable.

Age

The information in the 'age' column reveals a range from an infant born in the House to some aged over 100 years. If inmates are classified by decennial cohort, those aged from infancy to nine years (13 per cent), ten to nineteen years (13 per cent) and from sixty to sixty-nine (14 per cent) were more likely to be admitted than any other. The smallest cohort was aged between thirty and thirty-nine (9.5 per cent). Taken together, those up to the age of nineteen and those aged above sixty accounted for 58.2 per cent of all admitted. This suggests that the House consistently admitted those who through physical immaturity or decline were perhaps least capable of fending for themselves.

Although almost as many women as men were admitted, there was significant gender variation between age cohorts (fig. 2). Women outnumbered men in the twenty to twenty-nine, thirty to thirty-nine, forty to forty-nine and fifty to fifty-nine age cohorts. The largest differences appear for those aged between twenty and twenty-nine and between thirty and thirty-nine, when more than double the number of women than men were admitted. This was reversed for those aged between sixty and sixty-nine and seventy and seventy-nine, when men outnumbered women by two to one and three to one respectively. What is striking is not the number of women inmates aged between twenty and fifty-nine, but the smaller proportion of men of the same age. The under-representation of men in these cohorts may suggest that they were more likely to find employment than women of similar age. This is partly confirmed by the over-representation

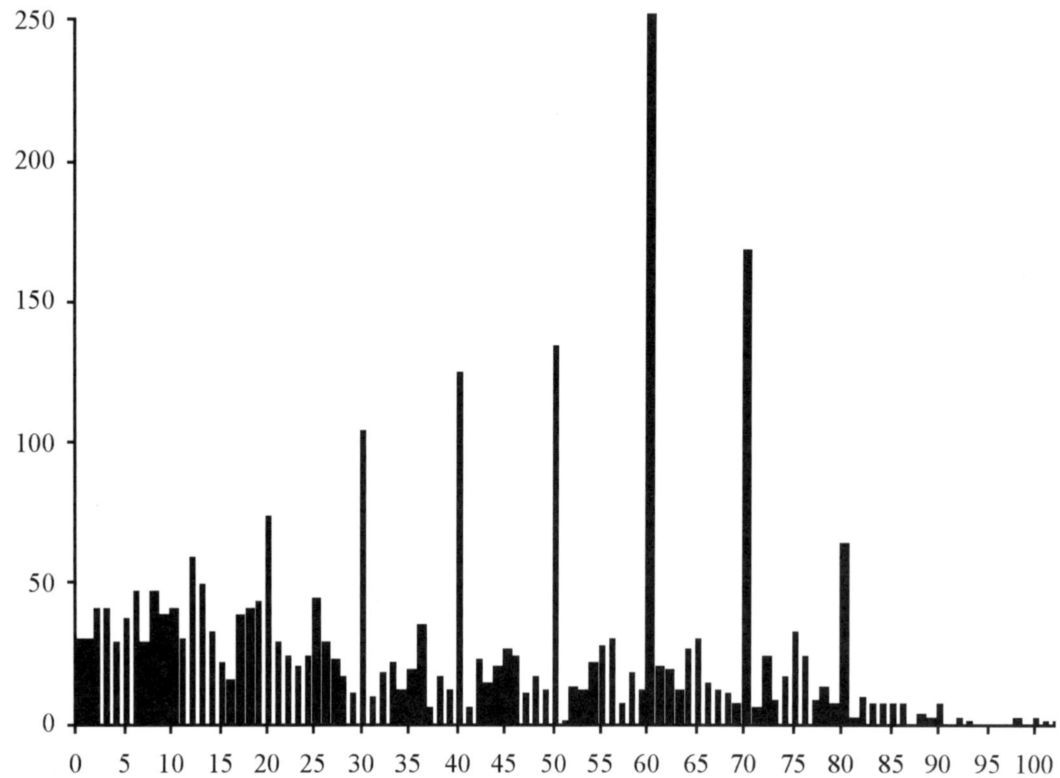

Fig. 3. Number of inmates by year of age, 1774–93
Source: The register

of men in the sixty to seventy-nine age cohort, who may have been no longer capable of manual work or unable to obtain any. For example, 109 of the 149 labourers admitted, seventy-one of the 108 weavers, ten of the eleven gardeners, and seven of the nine smiths were all aged sixty or above, while all three stay-makers were aged between seventy and seventy-nine.

The recording of ages was uneven. Heaping is evident from the over-recording of ages ending in zero or five and a consequent under-recording of adjacent ages (see fig. 3). The old were more likely to have their ages heaped in this way. The largest single year of age recorded is that of sixty-year-olds (9.2 per cent), followed by seventy-year-olds (6.1 per cent). The ages of the young were more evenly distributed.

Religion

The religious affiliation of inmates was recorded or can be ascertained for 2,551 (93 per cent) cases. No distinction was made between adherents of the various protestant denominations, except when James Nicholson (1758), a Quaker, was admitted on 28 August 1786. Somewhat fewer protestant women were admitted (43.2 per cent) than protestant men (56.8 per cent). In contrast, the balance of catholic men (50.1 per cent) and women (49.9 per cent) was more even. Why religious affiliation had to be recorded is not easily explained. The House did not subscribe to any particular official religious ethos, which in itself might reveal the wish to avoid the controversies associated with other institutions, such as the charter schools. While there is no evidence of chaplains being formally appointed, clergymen did attend the House.[46] Inmates were permitted temporary leave to attend religious services, notwithstanding the fact that sixteen used the occasion to escape.[47]

Catholics formed the largest religious group (2,080 or 81.3 per cent), followed by protestants (476 or

46 *LC*, 21 Feb. 1791.

47 See inmates 1649, 1690, 1853, 1947, 2168, 2177, 2388, 2464, 2476, 2479, 2772, 2514, 2550, 2554, 2569, 2720.

18.7 per cent). While there are no sources for determining the proportions of catholics to protestants in the late eighteenth century, an 1834 national survey of religious adherents provides a general, if somewhat unsatisfactory, measure. In that year, the percentage of catholics to protestants in the diocese of Limerick (for the most part coterminous with county Limerick) was 95.6 to 4.4. It is unclear to what extent this proportion might have changed since the late eighteenth century.[48] Excluding Limerick city's parishes, the percentage of catholics to protestants in the diocese in 1834 was 96.6 to 3.4. The percentage of catholic to protestant inmates giving their address as county Limerick was 90.9 to 9.1, which suggests that protestants may have been slightly over represented within the House. The difference was somewhat greater for those from Limerick city. The city's percentage of catholics to protestants in 1834 was 88.7 to 11.2, while the percentage of those admitted giving that place[49] as their residence was 81.7 to 18.3. There was also a difference in denominational breakdown between those who might be described as immigrants to Limerick and those ordinarily resident there. Of all protestants admitted to the House, 41.4 per cent had come from beyond the city or county. In contrast, just 28 per cent of all catholic inmates were immigrants. The networks that brought protestants together in late eighteenth-century Limerick, not least being members of the corporation or governors of the House may explain why the poor of that denomination appeared to be over represented there. Proportionately, protestants aged between ten and nineteen and catholics aged eighty and above were more likely to be admitted than their co-religionists, though the difference between the respective cohorts was not great (see Table 1).

Table 1. Religious affiliation of inmates by age cohort, 1774–93

	Catholic		Protestant			
Age at entry (years)	Number	Percentage	Number	Percentage	All denominations	Total inmates
0–9	237	78.0	67	22.0	304	373
10–19	264	77.0	79	23.0	343	378
20–29	233	83.5	46	16.5	279	298
30–39	201	80.1	50	19.9	251	260
40–49	215	79.9	54	20.1	269	281
50–59	220	80.3	54	19.7	274	284
60–69	327	83.4	65	16.6	392	410
70–79	259	84.4	48	15.6	307	313
80–89	101	89.4	12	10.6	113	113
90–99	14	100	0	0	14	14
100 +	5	100	0	0	5	5
Total	**2,076**	**81.4**	**475**	**18.6**	**2,551**	**2,729†**

Note:† Age was not recorded for an additional eighteen inmates.

Occupation

Entries were made in the 'occupation' column for a total of 2,361 cases (85.9 per cent), though a significant number of these cannot be readily identified with a specific economic activity. For example, the phrase 'bad woman' used in eight cases might well be a euphemism for prostitute, though it has to be considered alongside fourteen occurrences of 'bad girl' and two of 'bad boy'. If these too are imprecise, not revealing any obvious occupation, they hint at a deviant way of life that served to categorise them alongside other

48 S. J. Connolly, *Priests and people in pre-famine Ireland, 1780–1845* (Dublin, 1982), pp 24–5.

49 Includes those recorded as resident in 'Limerick'.

miscreants such as those who occupied themselves by begging or thieving. Some entries such as the five instances where an inmate's residence was recorded were probably a mistaken use of the occupation column, as was the entry giving details of an inmate's elopement, information usually recorded in the 'observations' column. Thirty-six entries described a disease or condition, and while thirty-two of these duplicate an entry in another column, their presence in the occupation column might be the result of a need to explain a person's inability to work. That too probably explains the adjective 'poor' in the case of 217 entries. While ninety-five of these were used with reference to a specific occupation, such as 'poor housekeeper', a total of 122 entries were used to qualify non-occupation descriptions such as 'woman' or 'child', perhaps to indicate a condition that identified them as helpless and deserving of whatever support the House could offer. Similarly, the use of terms that describe gender (boy, girl) and family or household status (orphan, widow, spinster) might also have been an attempt to record an inmate's circumstances, particularly if it explained their destitute state. When all such non-occupational terms are excluded, a total of 182 specific occupations may be identified. These, with the numbers engaged in them and the non-occupational descriptions are listed in Appendix 1.

For the purpose of description and analysis each specific occupation is allocated here to one of twelve general categories. Eight of these — agriculture, building, manufacturing, transport, distributive, labouring, personal services, and professional — following appropriate modification, are the categories of economic activity utilised by Professor Clarkson for his study of Carrick-on-Suir based on a census of 1799.[50] Some occupational categories not deployed by Clarkson, specifically those of housekeeper, entertainer and pupil, and those miscreants whose lives bordered on the delinquent and criminal, were well represented in the House. Rather than have them vanish under the heading of 'other', these four additional categories are utilised here of which 'miscreant' is sub-categorised into 'prostitute, 'vagabond and beggar' and 'delinquent' (see Table 2).

Table 2. Number of inmates in each occupational category, 1774–93

	Number	Percentage of all occupations	Percentage of all inmates
agriculture, horticulture, fishing and mining	48	2.5	1.8
building and allied trades	56	2.8	2
manufacturing: textiles and ropes	327	16.4	11.9
manufacturing: leather, bone and footwear trades	68	3.4	2.5
manufacturing: metalworking and clayworking	17	0.9	0.6
manufacturing: food, drink and tobacco processing	65	3.3	2.4
manufacturing: woodworking	14	0.7	0.5
transport	70	3.5	2.5
distributive	42	2.1	1.5
labouring	150	7.5	5.5
personal services	338	17	12.3
professional and administrative services	32	1.7	1.2
housekeeper	217	10.9	7.9
entertainer	17	0.9	0.6
pupil	11	0.6	0.4
miscreant: prostitute	68	3.4	2.5
miscreant: beggar and vagabond	388	19.5	14.1
miscreant: delinquent	65	3.3	2.4

50 L. A. Clarkson, 'The demography of Carrick-on-Suir, 1799', *Proceedings of the Royal Irish Academy*, C, 87 (1987), 2–36. Clarkson's general category of 'manufacturing' has been here subdivided into 'textiles and ropes', 'leather, bone and footwear trades', 'metalworking and clayworking', 'food, drink and tobacco processing' and 'woodworking'.

Despite the large number of specific occupations recorded, just five — servant, beggar, housekeeper, labourer and weaver — accounted for the majority of those recorded. The 338 inmates previously engaged in personal services — 331 described simply as 'servant' — constitute the largest single occupational category. Following closely were the 326 from the textile trades of whom weavers, at 110, were the largest specific occupation. Most of the other occupations listed — among them a priest, a potter, a fencing master, a lawyer and an embroiderer — were represented by just one or two cases. In 386 cases no entry was made in the occupation column and of those 82.4 per cent is accounted for by children aged thirteen or under. The earliest use of an occupational term is when two three-year-olds are described as 'beggar' and another as 'stroler'. Such occupational terms are rare amongst the very young, and of the 114 entries for those aged eight or under there are just seven beggars, two strollers and one lace maker. The earliest age at which 'idler' is used is in the case of nine-year-old William O'Nail (133) compelled to enter the House on 25 August 1775. From ten onwards the occurrence of a specifically occupational term becomes more frequent and by age thirteen is being used for the majority of entries.

Residence

As constituted, the House was intended for paupers residing in Limerick city and county. It is not surprising then that these two places together accounted for 1,916 (69.7 per cent) of all admitted. Limerick's economic hinterland which encompassed much of county Clare, parts of Tipperary and north Kerry meant that individuals were attracted to the city for its employment opportunities and for relief at times of dearth. Residents from these three counties accounted for a further 13.2 per cent of those admitted. Cork city and county made up 3 per cent, while those from Dublin followed with 2.9 per cent. Residents from twenty-six of Ireland's thirty-two counties were recorded (see Appendix 2).

Besides Irish residents, a small number came from England (26), Scotland (6), Jersey (3), France (4), Italy (1), Sweden (1), America (6) and the West Indies (1). The occupations of the twenty-six individuals from England varied from a mason (76) to a seventy-year-old fiddler (2341), as well as seven sailors, three servants, one cabinet-maker and one beggar. All six from Scotland (735, 736, 2258, 2292, 2710) were beggars. Those from Jersey were described respectively as beggar (2031 and 2136) and as a 'soldier's wife' (2905). The thirty-four-year-old Swedish sailor, Sevel Parson (492), was compelled to enter the House on 2 April 1778 but was discharged a day later. John Mathous (2187) a servant, from the West Indies, was admitted on 17 December 1789 and appears to have remained in the House until at least 1793. Four (180, 549, 836, 837) of the five Frenchmen were sailors. The six Americans included a soldier's wife (895) and two beggars (1581 and 1763). These examples suggest that those admitted from outside Ireland fit into one of three categories. Sailors who failed to leave with their ships, mostly due to some infirmity or illness, formed the largest number. Beggars formed the next largest group, and their number suggests that Limerick was part of a larger terrain travelled by the tramping poor. The third were women who were married to soldiers, deserted, perhaps, by them, or who could not find space in the barracks.

No residence was recorded or can be deduced for 109 inmates (4 per cent).

Terms of admission

Inmates either sought admission voluntarily or where compelled to enter the House. Terms of admission are known for 68.7 per cent of inmates. The completion rate of the two columns for recording this information reached or came close to 100 per cent in the first seven years. In 1781 the completion rate fell to 85.8 per cent, due perhaps to the unexpected influx in that year. By 1785, it had fallen to 55.8 per cent. Little or no attempt was made to enter information for the period between 1786 and 1790. By 1791 the completion rate had significantly increased to 86.7 per cent, though this spurt of clerical efficiency was brief. Thereafter the completion rate dropped to 54.5 per cent when the information appears to have been recorded only in the case of those compelled to enter.

Of 1,888 inmates whose term of admission was recorded, 1,207 (64 per cent) were voluntarily admitted, while 677 (36 per cent) were compelled. Almost equal proportions of males (50.6 per cent) and females (49.4 per cent) were compelled to enter the House. The old, aged eighty and above, were more likely to be compelled than any other age cohort. For example, 80 per cent of those aged between ninety and ninety-nine and 100 per cent of those aged over one-hundred had been compelled. Those least likely to be compelled were children aged up to nine (11.9 per cent). The percentages for those compelled from all other age cohorts ranged between 32 and 44 per cent. In the case of those compelled, a religious denomination is known for 652 cases. Of these, 581 (89.1 per cent) were catholic and 71 (10.9 per cent) protestant. Although the poor law specifically attempted to punish the migrant poor, the evidence from the register suggests a more complex approach as to how they were dealt with. For the most part, strangers or migrants to Limerick who entered the House did so voluntarily (see Appendix 2). Nonetheless, certain migrants, especially those from Connaught and outside Ireland, were as likely to be compelled as to be voluntarily admitted.

An occupation as well as the term of admission was recorded in 88.6 per cent of cases, which information can provide clues as to who the authorities wished to confine. Of those compelled, the majority had conventional economic occupations, ranging from schoolmasters (0.4 per cent), butchers (0.6 per cent), bakers (0.7 per cent), and farmers (0.9 per cent). Those further down the social scale included servants (11.9 per cent), labourers (4.6 per cent), housekeepers (2.5 per cent), weavers (1.8 per cent), spinners (1.9 per cent), and sailors (1.5 per cent). Those who can be identified as miscreants accounted for the rest (44 per cent). The largest single category of all those compelled was beggars and idlers, including 'shulers', 'strollers' and 'vagabonds' (35.3 per cent). Other miscreants included prostitutes – variously described as 'whore', 'strumpet' or 'harlot' (4.1 per cent), peddlers (1.5 per cent), ballad singers (1.2 per cent), thieves (0.8 per cent), rogues (0.7 per cent) and drunkards (0.4 per cent).

Those with perceived mental difficulties were more likely to be compelled than those with any other particular behavioural or medical condition. For example, out of a total of 181 cited as 'insane', information on terms of admission is given in seventy (38.7 per cent) cases. Of these, 65.7 per cent were compelled. Similarly 56.7 per cent of all thirty 'lunatics' admitted and 60 per cent of all ten described as 'mad' had been compelled to enter the House.

Health

Initially, the two columns that recorded whether those being admitted were healthy or sickly were filled in diligently, but clerical slackness in the summer months of 1777 and again in 1778 resulted in a completion rate for the first five years of 67.8 per cent. Thereafter entries were made less frequently and between 1 January 1783 and 1 September 1789, when this information was last recorded, entries were made for only 10 per cent of admissions. In all, 825 entries were made, equivalent to 46.6 per cent of those admitted during that period, of which 566 were returned as healthy and 259 as sickly. Even less attention was given to recording the health of a departing inmate. From the start entries under this heading were unusual and by 19 May 1781, when the last entry was made, had been completed for just 194 (22.2 per cent) of all those who by that date had departed the House. Of these 155 were classified as healthy and forty as sickly.

Information on specific conditions was recorded in a column headed 'disease'. This was completed correctly in the case of 969 (64.7 per cent) admissions, to which may be added the four diseased inmates whose condition was recorded in the occupation column but not repeated in the disease column. The terms deployed to describe a disease or illness may have reflected an inmate's own knowledge or that of the clerk or other official of the House. Not surprisingly, colloquial terms abound and descriptions of symptoms rather than underlying causes were common. Thus cases of 'yellow jaundice' and 'sore chest' were noted as were those who were 'insane', 'sick' or 'infirm', though, in an age before significant advances in identifying the nature and transmission of disease, a medical practitioner might have been no more informative. Nonetheless many of the entries reveal a determination to identify and classify: parts of body and limb are named, degrees of blindness specified, the extent of pain or discomfort noted, and had the authorities been asked to note each disease according to a contemporary nosology, or disease classification, they could probably have done so. Of the available systems, that developed by the Edinburgh physician William Cullen (1710–90) was then the most widely used. The subsequent growth in medical knowledge resulted in frequent revisions and elaboration. That adopted by the International Statistical Institute in 1893 as a universal standard was taken over by the World Health Organisation (WHO) at its foundation in 1948. Its tenth revision, in 1994, known as ICD-10, remains the most widely used.[51] For the purpose of description and analysis, each condition recorded in the register has been allocated to its WHO class and summarised in Table 3. A full list of all diseases and related health issues recorded in the register is provided in Appendix 3.

Table 3. Number of inmates in each disease class, 1774–93

		Number	Percentage of all conditions	Percentage of all inmates
1	Certain infectious and parasitic diseases	54	5.5	1.9
2	Neoplasms	1	0.1	0
3	Diseases of the blood and blood forming organs and certain disorders involving the immune mechanisms	3	0.3	0.1
4	Endocrine, nutritional and metabolic diseases	22	2.3	0.8
5	Mental and behavioural disorders	274	28.2	10.0
6	Diseases of the nervous system	29	2.9	1.0
7	Diseases of the eye and adnexa	85	8.7	3.1
8	Diseases of the ear and mastoid process	9	0.9	0.3
9	Diseases of the circulatory system	17	1.7	0.6
10	Diseases of the respiratory system	21	2.2	0.8
11	Diseases of the digestive system	23	2.0	0.7
12	Diseases of the skin and subcutaneous tissue	3	0.3	0.1
13	Diseases of the musculoskeletal system and connective tissue	157	16.1	5.7
14	Diseases of the genitourinary system	0	0	0
15	Pregnancy, childbirth and the puerperium	9	0.9	0.3
16	Certain conditions originating in the perinatal period	0	0	0
17	Congenital malformations, deformations and chromosomal abnormalities	2	0.2	0.1
18	Symptoms, signs and abnormal clinical and laboratory findings, not elsewhere classified	153	15.7	5.5
18	Injury, poisoning and certain other consequences of external causes	16	1.6	0.6
20	External causes of morbidity and mortality	0	0	0
21	Factors influencing health status and contact with health services	40	4.1	1.4
[–]	Inmates suffering more than one condition	55	5.7	2.0
	Total	**973**		**35.4**

51 World Health Organisation, *International statistical classification of diseases and related health problems* 10th revision (Geneva, 1994).

This classification suggests that of inmates whose condition was recorded, those afflicted by mental or behavioural disorders constituted the largest single category. They were followed by those whose degenerated muscles and limbs rendered them disabled and by an equal number of mostly aged inmates showing various symptoms of decline and infirmity. Together these three groups made up 61 per cent of diseased inmates.

Length of stay

Three columns recorded whether inmates were discharged, died, or escaped. Information of this type is available for 87.3 per cent of cases. No departure date was recorded for 342 cases. Many of these were still resident in the House when register entries end in May 1793.

The average length of stay for all inmates was 279 days (see table 4). Those aged between eighty and eighty-nine were more likely to stay longer (388 days) than others. The shortest average stay was 142 days reported for the twenty to twenty-nine age cohort, which suggests that they had or were considered to have had better opportunities than most for sustenance outside of the House.

Table 4. Number of inmates exiting and average length of stay (in days) by age cohort, 1774–93

Age at entry (years)	Discharged			Died			Escaped			All known outcomes	
	Number	Percentage	Days	Number	Percentage	Days	Number	Percentage	Days	Number	Days
0–9	266	79.2	268	42	12.5	393	28	8.3	397	336	353
10–19	216	64.5	195	13	3.9	797	106	31.6	94	335	362
20–29	173	66.0	135	16	6.1	217	73	27.9	73	262	142
30–39	161	71.6	132	17	7.6	417	47	20.8	73	225	207
40–49	172	71.0	133	19	7.9	420	51	21.1	89	242	214
50–59	162	65.9	145	40	16.2	506	44	17.9	200	246	284
60–69	205	58.6	148	87	24.9	696	58	16.5	144	350	329
70–79	157	59.9	157	82	31.3	410	23	8.8	273	262	280
80–89	55	53.4	97	38	36.9	740	10	9.7	327	103	388
90–99	6	46.2	124	6	46.2	330	1	7.6	20	13	158
100 +	3	60.0	25	2	40.0	904	0	0	0	5	310
Total	**1,576**	**66.2**	**168**	**362**	**15.2**	**530**	**441**	**18.5**	**140**	**2,379**	**279**

Inmates were more likely to be discharged from the House rather than to die there or escape. Even among the very young and the very old, discharge rather than death was the most likely form of exit, though death became an increasingly likely form of exit for those aged fifty and over (see table 4). Those discharged numbered 1,590 or 57.9 per cent of all admitted (see table 5). While a very small number (1.6 per cent) were discharged on the day of admission, most (12.3 per cent) were discharged between one day and a week of admission. A similar number (12 per cent) were discharged between a week and one month, while a slightly smaller percentage (11.4) left within two and three months of admission. A total of 196 (7.1 per cent) inmates were discharged more than one year after admission.

Table 5. Length of stay from admission to discharge, 1774–93

Discharged	Number	Percentage of all discharged	Percentage of all inmates
on day of admission	45	2.8	1.6
within two days and one week	339	21.3	12.3
within two weeks and a month	330	20.8	12.0
within two and three months	313	19.7	11.4
within four and six months	206	13.0	7.5
within seven months and one year	161	10.1	5.9
after more than one year	196	12.3	7.1
Total	**1,590**	**100**	**57.9**

The average stay of those discharged was 168 days, or just short of six months. Children up to the age of nine were more likely to be discharged (79.2 per cent) than any other cohort, but they tended to stay in the house for longer (268 days). For the most part, inmates across nearly all age cohorts could expect to be discharged sometime between 100 and 200 days after admission. This suggests that the governors sustained a regular policy of admission and discharge, one which provided temporary rather than long-term residence, thereby maximising the numbers obtaining relief.

Opportunities for employment, apprenticeship, or, in a small number of cases, education in a charity school, were offered to inmates. Peter Johnston (1950), a seventeen-year-old labourer secured his discharge on 11 March 1788 by becoming an indentured servant bound for America. He may well have encouraged two prostitutes, Norry Lynch (1918) and Catherine Creagh (1948), to do the same, as all three were discharged on the same day. Both Lynch and Creagh were admitted at different times in 1787 but seem to have emigrated together, which provides evidence of the interdependencies of inmates within the House. Likewise, in September 1789 three young boys who had escaped together from the House were, on their apprehension, discharged to the charity school at Shannongrove.[52]

Of all three ways to leave the House, death was the least likely and of those admitted, just 370 or 13.5 per cent died there (see table 6). The exact date of death was recorded in the case of 365 inmates. Of these, nearly two-thirds (239 or 66.0 per cent) died within a year of admission. The average length of stay for those who died in the House was 530 days (nearly 1½ years). The shortest period (217 days) between admission and death was for those aged between twenty and twenty-nine. Those aged between ten and nineteen were the least likely to die within the house. Those who did were likely to be long-term inmates. More inmates died in December than in any other month of the year (forty-seven or 12.8 per cent), though the next highest rate is for May (forty or 10.9 per cent), while September registered the fewest (fourteen or 3.8 per cent), suggesting that death struck indiscriminately. Those aged above fifty accounted for 70.2 per cent of all deaths, while children aged up to nine accounted for 12.5 per cent of deaths.

Cause of mortality was not recorded in the register though in some cases might be inferred from information recorded in the 'disease' column. A glimpse at a more unfortunate death was provided by the city's newspaper in October 1785. In that month, the fourteen-year-old Thomas Galvin (1583) suffocated and died when he 'fell into one of the sewers' of the House.[53] He may have been trying to escape.

Table 6. Length of stay from admission to death, 1774–93

Died	Number	Percentage of all deaths	Percentage of all inmates
on day of admission	2	0.5	0.1
within two days and one week	20	5.5	0.7
within two weeks and a month	52	14.2	1.9
within two and three months	58	16.1	2.1
within four and six months	56	15.3	2.0
within seven months and one year	51	13.9	1.9
after more than one year	126	34.4	4.6
Total	**365**		**13.3**

52 *Waterford Chronicle*, 2 Oct. 1789. Two of the three can be identified from the register: John Hallaran (1929) and John Ringrose (1899).

53 *LC*, 31 Oct. 1785.

Table 7. Length of stay from admission to escape, 1774–93

Escaped	Number	Percentage of all escaped	Percentage of all inmates
on day of admission	12	2.7	0.4
within two days and one week	103	23.4	3.7
within two weeks and a month	97	22.0	3.5
within two and three months	99	22.4	3.6
within four and six months	50	11.3	1.8
within seven months and one year	43	9.8	1.6
after more than one year	37	8.4	1.3
Total	**441**		**16.1**

Escape was the only other way of leaving the House (see table 7). Of all those admitted, 441 or 16.1 per cent escaped. Over a quarter of these escaped within a week of admission. In all over 70 per cent escaped within three months. Those who escaped in the greatest proportions (between 21 and 32 per cent) were aged between ten and forty-nine and did so soon after admission (within 100 days) (see table 4). The exception was the ninety-two-year-old labourer, Denis Kelly (2045) who was the only individual within his age cohort to escape, having spent only twenty days in the House. Those aged between ten and nineteen were more likely to escape than any other age cohort, and in all cases proportionately more males than females escaped. Those least likely to escape were children under the age of nine and those aged over seventy.

Most escaped over the garden wall or through the street door. At least eleven made their escape 'through the necessary house'. If they sought to escape, those classified as insane had first to break free of their handcuffs, chains or locked cells. Others having been given permission to leave for a short period never came back. Patrick Sheehan (1649) a seventy-two-year-old butcher was given permission to attend mass but did not return. Neither did Pierce Kelly (1113), a nine-year-old who went down to the Shannon to wash himself. The register may not have recorded all those who escaped and who were subsequently found or returned. For example, in 1789 a lunatic whose escape was reported in the *Limerick Chronicle* was returned to the House having reached Kilmallock in the county, 'after doing a good deal of damage', but his escape is not recorded in the register.[54]

Observations

The final column in the register, 'observations', was mainly used to provide information on the terms or circumstances of discharge, death or escape. Information is provided in 1,743 cases (63.5 per cent). The most frequent observation (42.9 per cent) recorded the order from the committee, governor, or other official who discharged the inmate. In fifty-one instances inmates paid for their release, fifty-five gave 'security' not to beg, eleven were 'to quit the town', twelve were found employment or an apprenticeship, four enlisted in the army, and four went to a charter school.

In the absence of minute books, the observations provide details on those who engaged in the administration of the House. The most active were the *ex-officio* governors including the mayor and the city sheriffs whose duties dovetailed with their civic obligations. While the governors had overall responsibility for the House, much of the work was performed by a committee and the treasurer.[55] In 1783 women were encouraged to visit the House, to take an interest in its arrangements and to subscribe

54 *Waterford Chronicle*, 2 Oct. 1789.
55 *LC*, 2, Apr. 1800.

to its upkeep.[56] In 1803 the governors appointed official visitors to inspect the House and in 1806 they agreed to perform this function in rotation.[57] Predictably, those who filled the offices of secretary and treasurer were most active and they directed the steward, who may well have been responsible for keeping the register. When the positions of steward and housekeeper were advertised in May 1774, it was stated that a 'man and wife' would not be appointed.[58] Later in the same year, doctors and apothecaries were given honorary appointments to the House, which they fulfilled without salary.[59] A bailiff had been employed by 1791, who, like the steward and housekeeper, received a 'small salary'.[60] (See Appendix 4 for list of governors and other officers mentioned in the observations column).

The activities recorded in the observations column reveal the outlook of these men and women. While attitudes varied with individual cases, in general they depended on whether an inmate was deemed 'helpless' and deserving of relief, or was a nuisance or menace and deserving of punishment and confinement. Thomas Kennedy (29), a fifty-one-year-old lunatic from Limerick was 'drove out of town' on 25 November 1774 after two days in the House. While no other information is given his case suggests that the authorities were incapable or unwilling to accommodate him further. Yet, in general, lunatics remained in the House for long periods. The unfortunate twelve-year-old 'insane' Thomas Galvin (1583), who had been admitted on 14 March 1784 and died while escaping on 30 October 1785 had spent over a year-and-a-half there. His mother bought his coffin and like other parents, she seems to have availed of the House to care for her helpless child.

The treatment of 'undesirables' reflected varying attitudes. Easther Condran (94), a forty-five-year-old ballad singer from Dublin was compelled to enter the House on 9 May 1775, but 'promised to leave the town' when discharged the same day. In this case the House acted as a mechanism through which the unwanted could be given a choice between incarceration or voluntary departure from the city. Prostitutes, especially those who had contracted venereal diseases, were feared for the perceived moral and physical contagion they brought. Elinor Hawksford (1155), a twenty-one-year old Dublin prostitute, voluntarily admitted herself on 24 September 1781, but was discharged after four days by the doctor 'she being rotten with the pox'. So too was another prostitute, Biddy Butler (1161), admitted two weeks later, whose condition was noted as 'poxed'. Although the House had been partly established as a means of removing prostitutes from the streets, there was a reluctance to confine women whose medical condition seemed incurable. In some cases the doctors were successful. Mary Hickey (1630), a nineteen-year-old prostitute, was 'cured of the bad disorder' and discharged in December 1785. A mortally-ill prostitute was not the only one who might be discharged. Francis Keeffe (1239), a thirty-six-year-old barber was 'turned out' in March 1782 because his cancer was 'incurable'.

If there was a sense of ill-fated inevitability there was also compassion. Michael Bourke (1246), a seventy-year-old comber from Limerick city, came to the House on 24 March 1782 because he 'was very ill' and he died there a week later. Eliza Headen (1502), a thirty-five-year-old seamstress from Tipperary and her two young children (1503, 1504), were allowed to stay in the House for a month when Sir Henry Hartstonge arranged to pay for them. There is no reason given for this, though it shows how charity could be extended by a governor. Children left orphaned or deserted by their parents could expect succour. John Industry (425), a two-year-old whose name evoked his foundling status, was 'left at the door' on 9 October

56 *LC*, 5 May 1783.

57 *LC*, 15 June 1803, 29 Feb. 1804, 10 Dec. 1806.

58 *LC*, 5 May 1774. The position was advertised again in 1782 — *LC*, 12 Dec. 1782.

59 *LC*, 21 November 1774.

60 *LC*, 25 Feb. 1791.

1777, and died in the House three months later. Compassion was also shown when an inmate died without anyone to arrange a funeral. In such instances — seventy-four of them recorded in the register — the governors agreed to buy a coffin. Among them was Thomas Geough (25), the twenty-fifth person admitted to the House in November 1774. He was then eighty years old and he remained there for eighteen years until his death in 1792.

Conclusion

Paupers in early modern Ireland took up a small part of the official record and rarely left their own personal accounts: there are now few traces of their individual experiences or of the specific conditions that they endured. However, the register of the Limerick House of Industy with its careful listing of name, age, religion, residence, health and occupation, provides an exceptional opportunity to identify and characterise a substantial number of the poor over two decades at the end of the eighteenth century. More particularly, it offers a great deal of information on how local functionaries and the charitably-minded attempted to implement the provisions of the 1772 poor law.

Those admitted to the House were drawn from every age group and they included almost as many men as women. While most were catholic, protestants were there in significant numbers. The majority came from Limerick and its hinterland but there were others from almost every part of Ireland and from England and Scotland and from places further away on the Atlantic edge. Thus in key respects they may have seemed like a cross-section of the population of a busy port city. They included several who in better times might have known a comfortable way of life, among them a priest, a lawyer, a gentlewoman and a gentleman. What the register does not reveal is the moment when their particular circumstances changed and they were forced to take a path that only a short time before might not have been anticipated. Many others had the knowledge and skills that had allowed them to earn a living in occupations as diverse as brewing, dressmaking, teaching, shopkeeping, shipbuilding, and milling. Against the background of increasing prosperity, such men and women might have expected a relatively good standard of living instead of having to seek admission to the House. Some were forced to go there because of a dramatic change in personal circumstances, such as failing sight or an illness that rendered them incapable of work. Others, having lost a parent or a spouse, were homeless and without access to the means of earning a living. The majority of those admitted, however, came from the ranks of the propertyless rural and urban poor whose livelihoods depended on a sustained capacity for manual work. At the best of times they had to work hard to attain the standards of shelter, diet and clothing that many took for granted. They could never be sure of securing a living and at times of crisis, such as when the cycle of the economy shifted downwards in the mid 1780s, their outlook became bleaker still. At such moments the House provided shelter and food and, if the numbers seeking help threatened to overwhelm its limited capacity, it was able to organise the distribution of food and clothes through the city.

Most of those admitted stayed but a short while. The sooner a pauper could leave, either to take up work or to go to another part of the country, the sooner another might be given a place. But there were some who never left the House, including the permanately disabled who lacked even the capacity to beg and the mentally ill who were perceived as being a threat to themselves and to others. For all, admission to the House meant disruption of a familiar routine and becoming subject to an impersonal rhythm that regulated each of the day's activities. This often meant the severing of personal ties and a loss of intimacy and many had to suffer criticism of a wayward life. On the other hand an inmate had the opportunity to avail of the sociability that living at close quarters brought and for as long as a pauper remained in the House, there was the guarantee of shelter, food, clothing and, when ill, the attention of a physician or surgeon. Notwithstanding its benefits and the extent to which some seemed content to remain under its regime, others set escape as their goal and they pursued that even at the risk of injury or death.

The erection of the House of Industry provided another sphere of activity for the charitable and the civic-minded. Some served by virtue of their office or calling; others dug into their pockets to contribute to its funds, sometimes anonymously. Priests preached on its behalf and newspaper proprietors publicised its good work and it was widely perceived and welcomed as a worthwhile, even fashionable, cause. Among those who lent their weight was Deane Hoare. In 1774 when the project was mooted he was a senior clergyman, already active on behalf of many of the city's charities and he was glad to turn his skills to the design of the House. Another was Lancelot Hill, recently retired from the army and having supervised the building of the House he went on to serve as its secretary and treasurer for many years. His wife Jane, a sister of Edmund Sexten Pery, was a frequent visitor to the House, a contributor to its funds and a source of consolation to the afflicted. So too was her sister Lucy Hartstonge, who contributed generously and became a life governor. Dymphna, the third Pery sister, may have urged her husband William Monsell to do the same. The governance of the House provided an opportunity for association in a project that most believed brought great benefits. As the city grew in wealth and the plight of the poor became every day more visible, it was a valued refuge for the most afflicted and deserving.

Some might have hoped that the erection of a house of industry with a strict work regime would lessen, or remove entirely, the burden that the poor presented. Notwithstanding its designation, the Limerick House of Industry, like most others at the time, functioned primarily as a place of refuge and confinement. Thus it was as likely to contain the orphaned and abandoned, the old and incapacitated, the lunatic and the miscreant, as to house the able-bodied, who, had they been there in sufficient numbers, might have justified its reorganisation as a self-supporting institution. During the period dealt with here it discharged a wider array of functions and in time other more specialised carcarel institutions such as the lunatic and the magdalen asylum, the industrial school and the reformatory, would emerge to replace it.

David Fleming
John Logan
Limerick, 2011

APPENDIX 1
Occupations of inmates, 1774–93

Agriculture, horticulture, fishing and mining

Farmer, poor farmer	34	Gardener	11	Miner	1
Fisherman	1	Husbandman	1		

Building and allied trades

Carpenter	12	Painter	2	Slater	6
Joiner	2	Paver	1	Sweep	1
Lime burner	1	Plummer	2	Wheelwright	3
Mason, stone cutter	10	Sawyer	6		
Nailor	9	Ship carpenter	1		

Manufacturing: textiles and ropes

Britches maker	2	Lace maker	12	Silk dier	1
Buttonmaker	4	Lawn maker	1	Silk weaver	4
Calico printer	2	Linen weaver	11	Silk winder	1
Card marker	2	Mantua maker	13	Spinner	28
Clothier	19	Mat maker	1	Stay-maker	3
Comber	10	Peruke maker	2	Stockingmaker	3
Cordwainer	8	Quilter	3	Tailor	23
Embroidrist	1	Quill winder	6	Threadmaker	7
Flax dresser	2	Ribbon weaver	3	Weaver	110
Hatter	2	Sail maker	1	Wigmaker	2
Hosier	3	Sempstress	22	Winder	1
Knitter	3	Serge weaver	4	Worsted spinner	3
		Shagg weaver	1		

Manufacturing: leather, bone and footwear trades

Blacker	1	Pattenmaker	3	Skinner	4
Combmaker	1	Saddler	5	Tanner	8
Cobbler	8	Shoe boy	4	Whipmaker	1
Glover	2	Broguemaker, shoemaker	34		

Manufacturing: metalworking and clayworking

Buckler maker	2	Gunsmith	1	Smith	9
Cutler	1	Pottermaker	1	Tinker	1
Founder	1	Sieve maker	1		

Manufacturing: food, drink and tobacco processing

Baker	14	Malster	6	Tobacco boy	1
Brewer, brewer's servant	4	Mealman	1	Tobacconist	6
Butcher	18	Mealwoman	1	Tripe woman	3
Cleeveboy	2	Miller	5		
Cook	3	Salt boiler	1		

Manufacturing: woodworking

Basketmaker	1	Cooper	6	Turner	1
Cabinetmaker	5	Corkcutter	1		

Transport

Boatman	5	Horse rider	1	Sailor, seaman,	
Chairman	13	Porter	16	poor seaman	32
Coachman	1			Turf porter	2

Distributive

Butter broker	1	Huckster, forestaller	4	Shopkeeper	3
Crier of news, news-seller	2	Merchant, poor merchant	2	Waterwoman	1
Dealer	9	Peddlar	18		
Grocer	2	Publican	1		

Labouring

Labourer	149	Workwoman	1		

Personal services

Barber	7	Servant	330	Steward	1

Professional and administrative services

Clerk, writing clerk	2	Priest	1	Schoolmaster	10
Dancing master	1	Process server	3	Schoolmistress	3
Fencing teacher	1	Proctor	1	Tutor	1
Constable	1	Soldier, old soldier, broken soldier	3	Toll gatherer	1
Marine, mariner	2			Weigh master	1

Housekeeper

Housekeeper	82	Reduced housekeeper, poor housekeeper	135

Entertainer

Actress	2	Mountebank	1	Thumbling girl	1
Balladsinger	9	Piper	2		
Fiddler	1	Sportsman	1		

Pupil

Apprentice	1	Poor scholar	9	Charity schoolboy	1

Miscreant: prostitute

Harlot	58	Strumpet	1	Whore	9

Miscreant: beggar and vagabond

Beggar	277	Traveller	1
Shuler, stroller, stroller vagabond, common stroller, strolling beggar	109	Vagabond	1

Miscreant: delinquent

Bad boy	2	Idle boy, idle bad boy	3	Rogue	8
Bad girl	12	Idle girl	1	Smuggler	1
Bad woman	6	Idle woman	1	Saucy fellow	1
Disobedient girl	1	Idler	17	Thief	7
Drunkard	4	Robber	1		

NON-OCCUPATIONAL DESCRIPTIONS

Residence

American	2	Frenchman	2	County Cork	1

Disease or behavioural condition

Bad disorder pox	3	Fool, foolish, strolling fool	15	Insane, mad, lunatic	6
Blindboy	1			Out of her senses	1
Cripple	5	Idiot	1	Drunkard	4

Household, gender, family or social status

Boy	3	Infant	1	Tailor's wife	1
Born in the House of Industry	1	Reduced gentleman, reduced gentlewoman	4	Butcher's son	1
Bastard	1	Spinster	10	Deluded from her parents	1
Child	71	Wife to named person	3	Had child by Mr Lynch	1
Child or grandchild to named person	11	Servant's child	2	Orphan and beggar	1
Orphan	54	Miller's wife	1	Widow	3
Girl	1	Soldier's wife	17		

The 'helpless' poor

Poor boy	39	Poor lad	1	Poor widow	1
Poor child	14	Poor man	9	Poor woman	25
Poor girl	39	Poor orphan	1	Reduced	2

APPENDIX 2

Residence of inmates by circumstances of admission, 1774–93

		Voluntary Number	Voluntary Percentage	Compulsory Number	Compulsory Percentage	Unknown terms of admission	Total
MUNSTER	Limerick City	594	69.5	261	30.5	450	1,305
	Limerick County	239	62.6	143	37.4	166	548
	Limerick	21	36.2	37	63.8	5	63
	Clare County	110	63.6	63	36.4	86	259
	Tipperary County	35	64.8	19	35.2	15	69
	Cork City	9	52.9	8	47.1	10	27
	Cork County	10	30.3	23	69.7	9	42
	Cork	9	100	0	0	4	13
	Kerry County	12	42.9	16	57.1	9	37
	Waterford County	4	57.1	3	42.9	1	8
	Total	*1,043*	*64.5*	*573*	*35.5*	*755*	*2,371*
LEINSTER	Carlow County	1	100	0	0	3	4
	Dublin City	26	78.8	7	21.2	10	43
	Dublin County	6	54.5	5	45.5	2	13
	Dublin	15	88.2	2	11.8	5	22
	Kildare County	1	100	0	0	0	1
	Kilkenny County	5	71.4	2	28.6	0	7
	King's County	7	77.8	2	22.2	3	12
	Leinster	0	0	1	100	0	1
	Longford County	2	66.7	1	33.3	0	3
	Meath County	1	50.0	1	50.0	0	2
	Queen's County	3	37.5	5	62.5	1	9
	Wexford County	1	25.0	3	75.0	4	8
	Total	*68*	*70.1*	*29*	*29.9*	*28*	*125*
ULSTER	Antrim County	9	90.0	1	10.0	0	10
	Armagh County	0	0	1	100	0	1
	Down County	2	50.0	2	50.0	0	4
	Cavan County	1	50.0	1	50.0	0	2
	Londonderry County	1	50.0	1	50.0	0	2
	Monaghan County	1	100	0	0	0	1
	North	12	80.0	3	20.0	9	24
	Tyrone County	0	0	2	100	0	2
	Total	*26*	*70.3*	*11*	*29.7*	*9*	*46*
CONNAUGHT	Connaught	0	0	2	100	2	4
	Galway County	12	60.0	8	40.0	2	22
	Mayo County	0	0	1	100	0	1
	Roscommon County	1	25.0	3	75.0	0	4
	Sligo county	0	0	2	100	2	4
	Total	*13*	*44.8*	*16*	*55.2*	*6*	*35*
OUTSIDE IRELAND	England	14	58.3	10	41.7	12	36
	North Britain	1	33.3	2	66.7	0	3
	Scotland	2	66.7	1	33.3	1	4
	Jersey	0	0	0	0	4	4
	France	1	25.0	3	75.0	1	5
	Italy	0	0	0	0	1	1
	Sweden	0	0	1	100	0	1
	America	2	40.0	3	60.0	1	6
	West Indies	0	0	0	0	1	1
	Total	*20*	*50*	*20*	*50*	*21*	*61*
	No residence recorded	37	58.0	29	42.0	43	109
	Total	*1,207*	*64.0*	*678*	*36*	*862*	*2,747*

APPENDIX 3

Classification of disease and related health condition of inmates, 1774–93

1	**Certain infectious and parasitic diseases**	
	Lax, laxative	4
	Venereal disease, bad disorder, pox, clap, inveterate pox, nose eaten off, jaws locked with the bad disorder	36
	Bloody flux	3
	Ague, shaking ague	3
	Fever, high fever, raging fever	6
	Impostume	1
2	**Neoplasms**	
	Cancer	1
3	**Diseases of the blood and blood-forming organs and certain disorders involving the immune mechanism**	
	Evil, running evil	4
4	**Endocrine, nutritional and metabolic diseases**	
	Scurvy, scorbutic, scorbutic face, scorbutic legs	22
5	**Mental and behavioural disorders**	
	Drunk, drunkard, dead drunk, given to drink, inebriated, loves liquor, full of whiskey	17
	Disordered in senses	4
	Dressed in boys clothes	1
	Fool, foolish	16
	Insane	182
	Lunatic	31
	Mad, stark mad	13
	Melancholy	1
	Naked	1
	Will eat nothing	1
6	**Diseases of the nervous system**	
	Falling sickness	1
	Fits	9
	Headache, pain in head	3
	Nervous disorder	1
	Palsy	12
	Dead palsy	1
	Dead at one side	2
7	**Diseases of the eye and adnexa**	
	Almost blind	3
	Blind, most blind, stone blind, want of sight, loss of sight	57
	Blind in one eye, most blind in one eye	13
	Dimness in sight	1
	Nigh sighted	3
	Pearl in one eye	1
	Sore eye, sore eyes	7
8	**Diseases of the ear and mastoid process**	
	Deaf, hard of hearing	5
	Dumb	4
9	**Diseases of the circulatory system**	
	Pain in heart	3
	Dropsy, dropsical	14
10	**Diseases of the respiratory system**	
	Asthma, asthmatic	19
	Consumption	1
	Cough	1
	Ptisick	1
11	**Diseases of the digestive system**	
	Costive	1
	Rupture, very large rupture	16
	Sore mouth	1
	Subject to worms	1
	Puking blood	2
	Yellow jaundice	1
	Canker	1
12	**Diseases of the skin and subcutaneous tissue**	
	Itch, violent itch	2
	Scald head	1
13	**Diseases of the musculoskeletal system and connective tissue**	
	Cripple, wants the use of limbs	36
	Lame	27
	Lame in left arm, lost use of one arm, lame in one arm, lame hand	8
	Lame in one leg, lame in both legs, lame step	14
	Pain in back	4
	Pain in leg, pain in legs	2
	Rheumatic, rheumatic pains, rheumatism	25
	Sore arm, sore hand, sore hands	6
	Sore leg, sore legs, desperate sore leg, swelled knee	33
14	**Diseases of the genitourinary system**	0
15	**Pregnancy, childbirth and the puerperium**	
	With child, big with child	6
	Sore breast	2
	Just brought to bed	1
16	**Certain conditions originating in the perinatal period**	0
17	**Congenital malformations, deformations and chromosomal abnormalities**	
	Chin and chest tied together	1
	Humpbacked	1
18	**Symptoms, signs and abnormal clinical and laboratory findings, not elsewhere classified**	
	Bedridden	1
	Decay	4
	Infirm	146
	Old age	3
	Sore chin	1
19	**Injury, poisoning and certain other consequences of external causes**	
	Broken leg, broke his leg	3
	Broken arm	1
	Broken back	2
	Broken bones	1
	Loss of foot, loss of feet, one leg, loss of toes	5
	Loss of hand, one hand, one arm	3

20 External causes of morbidity and mortality	0
21 Factors influencing health status and contact with health services	
Sick, sickly	40
[-] Inmates suffering more than one condition	
Asthmatic, rheumatic	1
Blind, decrepit	1
Dead drunk and bad disorder	1
Dropsical, rupture	1
Fits and blind in one eye	1
Fits and deaf	1
Fits and lame and rupture	1
Foolish and fits	1
Insane and blind	3
Lame and blind	1
Lame and deaf	1
Lame and dumb	2
Lame and paralytic	1
Land rupture	2
Old age and infirmity	1
Old age and sick	1
Pain in head and limbs	1
Rupture and asthmatic	2
Sick and infirm	27
Sick and sore breast	1
Sick and weak	4
Sickly and cripple	1
Most blind and lunatic	1

APPENDIX 4
Governors And Governesses, Visitors And Officers, 1774–93*

Acland, Lady Harriet, (1750–1815) dau. of Stephen Fox-Strangways, 1st Earl of Ilchester; married, 1771, Major John Dyke Acland, MP in Britain; governess of the House of Industry 1774.

Bassett, Mr, steward of the House of Industry *c.* 1782–1812.

Browne, James, woollen draper, of Main Street, Englishtown; founding governor of the House of Industry 1774.

Creagh, Andrew, MD, of St Mary's Abbey; physician to the House of Industry *c.* 1774–88.

Crosbie, Pyne, (d. 1812) dau. of Sir Henry Cavendish 1st Bt., and Anne Pyne; married, 1768, Maurice Crosbie, dean of Limerick; founding governess of the House of Industry 1774.

Davis, Samuel, (d. 1778) of Shamble Lane, Main Street; apothecary to the House of Industry 1774.

Dawson, Charles, surveyor of Limerick port; freeman 1784; founding governor of the House of Industry 1774.

Fitzgerald, William, sheriff 1775, mayor 1786; governor of the House of Industry *c.* 1786–92.

Ferrar, John, (1743–1804), printer and book seller, proprietor of the *Limerick Chronicle* 1768–81 and author of *The history of Limerick,* 1767; freeman 1768; founding governor of the House of Industry 1774, secretary and treasurer *c.* 1790.

Gore, William, (d. 1784) bishop of Limerick 1774–84, founding life governor of the House of Industry 1774.

Hassett, James, MD, of Mungret Street; physician to the house of Industry 1774 to *c.* 1792.

Hammond, John Dowdal, attorney, of Mungret Street; married, 1776, Arabella, dau. of William Minchin of Dublin; freeman 1747; attorney in the mayor's court 1754; founding governor of the House of Industry 1774.

Hartstonge, Sir Henry (*c.* 1725–1797), married, 1751, Lucy Pery; founding governor of the House of Industry 1774.

Hartstonge, Lady Lucy, (d. 1793), dau. of Rev. Stacpole Pery and Jane Twigg, and sister of Edmund Sexten Pery; married Sir Henry Hartstonge; founded St. John's Fever and Lock Hospital in Limerick 1781; visitor to the House of Industry *c.* 1784–92.

Hewson, Rev. Francis, (1738–89) of Woodford, Co. Kerry, son of John Hewson of Ennismore, Co. Kerry, and Margaret, dau. of Maurice FitzGerald, Knight of Kerry; entered TCD 1755, BA 1760; vicar of Cahir-Corney and Killkelane 1768, rector of Kilgibbin 1771, incumbent of Listowel; married, 1773, Margaret, dau. of Lancelot Sandes of Kilcavan, Queen's County; founding governor of the House of Industry 1774.

Hill, Jane dau. of Rev. Stacpole Pery and sister of Edmund Sexten Pery; married, 1774, Capt. Lancelot Hill; visitor to the House of Industry *c.* 1781.

Hill, Lancelot, (1734–1810) husband of Jane Pery; ensign in 55th regiment 1758, lieutenant 1760, captain 1768, resigned 1773; registrar of the diocese of Limerick 1773; freeman 1773; governor of the Blue School *c.* 1786; supervised the building and founding governor of the House of Industry 1774, secretary and treasurer *c.* 1779–86.

Hoare, Deane, (1724–1800), son of Robert Hoare of Cork and Jane Newenham; entered TCD 1740; vicar choral of Limerick 1755, sub-dean 1755, vicar general 1772, 1792; freeman of Limerick 1756; architect of the Limerick Assembly House 1770; overseer of Dr Jeremy Hall's charity; founder and treasurer of the County Limerick Infirmary 1759–96; founder and treasurer of the Limerick Society for the relief and discharge of persons confined for small debts 1775, 1779–88; married, 1757, Susanna, eldest dau. of Alderman John Ingram, and sister of Rev. Jacques Ingram, chancellor of St. Mary's cathedral, Limerick; architect and founding governor of the House of Industry 1774.

Howley, John, (1750–1825), of Rich Hill, Co. Limerick; married Amy, dau. of William Bourke of Pallas, Co. Tipperary; governor of the House of Industry *c.* 1783.

Ingram, Rev. Jacques, (d. 1793); entered TCD 1745, BA 1749; freeman 1746; vicar choral of Lismore 1746–72, of Limerick 1766–93; married, 1755, Jane daughter of Henry Ivers of Mount Ivers, Co. Clare, and secondly, Mary, dau. of Rev. John Smyth; founding life governor of the House of Industry 1774.

Johns, Joseph, (d. 1775); silversmith of Main Street; freeman 1731; sheriff 1755, burgess 1756, chamberlain 1769, mayor 1773–4; married, 1737, Ann Hincks; founding governor of the House of Industry 1774.

Lear, Dr, physician to the House of Industry *c.* 1791.

* Sources: J. Ferrar, *Directory of the city of Limerick* (Limerick, 1769); J. Ferrar, *The history of Limerick* (Limerick, 1787); P. Fitzgerald and J. J. McGregor, *The history, topography and antiquities of the county and city of Limerick* (2 vols, Dublin, 1827); M. Lenihan, *Limerick, its history and antiquities* (Cork, 1866); E. M. Johnston-Liik, *History of the Irish parliament, 1692–1800* (6 vols, Belfast, 2002); *Limerick Chronicle.*

Lefroy, Anthony Peter, (1743–1819), of 108 George's Street, Newtown Pery; lieut.-colonel of the 9th dragoons 1785; freeman 1794; married, 1765, Anne Gardiner, and secondly, Elizabeth Langlois; governor of the House of Industry *c.* 1785.

Mark, Mrs. Mary, née Fennell, married, 1774, Thomas Mark; governess of the House of Industry *c.* 1783.

Mark, Thomas, originally of Dublin, merchant of Main Street, Englishtown; married firstly, 1759, Mary Wheddon, and secondly, 1774, Mary Fennell; freeman 1759; governor of the House of Industry *c.* 1783.

Massy, Elizabeth, dau. of Hugh Baker of Lismacue, Co. Tipperary and Catherine Ryves; married, 1759, the Hon. John Massy, MP for Co. Limerick 1790–7; founding life governess to the House of Industry 1774.

McKeogh, John, of Main Street, Irishtown and later Broad Street; surgeon to the House of Industry 1774.

Maunsell George, (d. 1834) of Milford, Co. Limerick; collector of Limerick, 1784–*c.* 1811; governor of the House of Industry *c.* 1788.

Maunsell, Rev. Richard, (d. 1791) son of John Maunsell; chancellor of St. Mary's cathedral, Limerick, 1747–91; married a dau. of William Burscough, bishop of Limerick; founding governor of the House of Industry 1774.

Maunsell, Rev. Dr William, (d. 1804), son of Richard Maunsell, MP, and Jane Waller; married, Elizabeth, dau. of Rev. William Lyons; founding governor of the House of Industry 1774.

Monsell, William, (1706–*c.* 1788) son of Samuel Monsell of Tervoe, Co. Limerick, and [?] Webb; married firstly, 1731, Ann dau. of Rev. Richard Burgh, and secondly, 1751, Dymphna, dau. of Rev. Stacpool Pery and sister of Edmund Sexten Pery; founding governor of the House of Industry 1774.

Nash, James, founding governor of the House of Industry 1774.

Palmer, Rev. Edmond, (d. 1796) precentor of Ardfert 1789–91, prebendary of St. Munchin's, Limerick 1791–7; founder and president of the Limerick Benevolent Annuity Society 1769–96; founding governor of the House of Industry 1774.

Pery, Edmund Sexten, (1719–1806) MP for Wicklow 1751–60, Limerick, 1761–85; speaker of the House of Commons 1771–85; Viscount Pery of Newtown Pery 1786; founding governor of the House of Industry 1774.

Pery, William Cecil, (1721–94) bishop of Killaloe 1781, of Limerick 1781–94; Baron Glentworth 1790; founding governor of the House of Industry 1774.

Phillips, James Hill, (d. 1792); freeman 1773; married, 1769, Sarah dau. of William Richardson; governor of the House of Industry *c.* 1788–92.

Powell, Caleb, (1731–97) of Prospect Co. Limerick; collector of customs at Trim 1761, at Limerick 1766–81; founding governor of the House of Industry 1774.

Prendergast, John, (1742–1817) son of Charles Smyth Elizabeth dau. of Sir Thomas Prendergast, 1st Bt; sheriff 1763; MP for Carlow borough 1776–83, Limerick 1785–7; Baron Kiltarton 1810, Viscount Gort 1816; founding governor of the House of Industry 1774.

Rockfort, Michael, merchant, Exchange, Limerick; freeman 1794; governor of the House of Industry *c.* 1783.

Rose, George, of Morgans and Mount Pleasant, Co. Limerick, son of Lord Chief-Justice Henry Rose, MP for Ardfert, and Anne Crosbie; married, 1744, his cousin Catherine, dau. of Lancelot Sandes; sheriff of Co. Limerick 1766; founding life governor of the House of Industry 1774.

Seymour, Rev. John, (1728–95) of Pallace, Co. Limerick, son of William Seymour and Jane Wight; entered TCD 1745, BA 1749, MA 1752; chancellor of Emly 1765–6, precentor of Emly 1766; married his cousin, Griselda dau. of William Hobart of Highmount, Co. Cork; governor of the House of Industry *c.* 1784–6.

Shearer, Alexander, (d. *c.* 1802) MD, of Smyth Street and later Charlotte Quay; freeman 1762; married firstly, 1759, Margaret, dau. of William Stamer of Caherelly, Co. Clare and widow of Henry O'Brien of Stonehall, and secondly, 1767, Mrs D'Esterre, widow; founding governor and physician to the House of Industry 1774.

Shee, Stuart, MD physician to the House of Industry *c.* 1790–1.

Tunnadine, John, (1726–87) of Park, near Limerick, son of Rev. John Tunnadine; MP for Askeaton 1768–76, of Longford borough 1776–83; founding governor of the House of Industry 1774.

Vincent, John, merchant, son of Arthur Vincent; married firstly, 1759, Catherine, dau. of John Love of Castle Saffron, Co. Cork, and secondly, Lucy, dau. of Thomas Westropp of Ballysteen, Co. Limerick; freeman 1769; founding governor of the House of Industry 1774.

Watson, Andrew (d. 1834), printer and bookseller; succeeded John Ferrar as proprietor of the *Limerick Chronicle*; freeman 1781, sheriff 1796 and 1798, mayor 1812; secretary and treasurer of the House of Industry *c.* 1792–1834.

Widenham, Walter, merchant; sheriff 1759, burgess 1760, mayor 1777; married firstly, 1760, Ann dau. of Samuel Bindon, MP for Ennis, and secondly, 1795, Mrs Piercy; governor of the House of Industry *c.* 1778–88.

THE REGISTER OF THE LIMERICK HOUSE OF INDUSTRY, 1774–93

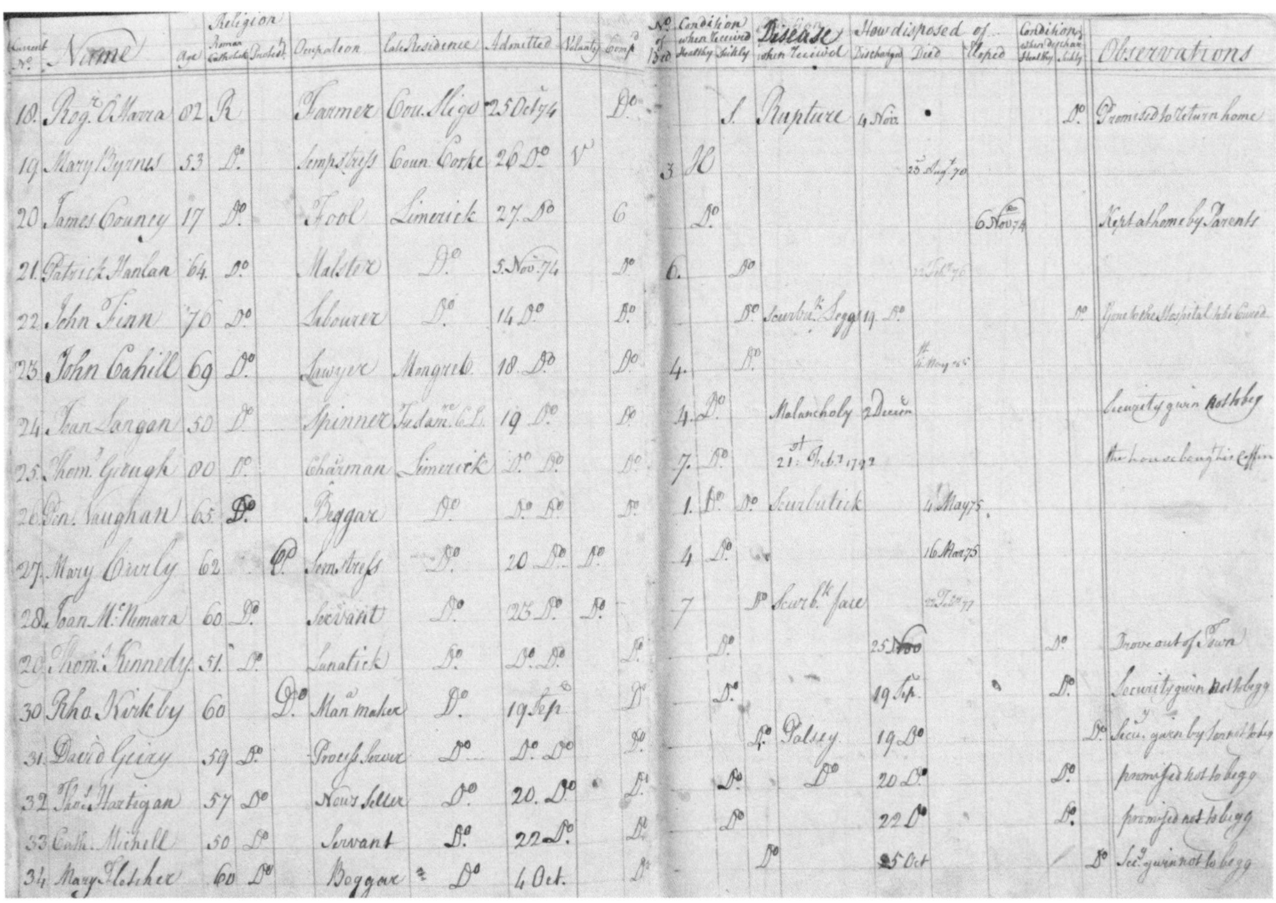

Current No.	Name	Age	Religion: Roman Catholick	Religion: Protest.t	Occupation	Late Residence	Admitted	Voluntary	Comp.d	No. of Bed	Condition when received: Healthy	Condition when received: Sickly	Disease when received	How disposed of: Discharged	Died	Eloped	Condition when discharged: Healthy	Condition when discharged: Sickly	Observations
18.	Rog.r O'Marra	82	R		Farmer	Cou. Sligo	25 Oct 74		Do.			S.	Rupture	4 Nov.				Do.	Promised to return home
19	Mary Byrnes	53	Do.		Sempstress	Coun. Corke	26 Do.	V		3	H				25 Aug.t 70				
20	James Couney	17	Do.		Fool	Limerick	27 Do.		6		Do.					6 Nov 74			Kept at home by Parents
21.	Patrick Hanlan	64.	Do.		Malster	Do.	5 Nov. 74		Do.	6.		Do.			22 Feb.y 76				
22	John Finn	70	Do.		Labourer	Do.	14 Do.		Do.			Do.	Scurbu.k Leggs	19 Do.				Do.	Gone to the Hospital to be Cured
23	John Cahill	69	Do.		Lawyer	Mongret	18 Do.		Do.	4.		Do.			[illegible] May 75				
24.	Joan Langan	50	Do.		Spinner	Tedam.re C.L.	19 Do.		Do.	4.	Do.		Malancholy	2 Decem.r					Security given not to beg
25.	Thom.s Grough	80	Do.		Chairman	Limerick	Do. Do.		Do.	7.	Do.		21st Feb.y 1792						the house bought his Coffin
26	Pen. Vaughan	65.	Do.		Beggar	Do.	Do. Do.		Do.	1.	Do.	Do.	Scurbutick		4 May 75				
27.	Mary Curly	62		Do.	Sem.stress	Do.	20 Do.	Do.		4	Do.				16 Mar 75				
28.	Joan McNemara	60	Do.		Servant	Do.	23 Do.	Do.		7		Do.	Scurb.k face		22 Feb.y 77				
29	Thom.s Kennedy	51	Do.		Lunatick	Do.	Do. Do.		Do.		Do.			25 Nov			Do.		Drove out of Town
30	Rho. Kirkby	60		Do.	Man.a maker	Do.	19 Sep.r		Do.		Do.			19 Sep.			Do.		Security given not to begg
31.	David Geiry	59	Do.		Process Server	Do.	Do. Do.		Do.			Do.	Palsey	19 Do.				Do.	Secu.y given by [illegible]
32	Thos. Hartigan	57	Do.		News Seller	Do.	20. Do.		Do.		Do.		Do.	20 Do.			Do.		promised not to begg
33	Cath. Michell	50	Do.		Servant	Do.	22 Do.		Do.		Do.			22 Do.			Do.		promised not to begg
34	Mary Fletcher	60	Do.		Beggar	Do.	4 Oct.		Do.			Do.		25 Oct				Do.	Sec.y given not to begg

Pages 4 and 5 of the Register of the Limerick House of Industry (by permission of Limerick City Archives).

Current No.	Names	Age	Religion Roman Catholic	Protestant	Occupation	Late residence	Admitted	Voluntary	Compulsory
1	William Brien	48	R		Cabint maker	Palas C Limk	19th Septr 1774		Comp
2	Michael Crosby	24		P	Beggar	Birr Ks County	19 *Do Do*		*Do*
3	Thoms Buckley	71		*Do*	Peruke Maker	Limerick	*Do*	Vol	
4	James Bourke	21	*Do*		Beggar	KMC Clare	*Do*		*Do*
5	James Finnessy	71	*Do*		Husbandman	Killy C Limerk	*Do*		*Do*
6	Barw Fitzpatrick	76	*Do*		Flax Dreser	B S C Kerry	*Do*		*Do*
7	Alice Malouny	82	*Do*		R Housek	Limerick	*Do*		*Do*
8	Cath Kennedy	75	*Do*		Servant	*Do*	*Do*		*Do*
9	Cath King	70	*Do*		Semstress	M S C Clare	23 Septr		*Do*
10	John McMahon	60	*Do*		Schoolmastr	P W Limerick	24 *Do*		*Do*
11	Brien Kelly	61	*Do*		Comber	Oran M C Galway	25 *Do*		*Do*
12	James Nash	57	*Do*		Redd housekeepr	Limerick	*Do Do*		*Do*
13	Henry Halfpenny	76		*Do*	Shoe Maker	*Do*	29 *Do*		*Do*
14	Cath Lahy	80	*Do*		Servant	N C C *Do*	*Do Do*		*Do*
15	Danl McNemarra	62	*Do*		Baker	Limerick	2 Octr 74		*Do*
16	Darby Ryan	85	*Do*		Labourer	County Clare	17 *Do*		*Do*
17	Thomas Nash	60	*Do*		Servant	Limerick	24 *Do*		*Do*
18	Rogr O'Harra	82	R		Farmer	Cou Sligo	25 Octr 74		*Do*
19	Mary Byrnes	53	*Do*		Semstress	Coun Corke	26 *Do*	V	
20	James Couney	17	*Do*		Fool	Limerick	27 *Do*		C
21	Patrick Hanlan	64	*Do*		Malster	*Do*	5 Novr 74		*Do*
22	John Finn	76	*Do*		Labourer	*Do*	14 *Do*		*Do*
23	John Cahill	69	*Do*		Lawyer	Mongret	18 *Do*		*Do*
24	Joan Langan	50	*Do*		Spinner	Fedamre C L	19 *Do*		*Do*
25	Thoms Geough	80	*Do*		Chairman	Limerick	*Do Do*		*Do*
26	Pen Vaughan	65	*Do*		Beggar	*Do*	*Do Do*		*Do*
27	Mary Curly	62		P	Semstress	*Do*	20 *Do*	*Do*	
28	Joan McNamara	60	*Do*		Servant	*Do*	23 *Do*	*Do*	
29	Thoms Kennedy	51	*Do*		Lunatick	*Do*	*Do Do*		*Do*
30	Rho Kirkby	60		*Do*	Mana maker	*Do*	19 Sep		*Do*
31	David Geiry	59	*Do*		Process Server	*Do*	*Do Do*		*Do*
32	Thos Hartigan	57	*Do*		News Seller	*Do*	20 *Do*		*Do*
33	Cath Michell	50	*Do*		Servant	*Do*	22 *Do*		*Do*
34	Mary Fletcher	60	*Do*		Beggar	*Do*	4 Oct		*Do*
35	Margret Lacy	57	R		Beggar	Limerick	20 Octr		*Do*
36	Penely McDermot	60	*Do*		*Do*	*Do*	25 *Do*		*Do*
37	Briget Hill	45	*Do*		*Do*	*Do*	9 Nov		*Do*
38	Hugh Maguire	61		P	Servant	Ennis C C	28 *Do*		*Do*
39	John Fitzgerald	89	*Do*		Cork Cutter	Limerick	2 Decemr		*Do*
40	Winny Grady	68	*Do*		Servant	Dromr C C	3 *Do*		*Do*
41	Margret Dundon	56	*Do*		*Do*	*Do Do*	4 *Do*		*Do*
42	Elinor O'Brien	55	*Do*		Spinner	C Limerick	*DoDo*		*Do*
43	Catherine O'Daniel	45	*Do*		Wosd Spiner	C Clare	*Do Do*		*Do*
44	James Kearny	76	*Do*		Labourer	*Do Do*	*Do Do*		*Do*
45	Margret Griffin	92	*Do*		Beggar	Limerick	5 *Do*		*Do*
46	James Duggan	82	*Do*		Servant	Gli Omte C C	10 *Do*		*Do*
47	Carrol Daly	80	*Do*		Labourer	C Limk	14 *Do*		*Do*
48	Timothy Mulcahy	61	*Do*		Labourer	Limerick	17 *Do*		*Do*
49	John Lynch	88	*Do*		*Do*	C Limerk	*Do Do*		*Do*
50	James Hays	16	*Do*		P Scholar	*Do Do*	*Do Do*		*Do*
51	John O'Connor	79	*Do*		Labourer	*Do Do*	*Do Do*		*Do*
52	Timothy Donovan	18	*Do*		Pr Scholar	C Cork	19 *Do*		*Do*
53	Connor O'Brien	101	*Do*		Miner	Limerick	20 *Do*		*Do*
54	Margt Sulivan	16	R		Beggar	Penywill	22 Decr 74		Comp
55	Timo Cavanagh	86	*Do*		Pedlar	C Clare	*Do Do*		*Do*
56	David Geiry	59	*Do*		Pro Server	Limerick	*Do Do*		*Do*
57	Rhody Kirkby	60		P	Mana maker	*Do*	23 *Do*		*Do*
58	John Merrit	64		*Do*	Carpenter	P Kilmurry	1 Jany 75		*Do*
59	John Murphy	13		*Do*	Poor Scholar	Ladoone	3 *Do*		*Do*

No. of bed	Condition when received Healthy	Condition when received Sickly	Disease when received	How disposed of Discharged	Died	Eloped	Condition when discharged Healthy	Condition when discharged Sickly	Observations
3	H		Blind	22 Feb 75			H		To Quit the Town
1			*Do*	5 Jan 76			H		To Quit the Town
8	*Do*					2 Feby 75	H		
1			Lame	9th Feby 79					To go to Mr Daffy
2		S	*Do*			29 Octr 75	H		
3	*Do*				19th Octr 1781				
1	H			1 Augt 75			H		Security not to begg
2					9 Octr 1781				
2		*Do*		12 June 75			H		Security not to begg
	Do			27 Sepr 74			H		Security given not to Begg
5		*Do*			2d Novr 82				
5		*Do*				29th Apr 1784			the door keeper's fault by letting him out without Leave
8	*Do*			25 March 76			*Do*		By order of the Corporation, Without fees
3	*Do*				23 May 76				
	Do			9th Octr 74			*Do*		Security given to labour
2		*Do*			4 July 76				
6		*Do*			12th April 79				
		S	Rupture	4 Nov				*Do*	Promised to Return home
3	H				23d Augt 78				
	Do					6 Novr 74			Kept at home by Parents
6		*Do*			22 Feby 76				
		Do	Scurbuk Leggs	19 *Do*				*Do*	Gone to the Hospital to be Cured
4		*Do*			4th May 85				
4	*Do*		Malancholy	2 Decemr					Security given not to beg
7	*Do*		21st Feby 1792						the house bougt his Coffin
1	*Do*	*Do*	Scurbutick		4 May 75				
4	*Do*				16 Mar 75				
7		*Do*	Scurbk Face		22 Feby 77				
	Do			25 Nov			*Do*		Drove out of Town
	Do			19 Sept			*Do*		Security given not to begg
		Do	Palsey	19 *Do*				*Do*	Secuy given by son not to beg
			Do	20 *Do*			*Do*		promised not to begg
	Do			22 *Do*			*Do*		promised not to begg
		Do		25 Oct				*Do*	Secy given not to begg
	Do			24 Oct			*Do*		Security given not to beg
		Do	Fitts	26 *Do*				*Do*	Security not to beg
	Do			9 Novr			*Do*		Security not to beg
4		*Do*			3d March 83				
7	*Do*				27 Decr 76				
		Do	*Do*	5 Decr				*Do*	Bond of Fifty pounds given not to Beg
	Do			5 *Do*			*Do*		*Do Do Do*
	Do			*Do Do*			*Do*		*Do Do Do*
	Do			*Do Do*			*Do*		*Do Do Do*
	Do			*Do Do*			*Do*		*Do Do Do*
4	*Do*			16 *Do*			*Do*		*Do Do Do*
	Do				18th March 78				
9	*Do*				27th May 83				
10	*Do*				26th April 79				
10	*Do*			22 *Do*			*Do*		*Do Do Do*
		Do	Dropsy	28 *Do*				*Do*	Sent to the Infirmery
11	*Do*			*Do Do*			*Do*		*Do Do Do*
	Do		Scurbutick	*Do Do*			*Do*		promised to Return home
	Do				16th Feby 77				
	H		a Criple		16th March 78				
	Do			6 Jany 75			H		Security not to begg
10	*Do*		Palsey	7 Mar					his Daughter having promised to maintain him
	Do			30 Decr 74			H		Security not to Begg
	Do		Asmatick		12 Mar 75				
		S	Scurbutick	28 Jany 75				S	Sent to the Infirmery

Current No.	Names	Age	Religion Roman Catholic	Protestant	Occupation	Late residence	Admitted	Voluntary	Compulsory
60	Mary Cavanagh	60	*Do*		Semstress	Cu C L	4 Jany 75		*Do*
61	John Gleeson	35	*Do*		Slater	C C L	8 *Do*		*Do*
62	Sarah Wolock	61	*Do*		Beggar		11 *Do*		*Do*
63	Elinr Fitzgerald	25	*Do*		Beggar	R D Qs C	15 *Do*		*Do*
64	Patrick Keefe	70	*Do*		Weaver	Limerk	16 *Do*	V	
65	Luke Conway	74	*Do*		Labourer	Mongret	24 *Do*	*Do*	
66	John Collins	61		*Do*	Coachman	Cou Clare	31 *Do*	*Do*	
67	Patt Fox	34	*Do*		Servant	*Do Do*	5 Februy		*Do*
68	Mary Calfield	55	*Do*		Wosted Spiner	Penywill	9 *Do*	*Do*	
69	William Orr	52		*Do*	Shoemaker	Cou Antrim	11 *Do*	*Do*	
70	Margt Fitzgerald	90	*Do*		Spinner	Mayr Stone	14 *Do*		*Do*
71	Denis Cane	65	*Do*		Labourer	C Limk	*Do Do*		*Do*
72	John Teirny	63	*Do*		Tobaconist	Limk	15 *Do*		*Do*
73	Paul Murphy	68	*Do*		Labourer	C Clare	25 *Do*	*Do*	
74	John Murphy	13		P	poor Scholar	Likadoone	26 Feb 75	Vol	
75	Margt Costola	60	R		Servant	Cou Clare	2 March		C
76	Edwd Davis	31		*Do*	Mason	Glr England	4 *Do*	V	
77	John Hays	75	*Do*		Labourer	Ci Limerick	*Do Do*		*Do*
78	John King	74		*Do*	Baker	City Limerick	14 *Do*	*Do*	
79	Mary Cutler	30		*Do*	Pl Workwoman	City London	14 *Do*	*Do*	
80	Honor Slattery	70	*Do*		Housekeeper	City Limerick	25 *Do*		*Do*
81	John Murphy	13		*Do*	Poor Scholar	Likadoone	28 *Do*	*Do*	
82	Mary Ryan	70	*Do*		Servant	Co Limerick	2 Apr		*Do*
83	Corns Flanagan	70	*Do*		Weaver	Cou Clare	3 *Do*		*Do*
84	Thoms Downes	75	*Do*		Weaver	City Limerick	7 *Do*	*Do*	
85	Hugh Hays	70	*Do*		Labourer	Cou Clare	9 *Do*		*Do*
86	Margret Cirly	52	*Do*		Begar	City Limerick	12 *Do*		*Do*
87	Thoms Consadine	92	*Do*		Labourer	*Do Do*	*Do Do*		*Do*
88	Brien Daniel	81	*Do*		Malster	*Do Do*	22 *Do*		*Do*
89	Margt Shea	55	*Do*		Servant	*Do Do*	26 *Do*		*Do*
90	Morlin Chadock	80	*Do*		Servant	Cou Clare	28 *Do*		*Do*
91	Char McCarthy	60	*Do*		Dealer	Balinacuragh	3 May		*Do*
92	Abigail Devit	60	*Do*		Begar	Cou Clare	9 *Do*		*Do*
93	John McMahon	60	R		Schl Master	Penny Wellroad	9 May 75		C
94	Easther Condran	45		P	Balld Singer	City of Dublin	*Do Do*		*Do*
95	Marg Jordan		*Do*		*Do Do*	*Do Do*	*Do Do*		
96	Mary Donaghue	70	*Do*		Spiner	City of Limk	16 *Do*		*Do*
97	Elinor Kinnely	67	*Do*		Begar	Cou Clare	3 Jun		*Do*
98	Honor Slattery	80	*Do*		Servant	City Limerick	*Do Do*		*Do*
99	Margret Malouny	90	*Do*		Spinner	County Limerick	*Do Do*		*Do*
100	Thomas Noonane	88	*Do*		Smith	City of Limk	6 *Do*		*Do*
101	Darby Croneen	11	*Do*		An Idler	*Do Do*	9 *Do*		*Do*
102	Margret Jones	80		*Do*	Card maker	*Do Do*	10 *Do*		*Do*
103	Edward Malouny	40	*Do*		Weaver	*Do Do*	10 *Do*		*Do*
104	Mary Purcell	33	*Do*		Servant	*Do Do*	13 *Do*		*Do*
105	Mary Shea	80	*Do*		*Do*	*Do Do*	14 *Do*		*Do*
106	Michael Casey	74	*Do*		Constable	Kilfa C Clare	16 *Do*	V	
107	Honor Magrath	80	*Do*		Spinner	Cou Limerick	26 *Do*		*Do*
108	Joan Bagwell	50	*Do*			City of Limerick	2 July		*Do*
109	Willm Montford	9		*Do*		Citty London	*Do Do*		*Do*
110	John Downes	80	*Do*		Brewer	City Limerick	6 *Do*		*Do*
111	Ann Stokes	54		P	Sempstress	City Limerick	12 July 75		C
112	Mary Jones	55	R		Servant	Cou Clare	20 *Do*	V	
113	James Roch	64	*Do*		Skiner	Cou Limk	29 *Do*		C
114	James Hamilton	62	*Do*		Sailor		6 Augt		*Do*
115	John Tankard	13	*Do*		Idler	City Limk	11 *Do*		*Do*
116	Mary Lyons	80	*Do*		Servant	*Do Do*	12 *Do*		*Do*
117	Prudence Bourke	80	*Do*		Baker	*Do Do*	*Do Do*		*Do*
118	Briget Quin	24	*Do*		Servant	*Do Do*	*Do Do*		*Do*
119	Denis Hays	52	*Do*		Weaver	*Do Do*	*Do Do*		*Do*
120	Joan Magrath	82	*Do*		Spiner	C Limk	*Do Do*	*Do*	

No. of bed	Condition when received Healthy	Sickly	Disease when received	How disposed of Discharged	Died	Eloped	Condition when discharged Healthy	Sickly	Observations
	Do			7 Jany 75			*Do*		Security not to begg
		Do	Criple	2 Feby *Do*				*Do*	
	Do	*Do*	Lunatick	2 Feby *Do*				*Do*	
	Do			25 *Do*			*Do*		
	Do				28th April 79				
			Rhumatism	17 Mar 75			*Do*		Gone to labour
				Do Do				*Do*	
	Do		Lunatick	7 *Do*			*Do*		
5				5th May 77			*Do*		
8	*Do*			7 Jany 76			*Do*		Gone to follow his Trade again
			Blind	14 *Do*			*Do*		
			Scurbutick		12th Jany 77				
	Do			27 July 75			*Do*		Security not to begg
	Do		Sore Legs	26 Oct *Do*			*Do*		Security not Begg
		Sickly	Scurbutick	27 Feb 75	*D*			Sickly	Sent back to the Infirmery
	H			21 June 75			H		Security not to begg
	Do		Sore Eye	11 March			H		Sent to the Infirmery
	Do			On Leve					
	Do			Discharge					
	Do		Lunatick	15 *Do*			*Do*		
	Do			26 *Do*			*Do*		Security not to Begg
	Do			22 June 77			*Do*		At his one Request
		Do		3 April				*Do*	Security not to Begg
		Do	Scurbutick	25 Apl 1776					Discharged without Fees
	Do					5th April 78			
	Do			13 *Do*			*Do*		Security not to beg
	Do			*Do Do*			*Do*		*Do Do*
	Do			*Do Do*			*Do*		*Do Do*
	Do			1 Feby 1776					By order of the Corporation without paying anything
	Do			27 *Do*			*Do*		*Do Do*
	Do				15 April 76				
	Do		Dropsical		18 June 75				
	Do		Blind	9 May					*Do Do*
	H					E 10 May	H		
	Do			9 May 75			H		Promised to leave the town
	Do			*Do Do*			H		*Do Do*
	Do		Palsey	118 [sic] *Do*			H		Security not to beg
	Do		a Criple	6 June			H		Security not to beg
	Do			*Do Do*	25 July 76		*Do*		Security not to begg
	Do			2 July			*Do*		Security not to beg
	Do			7 *Do*			*Do*		Security not to begg
	Do			*Do Do*			*Do*		Security to Labour
	Do			8 Mar 76			*Do*		By order of the corpn without Fees
	Do		Ripture		25 Feby 76				
	Do		a Criple	14 June 75			*Do*		Security not to begg
	Do			15 *Do Do*			*Do*		Security no to begg
		S	a Criple		1st Feby 77				
				8th Feby 78					
	Do		a Lunatick			2 Sept 1775	*Do*		Went out the street door [referring to second eloped date 14th July 86]
	Do					31 Augt 76			
	Do			10th March 79					
	H				D 27 Sep				
	Do			5 May 77			*Do*		
	Do					24 Sept 75	H		
	Do		Dumb			10 Augt 75	H		
	Do					15 *Do*	*Do*		
	Do			16 Augt 75					Security not to Beg
	Do			*Do Do*					*Do Do Do*
	Do		Lame	23 *Do*			*Do*		*Do Do Do*
	Do		Blind	*Do Do*			*Do*		*Do Do Do*
	Do			23 Novr 75			*Do*		

Current No.	Names	Age	Religion Roman Catholic	Protestant	Occupation	Late residence	Admitted	Voluntary	Compulsory
121	Luke Harwell	40		*Do*	Weaver	*Do Do*	12 Augt 75		*Do*
122	Alice Malouny	82	*Do*		Begar	*Do Do*	*Do Do*		*Do*
123	Mary Farguson	64	*Do*		*Do*	*Do Do*	14 *Do*		*Do*
124	Elinor Hehir	56	*Do*		*Do*	*Do Do*	*Do Do*		*Do*
125	Patt Sulivan	12	*Do*		Idler	*Do Do*	19 *Do*		*Do*
126	Danl Grady	80	*Do*		Dealer	C Clare	15 *Do*		*Do*
127	Felix Size	12	*Do*		Idler	C Limk	17 *Do*		*Do*
128	John Cusheen	13	*Do*		*Do*	*Do Do*	17 *Do*		*Do*
129	James Couney	17	*Do*		Begar	City Limk	20 *Do*		*Do*
130	Denis Ready	85	*Do*		Labourer	*Do Do*	22 *Do*		*Do*
131	Arthur McDaniel	82	*Do*		Farmer	Co *Do*	*Do Do*		*Do*
132	Mary Bearman	80	*Do*		Spiner	City *Do*	*Do Do*		*Do*
133	William O'Nail	9	*Do*		Idler	*Do Do*	25 *Do*		*Do*
134	John Dogherty	20	*Do*		Cleeveboy	*Do Do*	*Do Do*		*Do*
135	Owen Daly	42	R		Broguemaker	County Clare	8 Sepr 75	V	C
136	Aristatia Nash	60		P	Redu Gentlewoman	City Limerick	13 *Do*	*Do*	
137	Hugh Hays	70	*Do*		Labourer	County Clare	16 *Do*		*Do*
138	William Grady	76	*Do*		Mason	Citty Limerick	18 *Do*		*Do*
139	Patrick Lynch	42	*Do*		Weaver	County Kerry	24 *Do*		*Do*
140	Timothy Ryan	76	*Do*		Labourer	City Limerick	25 *Do*	*Do*	
141	Michael O'Harra	70	*Do*		*Do*	*DoDo*	27 *Do*		*Do*
142	Sarah Ryan	70	*Do*		Knitter	Cou Tipperary	29 *Do*		*Do*
143	Paul Connors	77	*Do*		Butcher	City Limerick	4 Octr 75		*Do*
144	Mary Fitzgerald	50	*Do*		Spinner	County Clare	6 *Do Do*		*Do*
145	Susanah Wescott	9		*Do*	an Orphan, and a Beggar	City Limerick	7 *Do Do*	*Do*	
146	Margt Brotherton	53	*Do*		Redud Housekeepr	*DoDo*	*Do Do Do*		*Do*
147	Elizabeth Sorrell	70	*Do*		Redud Hokeeper	County *Do*	9 *Do Do*		*Do*
148	William Garrett	25		*Do*	Stroler	Bandon	12 *Do Do*		*Do*
149	Margret Kennedy	55	*Do*		Spinner	City Limk	20 *Do Do*		*Do*
150	John Minahan	74	*Do*		Beggar	*Do Do*	23 *Do Do*	*Do*	
151	John FitzGerald	56	*Do*		Servant	*Do Do*	24 *Do Do*	*Do*	
152	Jane Russell	43		*Do*	*Do*	City Cork	27 *Do Do*		*Do*
153	Patrick Flannery	70	*Do*		Idler	Cou Limerk	30 *Do Do*		*Do*
154	Joan Bagwell	50	*Do*		Spiner	City Limk	2 Novr 75		*Do*
155	Richd Maloy	60		P	Sail Maker	Kilworth	3 Novr 75	V	
156	Mary Downes	60	R		Wosted Spinner	Coun Limerick	4 *Do Do*		C
157	Patrick Maroney	48	*Do*		Porter	City of *Do*	17 *Do Do*	*Do*	
158	Abigail Devitt	60	*Do*		Begar	*Do Do*	18 *Do Do*		*Do*
159	Sarah Tierny	60	*Do*		Servant	*Do Do*	*Do Do*		*Do*
160	Jane Morgan	80	*Do*		*Do*	*Do Do*	*Do Do*		*Do*
161	Daniel Gonan	67	*Do*		Weaver	*Do Do*	23 *Do*	*Do*	
162	Elizabeth Butler	30	*Do*		Begar	Cou Longford	25 *Do*	*Do*	
163	Mary McNamarra	75	*Do*		Servant	City Limerick	28 *Do*	*Do*	
164	Michael Conway	62	*Do*		Salt Boiler	*Do Do*	1st Decemr 75	*Do*	
165	Catherine Hurly	13	*Do*		Idler	Cou Limerick	2 *Do*		*Do*
166	Peter Murnane	93	*Do*		Taylor	*Do Do*	5 *Do*		*Do*
167	Cath Morrisson	78	*Do*		Servant	City Limerk	8 *Do*	*Do*	
168	Patrick Dunworth	77	*Do*		Writing Clerk	Cou *Do*	11 *Do*	*Do*	
169	Michael Shaughnesy	64	*Do*		Weaver	*Do Do*	12 *Do*	*Do*	
170	Darby Long	14	*Do*		*Do*	City Limerick	16 *Do*		*Do*
171	Patt Bourke	70	*Do*		Miller	County *Do*	22 *Do*	*Do*	
172	John Crawly	71	*Do*		Labourer	County Clare	29 *Do*	*Do*	
173	Mary Purcell	33	*Do*		Servant	City Limerick	*Do Do*		*Do*
174	Michael Mulvihil	65	*Do*		Labourer	County Kerry	31 *Do*		*Do*
175	Judith Daly	50	*Do*		Mantua maker	City Dublin	31 *Do*		*Do*
176	Jane Daly	12	*Do*		Stroling begar	*Do Do*	31 *Do*		*Do*
177	Margret Costola	60	R		Servant	County Clare	5 Jany 76		C

No. of bed	Condition when received Healthy	Sickly	Disease when received	How disposed of Discharged	Died	Eloped	Condition when discharged Healthy	Sickly	Observations
	Do			31 Jany 77					Without Fees
	Do		Deaff	12 Feby 76					Without Fees
	Do		Lunatick		16 Sepr 76				
		S	Fitts	23 Novr 75				S	Security not to Beg
	Do					19 *Do*	*Do*		
	Do				27th Decr 86				
	Do					*Do Do*			
	Do					*Do Do*			
	Do		Lunatick	*Do*					
	Do				30 Augt 75				
	Do			25 Augt 75			*Do*		Security not to beg
	Do			20 Feby 76					
	Do					10 Sepr 76			
	Do			Sepr 18 *Do*			*Do*		Never to forestall
	H		Disordered in his senses			26 May 76	*Do*		
	Do				21 Decr 75				
		Do		23 Novr 75				S	
	Do				30th July 79				
	Do		Lame	28 Sepr 75			*Do*		Security given not to beg
		Do	Rupture			19 May 76			
		Do		23 Novr 75			*Do*		Security not to beg
		Do		5 Octr *Do*				*Do*	Security not to beg
	Do		Sore leg		16 Decr 75				
	Do			13 *Do Do*			*Do*		Security not to beg
	Do			14 June 80, 21 June 84					Went Servt to the thread Maker
	Do			24 Apl 76	1st Jany 77				To be Dischargd without Fee
		Do	Laxative		14 Decer 75				
	Do		Dumb		Died 12th Decr 1775				
	Do			26 Octr 75			*Do*		Security not to Begg
	Do				19th Augt 76				
		Do		*Do*					
	Do			3 Novr 75			*Do*		Promised to leave the Town
	Do					5 of Augt 76			
	Do		Lunatick			14th July 86			Went out for a can of water
	H		Scurbutick			9 June 76	*Do*		
	Do			6 Novr 75					Security not to Beg
		S	Scurbutick	D 100 [sic]					
	Do		Blind	23 Novr 75			*Do*		Security not to beg
		S	*Do*	*Do Do*			*Do*		*Do Do Do*
		Do	Blind	*Do Do*			*Do*		*Do Do Do*
	Do				16 Decr 75				
	Do			26*Do*			*Do*		
	Do			19 July 76					Without fees
		Do		*D*					
		Do	Venerial Disease	3 April 76				*Do*	Discharged without Fees and sent to infirmery
	Do				14 April 76				
	Do			15 June 76					Discharged at her own request without fees
	Do		Almost Blind	*D*					
		S	Palsey	9 Augt 76				*Do*	Discharged without Fees & sent to the infirmery
	Do			19 Decr 75			*Do*		
		Do		15th Novr 77					And sent to the Gaol by the mayor
		Do		26 Augt 76			*Do*		
		Do	A Criple	*D*			*Do*		Security not to beg
		Do	Scurbutick			4th Jany 76		*Do*	
	Do			4th Jany 76			*Do*		To Quit the town without Fees
	Do			4th Jany 76			*Do*		To Quit the town *Do*
	H			24 Feby 76			H		By order of the Corporation on paying 1/1

Current No.	Names	Age	Religion Roman Catholic	Protestant	Occupation	Late residence	Admitted	Voluntary	Compulsory
178	John Cooper	5		P	A poor Orphan	City Limerick	4 Jany 76	V	
179	John Hartigan	50	*Do*		Brewers Servt	*Do Do*	12 *Do*	*Do*	
180	James Duprey	48	*Do*		Sailor	France	15 *Do*		*Do*
181	Judith Daly	50	*Do*		Mantua Maker	City Dublin	17 *Do*		*Do*
182	Patrick Lynch	42	*Do*		Weaver	Cou Kerry	18 *Do*		*Do*
183	Jane Daly	12	*Do*		Stroling Begar	City Dublin	23 *Do*	*Do*	
184	John Wayre	86	*Do*		Sadler	Tarbert C Kerry	26 *Do*	*Do*	
185	Timothy Sulivan	67	*Do*		Porter	City Limerick	4 Feby 76	*Do*	
186	Honor Cormackan	55	*Do*		Servant	Cou Clare	4 *Do Do*	*Do*	
187	Matthew Malouny	76	*Do*		Weaver	*Do Do*	9 *Do Do*	*Do*	
188	Morris Geiry	14	*Do*		Stroler	Count Limerick	11 *Do Do*		*Do*
189	Hanah Coffee	50	*Do*		Servant	*Do Do*	15 *Do Do*	*Do*	
190	Mary Hurly	20	*Do*		Stroler	*Do Do*	17 *Do Do*		*Do*
191	Simon McMahon	80	*Do*		Labourer	Cou Clare	22 *Do Do*	*Do*	
192	Elinor Fitzgerald	46	*Do*		Pedlar	*Do Do*	27 *Do Do*	*Do*	
193	Daniel Marony	20	*Do*		Butcher	Cou Limerick	28 *Do Do*	*Do*	
194	Mary Norton	18	*Do*		Servant	*Do Do*	29 *Do Do*	*Do*	
195	Mary O'Hearne	55	*Do*		Forestolar	*Do Do*	2 Mar 76		*Do*
196	Mary Holmes	45	*Do*		Servant	*Do Do*	7 Mar *Do*		*Do*
197	William Downes	70		*Do*	Gardiner	Coun Waterford	9 *Do Do*	*Do*	
198	Joan Halleran	100	R		Servant	Ballymorris C Clare	15 Mar 76		C
199	Eliz Wheeler	38		P	*Do*	City Limerick	*Do Do*		*Do*
200	James Frost	6		*Do*		*Do Do*	*Do Do*	V	
201	Garret Farrel	102	*Do*		Labourer	County Longfd	16 *Do Do*		*Do*
202	Mary Kennedy	80	*Do*		Calico printer	County Limerick	26 *Do Do*		*Do*
203	Ann Finucan	10		*Do*		City *Do*	28 *Do Do*	*Do*	
204	Jane Finucan	4		*Do*		*Do Do*	*Do DoDo*	*Do*	
205	William Finucan	2		*Do*		*Do*	*Do DoDo*	*Do*	
206	Miles Grady	80	*Do*		Reduced Farmer	Bruff C Limerick	6 April 76		*Do*
207	Timothy Marony	20	*Do*		Shoe boy	City Limerick	7 *Do Do*		*Do*
208	Margret Jones	80		*Do*	Cardmaker	*Do Do*	9 *Do Do*		*Do*
209	Mary Shaughnesy	80	*Do*		Servant	County *Do*	11 *Do Do*		*Do*
210	William Shaughnesy	78		*Do*	Boatman	*Do Do*	17 *Do Do*	*Do*	
211	Martin Noonane	70	*Do*		Labourer	*Do Do*	21 *Do Do*	*Do*	
212	James Lombert	72	*Do*		Weaver	City *Do*	22 *Do Do*	*Do*	
213	Henry Greene	70		*Do*	Labourer	County *Do*	25 *Do Do*	*Do*	
214	Michael Costola	2				*Do Do*	25 *Do Do*		
215	Darby Malouny	78	*Do*		Labourer	City Limerick	28 *Do Do*	*Do*	
216	Alice Malouny	83	*Do*		Begar	*Do Do*	29 *Do Do*		*Do*
217	Cath Tranor	54	*Do*		Servant	County *Do*	29 *Do Do*	*Do*	
218	Mary Norton	18	*Do*		*Do*	*Do Do*	3 May 76	*Do*	
219	Patrick Sulivan	76	R		Comb maker	County Clare	6 May 76	V	
220	Mary Kennedy	80	*Do*		Calico Printer	County Limerick	8 *Do Do*		C
221	Morris Dee	54	*Do*		Redud Shopkeeper	County Kerry	9 *Do Do*	*Do*	
222	Edmond O'Dwyer	62		P	Redud Gentleman	County Clare	10 *Do Do*	*Do*	
223	Mary Corkery	44	*Do*		Sempstress	City of Limerick	14 *Do Do*	*Do*	
224	Patrick Corkery	5	*Do*			*Do Do*	*Do DoDo*	*Do*	

No. of bed	Condition when received Healthy	Sickly	Disease when received	How disposed of Discharged	Died	Eloped	Condition when discharged Healthy	Sickly	Observations
	Do								
		S	Scurbutick		14th Decr 77				By order of the Corporation without Fees
	Do			1 Feby 1776					By order of the Corporation without Fees
			Do Do	8 Feby 76					
	Do		Lame	3 Feby 76			*Do*		
	Do			8 Feby 1776					By order of the Corporation without Fees
	Do			8 Feby 1776					by order of the Corporation without Fees
	Do			31st May 78					By the Mayor and Dr Creagh and gon to servas to Mr Hulet
	Do					20 Augt 76	*Do*		
	Do				19 April 76				
	Do			11 Feby					Without Fees To Quit the town
	Do		a Lunatic	9th Octr 83					By a committee
	Do			19 Feby 76			*Do*		Without Fees
		Do	Dropsical	8 March 76				*Do*	Discharged without Fees and sent to Infirmery
		Do	Pain in head & limbs	17 June 76				*Do*	Discharged without Fees and sent to Infirmery
		Do	Falling Sickness			9 Augt 76			
		Do	Foolish			30 April 76	*Do*		
		Do	Fitts & blind of Eye	21 Mar 76				*Do*	Discharged on Bail & on paying 3/8
	Do		Lame	21 *Do Do*			*Do*		Discharged on Bail & on paying £0 2 10
	Do		Blind		Died 12th April 1777				
		S			28th Decr 1776				
		Do	Almost Blind	15 June 1776					Discharged without Fees, gone to Cork
	H			*D*					*Do*
		Do	A Ripture	20 March 76				*Do*	Discharged without Fees Security not to beg
		Do		*Do*					Discharged on paying 1/7 with security not to Beg
	Do			*Do*					
		Do		*Do*					
		Do			2d Novr 77				
		Do	Rhumatic pains	15 June					Discharged on giving security not to beg & on paying 1/5
	Do		Lame			9 April 76	*Do*		
	Do				1st March 77				
	Do		Blind of One Eye	14 April 76			*Do*		Constable & Diet 2s 1d Security not to beg
		Do	Ripture & Asmatick	20th Jany 79					
		Do	Blind		7 May 76				
		Do			*D*				
		Do	Blind of One Eye	26 April 76				*Do*	Without Fees
						14th July 87			Went Out the street door
		Do			29th Decr 76				
		Do	Deaff	11 Jany 1777					without Fees
	Do				Died 24th Decr 1776				The house bougt her coffin
		Do	Foolish & Fitts			20 Jun 76			
		S	Blind	6 May 76				S	Without Fees
		Do		15 Aug					Discharged on paying 5 5
		Do	Asmatick			19 May 76			
		Do	Lame	11 July 76			*Do*		By order of the corpn without fees
	H				3d May 77				
	Do			Octr 4th 84 Discharged					

Current No.	Names	Age	Religion		Occupation	Late residence	Admitted	Voluntary	Compulsory
			Roman Catholic	Protestant					
225	Margret Gleeson	100	*Do*		Servant	County Clare	22 May 76		*Do*
226	Jane Duehig	64		*Do*	Sempstress	Northamton England	25 *Do Do*	*Do*	
227	William Edge	83		*Do*	Broken Soldier	County of Limerick	25 *Do Do*		*Do*
228	Catherine Brien	50	*Do*		Sempstress	*Do Do*	25 *Do Do*	*Do*	
229	Patrick Hallinan	9	*Do*			*Do Do*	25 *Do Do*	*Do*	
230	James Couney	70	*Do*		Weaver	City of Limerick	5 June 76	*Do*	
231	Michael Whealan	65	*Do*		Labourer	County Clare	6 *Do Do*	*Do*	
232	Mary Roch	29	*Do*		Servant	County Kilkeny	12 *Do Do*	*Do*	
233	Daniel Lyndon	69	*Do*		Labourer	County Clare	15 *Do Do*	*Do*	
234	Michael Nevill	78	*Do*		*Do*	County Kerry	17 *Do Do*		*Do*
235	Patrick Halinan	9	*Do*			County Limk	17 *Do Do*	*Do*	
236	Daniel Parsley	12		*Do*	a Charr Schoolboy	Dunkerin School	18 *Do Do*	*Do*	
237	Francis Taylor	76		*Do*	Weaver	County Limerick	19 *Do Do*	*Do*	
238	Owen Daly	42	*Do*		Brogue maker	County Clare	19 *Do Do*	*Do*	
239	Briget Ryan	46	*Do*		Spinner	*Do Do*	22 *Do Do*		*Do*
240	Thomas Shea	25	*Do*		Labourer	County Limerick	24 *Do Do*	*Do*	
241	Honor Daly	36	*Do*		Servant	*Do Do*	26 *Do Do*	*Do*	
242	William Murphy	76	*Do*		Taylor	County Limerick	26 June 76	*Do*	
243	Thomas Bourke	60	*Do*		Dealer	*Do Do*	*Do Do Do*	*Do*	
244	Margret Brotherton	53	*Do*		Redud Housekeeper	City Limerick	27 June 76	*Do*	
245	Mary McInerny	60	*Do*		Poor Widow	County Clare	29 June 76	*Do*	
246	Briget Cane	38	*Do*		Servant	County Limerick	1 July 76		*Do*
247	Margret Miller	26	*Do*		*Do*	County Kery	6 *Do Do*		*Do*
248	Honor Daly	36	*Do*		*Do*	County of Limerick	6 *Do Do*	*Do*	
249	Patrick Calaghan	98	*Do*		Chairman	*Do Do*	11 July 76		*Do*
250	Margret O'Laughlin	9	*Do*			City Limerick	11 *Do Do*		*Do*
251	Andrew O'Laughlin	5				*Do Do*	11 *Do Do*		*Do*
252	Catherine O'Laughlin	2				*Do Do*	11 *Do Do*		*Do*
253	Alice McDaniel	51	*Do*		Spiner	County Tyrone	15 *Do Do*		*Do*
254	Mary McNamarra	25	*Do*		*Do*	County Clare	16 *Do Do*	*Do*	
255	Thomas Shea	25	*Do*		Labourer	County Limerick	18 *Do Do*	*Do*	
256	Mary Millerd	76	*Do*		Servant	City Limerick	20 *Do Do*		*Do*
257	Simon Browne	76		*Do*	Gunsmith	*Do Do*	23 *Do Do*	*Do*	
258	John Slattery	25	*Do*		Labourer	Cou Limerick	24 *Do Do*		*Do*
259	James Malouny	37	*Do*		*Do*	Cou Clare	27 *Do Do*	*Do*	
260	Thomas Hamilton	30	*Do*		Stroler	Newry	29 *Do Do*		*Do*
261	Philip Molan	75	*Do*		Taylor	City Limerick	29 *Do Do*	*Do*	
262	Egmond m Ryan	70	*Do*		Stay-Maker	Cou Tiperary	29 *Do Do*	*Do*	
263	Daniel McNamara	63	*Do*		Baker	City Limerick	5 Augt 76		*Do*
264	Daniel Magrath	78	*Do*		Wheelwright	Rathkale C L	8 Augt 76	*Do*	
265	Darby Kenely	70	*Do*		Labourer	Cou Limerick	10 July 76		*Do*
266	Ignatious Ryan	70	*Do*		Stay-maker	C Tipperary	15 Augt 76	*Do*	
267	Catherine Moore	25	*Do*		Stroler	Cou Limerick	20 *Do Do*		*Do*
268	Elizabeth Barry	30		*Do*	Servant	Cou Cork	21 *Do Do*		*Do*
269	Michael Shaughnesy	64	*Do*		Weaver	Cou Limerick	21 *Do Do*	*Do*	
270	Margret Barnwell	60	*Do*		Spinner	City Dublin	24 *Do Do*		*Do*
271	Paul Murphy	73	*Do*		Labourer	Cou Clare	30 *Do Do*	*Do*	
272	Elinor Hays	30	*Do*		Servant	Cou Limerick	4 Sepr 76	*Do*	
273	Elizabeth Hays	9	*Do*			*Do Do*	*Do Do Do*	*Do*	
274	Timothy Hays	3	*Do*			*Do Do*	*Do Do Do*	*Do*	
275	Mary Hays	Monhs 4				*Do Do*	*Do Do Do*	*Do*	
276	Owen Daly	42	*Do*		Bromaker	Cou Clare	9 Sepr 76	*Do*	
277	Timothy Fahy	86	*Do*		Fisher-man	Cou Limerick	17 Sepr 76	*Do*	
278	John Murphy	10		*Do*		City Limerick	26 *Do Do*	*Do*	
279	Arthur Murphy	8		*Do*		*Do Do*	26 *Do Do*	*Do*	
280	Philip Shane	72	*Do*		Linen Weaver	Cou Limerick	2 Octr 76	*Do*	
281	Thomas Welsh	75	*Do*		Labourer	*Do Do*	5 Octr 76		*Do*

No. of bed	Condition when received Healthy	Sickly	Disease when received	How disposed of Discharged	Died	Eloped	Condition when discharged Healthy	Sickly	Observations
		Do		15 Aug					Discharged on paying 1/1 for the Constebles & giving security
	Do				Died 2d Octr 1792				The house bougt her coffin
	Do				22d Jany 77				
	Do		Blind	3 June 76			*Do*		Discharged without (erased) Security not to beg. fees 1/1
		Do	Dropsical & Ripture	27 May 76				*Do*	And sent to the Infirmery
		Do			3d Octr 76				
		Do	a Ripture		17th Octr 82				
		Do	a high Faver	1 July 76					By order without fees
		Do	Lame & a Ripture	10th Novr 78					By order of the Mayor
		Do	Lame			19 Augt 76		*Do*	
		Do	a Ripture		8 Feby 83				
	Do					20 June 76	*Do*		
		Do	Scurbutick	20 June 76				*Do*	Discharged without Fees
	Do		Disordered in his senses			17 July 76	*Do*		
	Do					13 Octr 76	*Do*		
	Do		Lame & Dumb			15 July 76		*Do*	
	Do		Lunatick	27 June 76				*Do*	Discharged without fees
		Do	a Ripture		20th May 79				
	Do				2d July 86				
		Do			Died				
		Do	Blind of one eye	18 July 76				*Do*	Without fees
	Do		Lunatick			3 July 76	*Do*		
		Do	a Criple	*Do*					
	Do		Lunatick	*Do*					
			a Ripture	11 July					On paying 1/1
	Do			18 July 76			*Do*		Without Fees
	Do			18 July 76			*Do*		Without Fees
	Do			18 July			*Do*		Without Fees
		Do		18 July 76				*Do*	On paying Two Shillings & One peny
	Do		Broken back	5th May 77			*Do*		
	Do		Lame & Dumb	*Do*					
		Do		~~15th August~~ 13th Oct 78	13th Oct 78				Discharged without Fees
		Do	a very Larg Ripture		25 Augt 76				
	Do		a Lunatick			13 Augt 76	*Do*		
		Do				4 Augt 76		*Do*	
	Do		Lame			2 Augt 76	*Do*		
		Do	Blind		Died				
		Do		30 July 76				*Do*	Without Fees
	Do			13 July 76			*Do*		On paying Three Shillgs & 1 peny
		Do	Ripture and Lame	*Do*					
		Do	Lame & Deaf		15th Feby 77				
		Do				7th July 77			
		Do	Fitts & Lame			*Do*			
	Do			11th May 77					
		Do	Palsey		Died				
		Do		31st Jany 76					
		Do	Sore Legs		Died				
	Do			22d May 77					Without Fees
	Do			*Do*					*Do*
	Do			*Do*					*Do*
				Do					*Do*
	Do		Disordered in his Senses			13 Octr 76	*Do*		
		Do	Rhumatick pains		12th Novr 86 Aged 96				Died 96 years of his Age
	Do			3 Octr 76			*Do*		Without Fees
	Do			25th Oct 78					By order and gon to a Trad
		Do	Asmatick			13th Octr 76		*Do*	
		Do	Paraletick & Lame	20 Decr					On paying 1/1

Current No.	Names	Age	Religion Roman Catholic	Protestant	Occupation	Late residence	Admitted	Voluntary	Compulsory
282	Winny Gavan	72	*Do*		Servant	*Do Do*	5 Octr 76		*Do*
283	Elizabeth Mahony	53		*Do*	Lace-maker	*Do Do*	8 Octr 76	*Do*	
284	James Mahony	11		*Do*		*Do Do*	8 Octr 76	*Do*	
285	Giles Quane	76	*Do*		Servant	*Do Do*	8 Octr 76	*Do*	
286	Patrick Kelly	75		*Do*	Tobaconist	City Limerick	17 *Do Do*	*Do*	
287	Owen Daly	42	*Do*		Broguemaker	Cou Clare	19 *Do Do*	*Do*	
288	Mary Malacky	82	*Do*		Servant	City Limerick	27 *Do Do*	*Do*	
289	Susanah Ryan	25	*Do*		Spinner	City Limerick	28 Octr 76	*Do*	
290	Elizth McNaile	43		*Do*	Spinster	City Limerick	3th Novr 76	*Do*	
291	Margt McNaile	5		*Do*		City Limerick	3th Novr 76	*Do*	
292	Nickls Hays	10	*Do*			Cou Limerick	5 Novr 76	*Do*	
293	Mathw Harthney	70	*Do*		Sarvt	Cou Clear	14 Novr 76	*Do*	
294	Edmond Scanllon	68		*Do*	Pumbouor	City Limerick	19 Novr 76	*Do*	
295	Roger Hynes	73	*Do*		Bucher	City Limerick	20 Novr 76	*Do*	
296	Patrick Regan	76	*Do*		Labor	City Limerick	22 Novr 76	*Do*	
297	Michl Ryan	75	Rom		Bucher	City Limerick	23 Novr 76		
298	John FitsGibbon	12	*Do*		Stroler	Cou Limk Frierstown	24 Novr 76		*Do*
299	John Hays	75	*Do*		Labourer	City Limerick	24 Novr 76	*Do*	
300	Henry Cornwell	17		*Do*	Stroler	Gallway	25 Novr 76		*Do*
301	Darby Sullavan	70	*Do*		Labourer	Cou Limk Castl Gaine	29 Novr 76	*Do*	
302	John Crawly	71	*Do*		Labourer	Cou Clare	29 Novr 76	*Do*	
303	Thos Welch	19	*Do*		Labourer	Cou Limerick	3th Decm 76		*Do*
304	Judy Dougherty	50	*Do*		Sarvt	Cou Limerick	7th Decm 76		*Do*
305	Wenney Dwyer	50	*Do*		Sarvt	Cou Clare	7th Decm 76	*Do*	
306	Willm Thomson	16		*Do*	Sweep	City Limerck	10th Decm 76	*Do*	
307	John Driskel	53	*Do*		Baker	City Limk	11th	*Do*	
308	Winny Gavan	72			Sarvt	Cou Limk	23th Decm 76		*Do*
309	Philip Clary	60	*Do*		Labor	Cou Limk Newcastle	24th Dem 76	*Do*	
310	Margt Crookes	50	*Do*		Dealer	City Kilkenney	27th Der 76	*Do*	
311	Elenr Kennely	68	*Do*		Beger	City Limerick	29th Decr 76		*Do*
312	Ann Bayly	30		*Do*	Imbrodrest	Cootehill	30 Decr 76	*Do*	
313	Elezth Ryan	4					31 Decr 76		
314	Jams McDanel	72		*D*	Brithis's maker	City Limerick	4th Jany 77	*D*	
315	Cathn Pickmar	60	*D*			City Limerick	5 Jany 77	*D*	
316	Ann McNeal	19		*D*	Servant	City Limerick	8th Jany 77	*D*	
317	Alexr Quin	70		*D*	Nealer	City Limerick	11th Jany 77	*D*	
318	Thoms Cowny	15					24 Jany 77		*D*
319	Dins Bryan	75	*D*		Butcher	City Limerick	31 Jany 77	*D*	
320	John Dillon	30	*Do*		Marrinor	County Limerick	4 Feby 77	*D*	
321	Cath Cloghesy	30	*D*		Servant	County Clear	4th Feby 77		
322	John Cloghesy	2					4th Feby 77		
323	Thoms Cowney	15					7th Feby 77		*D*
324	John Commens	60		*D*	Labr	County Tipy	10th Feby 77	*D*	
325	Davd Ellison	10			IdleBoy	City Limerick	16th Feby 77		*D*
326	Cathn Ellison	40	*D*		Servant	City Limerick	20 Feby 77		*D*
327	Mary Gidmore	19		*D*	Servant	City Limerick	26th Feby 77	*D*	
328	Nathl Gidmore	4 months				*D*	*D*		
329	Thoms Butler	46	*D*		Waver	City Limerick	27th Feby 77	*D*	
330	Margt Bridgman	38	*D*		Servant	County Limk	3rd march	*Do*	
331	Danl McNamara	63	*D*		Baker	City Limerick	18th march		*Do*
332	Wm Hines	10	*D*			*D*	25th March		*D*
333	Jams Dugan	17	*D*		Poor Scholer	County Limerick	28th March	*D*	
334	Mary Godfree	26	*D*		Spinster	City Limerick	2nd April		*D*
335	Chars Smith	12		*D*		*D*	5 Apr	*D*	
336	Pat Kelly	17	*D*		Poor scholer	County Galway	13th April	*D*	
337	Michl Skiddy	82	*D*		Labr	City Limk	14th April	*D*	
338	Sera Dunn	60	*D*		Servant	Kings County	15 April 77		*D*
339	Pat Purssel	70	*D*		Labr	County Limk	17 April 77		*D*

No. of bed	Condition when received Healthy	Sickly	Disease when received	How disposed of Discharged	Died	Eloped	Condition when discharged Healthy	Sickly	Observations
		Do		17 Octr 76				*Do*	On paying 4s 4d fr Fees & Constables
	Do			23 Decr					Without Fees
	Do			8 Octr 76					
		Do	Asmk & Rhumatick	25 Jany 77			*Do*		On paying 2s 6d for a shirt he lost
		Do	A very large Ripture	3 Augt 78					
	Do		Disordered in his senses			25th Decr 76			
	Do			31 Jany					Without Fees
	Do			23 Decr					Without Fees
	Do			15th Jany 78					By order of a Committee
	Do				27th May 78				
	Do			22 May 77					
	Do			27 Sepr 78					By order of a Committee
			Palsey	18 Apl 78					by his own Desire he having got a freehold from Mr Odle at Ballingarry
			Ruptuer & Asmatik			Eloped			
			Ruptuer	23 Decr					without without (sic) Fees
	Do			*D*					
			Lame Left Arm	*D*					
	Do			*Do*					
			Cripel			Eloped			
		Sickly		*Do*					
		Sickly		31s Jany 77			H		without Fees
		Sickly	Eavel			15th April 77			
			hard of hearing	31 Jany 77					without Fees
				22 June 77					At her one Request
	Do					*Do* 7th Feby 77			
	Do					12th March 77			
		Do		31st Jany 77					
					4th Feby 83				
		Do	Almost Blind	2nd Jany 77					
			Cripel	9th Jany 77				Sickly	
		D		20 Augt 77			H		
				29th Sepr 77					and Given to her mother
	D		Most Blind		2d Octr 82				
		D			25th Jany 77				
	D			7th March					Let her hire with the steward
		D		DO	20th Feby 77				
				31 Jany 77					
				Do					
		Dropsy	Dropsy		14th April 77				
	D			29th June 77			*D*		
				29 June 77			*D*		
				15 march 77					
				7 March					Discharged without Fees
				29 Augt 78					and gon to Dins Daffey
		Lame	Lame			7th June 78			
				12th Augt 78					By order of a Committee without fees and got the Clothes
	D			*Do*					
			Palsey		28-May-78				
			Rheumatism		6th March 1789				
	Do					31st May 81			with a New Shirt and Shoes he was Confind and broke out
						15th April 77			returned in 4 days and was discharged 11th Octr 1783
		D				31st March 77			
			Dropsey	12th April 77					
	D			26 April 77					to go to the Salt Water
			Lame	12 June 77					
			Rheumatisam			8th Octr 83			
		D		20th April 77					
			Palsey	22d May 77					paying 2s 2d

Current No.	Names	Age	Religion Roman Catholic	Protestant	Occupation	Late residence	Admitted	Voluntary	Compulsory
340	Elenr Heaphy	30				County Limk	22 April 77	*D*	
341	Mary Heaphy	19				*D*	22 April 77	*D*	
342	Jams Noonan	45		*D*	Sailor	*D*	25 April		*D*
343	Wm Walker	30	*D*		Stroler	County Limk	1st May 77		*D*
344	Cathn Lite	16	*D*		Servant	City Limerick	1st May 77		*D*
345	Martin Maguier	40	*D*			*D*	12th May 77	*D*	
346	Jos Dallehunty	66	*D*		Selor	County Tipy	12th May 77	*D*	
347	Pat Ryan	60	*D*		Garner	County Limk	14 May 77	*D*	
348	Owen Daly	43	*D*		Broguemakr	County Clare	19 May 77	*D*	
349	Jane Barrey	40	*D*		Stroler	Dublin	19 May 77		*D*
350	Wm Dwyer	60	*D*			County Clear	20 May 77		*D*
351	Rebeca Vaile	35		*D*	Servant	City Limerick	28th May 77	*D*	
352	Mortg Kerley	83	*D*		Miller	Libys Limk	28 May 77		*D*
353	Thoms Campble	62	*D*		Labr	*D*	28 May 77		*D*
354	Margt O'Brian	80	*D*		Spinster	City Limk	28 May 77		*D*
355	Mary McDonough	60	*D*		Servant	County Limk	28 May 77		*D*
356	Mary Deay	50	*D*		*D*	County Clear	28 May 77		*D*
357	Pat Pursel	70	*D*		Labr	County Limk	30 May 77		*D*
358	Davd Geiry	60	*D*		Pro Server	City Limerick	377		*D*
359	Elenr FzGerald	46	*D*		Pedlor	County Clear	3 June 77		*D*
360	Bridget Mckinsey	70	*D*		Servent	*D*	9th June 77		*D*
361	John Conner	12	*D*		Stroler	*D*	12th June 77		*D*
362	Elizth Finan	60		*D*	*D*		15 June 77		*D*
363	Wm Dunmade	7			Child	City Limk	21 June 77	*D*	
364	Bridget Hill	65		*D*	Servent	*D*	27 June 77		*D*
365	Bridget Barret	50	*D*		Stroler	Galway	2 July 77		*D*
366	Isac Stokes	40		*D*	Nailer	City Limk	2 July 77	*D*	
367	John Stokes	8		*D*	Child	*D*	*D*	*D*	
368	Josep Stokes	6		*D*	*D*	*D*	*D*	*D*	
369	ThomsCowny	15				*D*	D 77		*D*
370	Robert Heher	7			Child	*D*	18 July 77	*D*	
371	Cathn Healy	40	*D*		Servant	County Limk	24th July 77		*D*
372	Mary Healy	13			Child	*D*	*D*		*D*
373	Jno Healy	2			*D*	*D*	*D*		*D*
374	Eals Mallony	83	*D*		Begar	City Limk	25 July 77		*D*
375	Mary Homes	50	*D*		Servent	County Limk	27th July 77	*D*	
376	Mary Homes	8	*D*		Child	*D*	*D*	*D*	
377	Michl Homes	6	*D*		*D*	*D*	*D*	*D*	
378	Jane Leacy	55		*D*	Servent	City Cork	30 July 77		*D*
379	Tim Marony	21	*D*		Shoeboy	City Limk	31st July 77		*D*
380	Edmd Gail	26	*D*		Poorboy	County limk	1st Augt 77	*D*	
381	Jno Clark	3			Child	City Limk	*D*	*D*	
382	Darby Murnane	22	*D*		a Cleefboy	*D*	2nd Augt 77		*D*
383	Hana Fosett	78		*D*	Redud housekeeper	*D*	6 Augt 77	*D*	
384	Margt McCoy	28	*D*		Servant	*D*	*D*	*D*	
385	Cathn McCoy	7	*D*		Child	*D*	*D*	*D*	
386	Gart Cavanaugh	56	*D*		Treadmaker	City Dublin	8th Augt	*D*	
387	Mary Spelesy	11			Child		9 Augt		*D*
388	Dines Healy	64	*D*		Shoemaker	City Limk	16 Augt	*D*	
389	Mary Naughton	19	*D*		Servent	County Limk	17th *D*	*D*	
390	Edmd Collepy	4			Child	City Limk	17 *D*		*D*
391	Jno Maly	75	*D*		Weaver	*D*	21 *D*	*D*	
392	Ann Nevel	50	*D*		Cook	County Limk	23		*D*
393	Mary Carr	28		*D*	Servent	City Limk	26 *D*	*D*	
394	Honr Mourarty	32	*D*		*D*	*D*	31 *D*	*D*	
395	Ann Mourarty	1			Child	*D*	*D D*	*D*	
396	Mary Mourarty	8	*D*		*D*	*D*	*D*	*D*	

No. of bed	Condition when received Healthy	Sickly	Disease when received	How disposed of Discharged	Died	Eloped	Condition when discharged Healthy	Sickly	Observations
			Foolish	14th July 81					By 3 Governors she having the bad disorder
			Foolish						
			Dropsey		19th May 77				
	D					18th May 77			
			Lunatick	19th Sepr 77					By order of the mayor
			D			8-Mar-78			
			Sore Legg	11th Augt 78					To go to the Infermory
			Asmatick	16th Sepr					By order of the mayor & Mr Widenham
			Lunatick			30 Augt 77			
			D	22 May 77					
				22d May 1777					Paying 1s1d
			Lunatick	23 Sepr 1777					
	D					8th April 78			When at Labour abroad
			Palsey	28 May 77					Paying 1s 3p
			Most Blind	30 May 77					Paying 1s 3p fees & 6 Diet
	D			3 June 77					Paying 3s 1p
	D			28 May 77					Paying 1s 3p
			Palsey		29th July 77 & Confind by				
			D		6th April 78				
			Dropsical	11 July 77					
	D			28th June 77					On paying the Consle 1 1
	D					19th Sepr 77			
	D			21st June 77					To Quit the Town & County
	D				2nd June 79				
			Blind	27th June 77					on paying 1s-1d
				25th July 77			*D*		on paying 1-1
		D	Lunatick		18th Sepr 77				
				3 Jany 78					By order and gon to the Blue school
	D			5 March 79					By order of mayor and to go to the Blue School
			a Fool	~~3 Jany 78~~ 1st June 81					By order of a Committee
				29th Sepr 82					by 3 Governors
	H			28th Augt 77			*D*		paying 1-1
	D		Fool	*D*					*Do* 1-1
	D		Blind	*D*					
		D	Deaff	5th Novr 77					By order of a committee
			Lame	5th June					By order of a commitee
	D			*D D*					By order of a commitee
	D			*D D*					By order of a commitee
		D	Lame & Blind			31 July 77			
	D		Lame			31 Augt 77			
	D		Blind	10th Sepr 77 B.W.W order					
	D				30th June 1779				
	D		Rheumatisam			11 Sepr 77			
			Rheumatisam			28th June 1781			
	D				*Do*				Prosecutd & convicted for ye murder of her child
	D					*Do* 28th June 1781			
			Most Blind of one Eye			6 Jany 78			
	D					12th May 79			
	D			3 Jany 78		3rd Jany 78			By order of a Committee
			Foolish			19th Sepr 77			
	D			22 Octr 77					by order of the coporation
	D			21st Decr 77					and gon home to his son sick
		D	Lame	15 June 78					
			Lunatick	29th Augt 77					
	D			11th octr 77					
	D			*D*					
	D			*D*					

Current No.	Names	Age	Religion Roman Catholic	Protestant	Occupation	Late residence	Admitted	Voluntary	Compulsory
397	Pat Mourarty	3	*D*		*D*	*D*	31 Augt 77	*D*	
398	Michl Mourarty	5	*D*		*D*	*D*	*D*	*D*	
399	Michl Hanrehan	13	*D*			*D*	Sepr 3		
400	Elenr Fish	48		*D*	Servant		*D*	*D*	
401	Greas Fish	17		*D*	*D*		*D*	*D*	
402	Owen Dealy	43	*D*		Cobler	County Clear	8th Sepr	*D*	
403	Ann Night	30		*D*	Foolish	City Limk	8 *D*		*D*
404	Elenr Finnel	21	*D*		Servent	County Clear	10 Sepr		*D*
405	Mary Charlton	11	*D*		Child	City Limk	10 Sepr	*D*	
406	Honr Markaham	61	*D*		Servant	County Clear	13th *D*	*D*	
407	Tim Morony	21	*D*		Shoeboy	City Limk	14 *D*		*D*
408	Thoms Hall	46	*D*		Servent	County Clear	15 *D*	*D*	
409	James Hickey	46	*D*		Buckelmaker	City Limk	16 *D*		*D*
410	Margt Brian	30	*D*		Servant	County Limk	*D*		*D*
411	Mary Brian	6				*D*			*D*
412	John Brian	3				*D*			*D*
413	W Hayes	65	R			County Limk	22nd Sepr 77		*D*
414	Michl Towney	65	*D*		Labourer	*D*	*D*		*D*
415	Cathn Clohesey	30	*D*		Servant	County Clear	*D*	*D*	
416	Jno Clohesey	2					*D*	*D*	
417	Edmd Bannen	20	*D*		Servant	County Tipy	*D*	*D*	
418	Elenr Cahil	20	*D*		*D*	County Limk	23rd Sepr 77	*D*	
419	Ann McNeal	19		*D*	*D*	City Limk	24th Sepr 77	*D*	
420	Mary Naughton	19	*D*		Servant	County Limk	24th Sepr 77	*D*	
421	Jno King	60	*D*		Labourer	*D*	28 Sepr 77	*D*	
422	Cath Saeymor	65		*D*	Servent	City Limk	29th *D*	*D*	
423	Ann Ripton	40		*D*	Schoolmistris	County Waxford	8th 8ber	*D*	
424	Jno Peevers	50	*D*		Sawier	County Limk	8 octr		*D*
425	Jno Industry	2					9th octr	Left at door	
426	Tobias Roche	84	*D*		Schoolmaster	County Kildear	11 *D*	*D*	
427	Honr Morearty	32	*D*		Servant	City Limk	15 Octr	*D*	
428	Ann Morearty	1	*D*		Child	*D*	*D*	*D*	
429	Mary Morearty	8	*D*		*D*	*D*	*D*	*D*	
430	Michl Morearty	5	*D*		*D*	*D*	*D*	*D*	
431	Pat Morearty	3	*D*		*D*	*D*	*D*	*D*	
432	Mary Flarty	68	*D*		a Redud housekeepr	City Limk	19th octr	*D*	
433	Pat Flarty	70	*D*		Garner	County Galway	25th Octr	*D*	
434	Margt Mullens	2	*D*		Child		31st Octr 77	Left at door	
435	Martin Garlin	68	*D*		Weaver	County armagh	Novr 2 77		*D*
436	Jas McCluard	70		*D*	Cutler	City Limk	29th Novr 77	V	
437	Richd Jackson	12		*D*		*D*	1st Decr 77	*D*	
438	Elizth Woulf	46	*D*		Stroler	*D*	6 Decr 77		*D*
439	Elenr Fish	48		*D*	Servant	Tiparery	*D*	*D*	
440	Wm Ellison	20	*D*		*D*	City Limk	8 Decr 77		
441	Mary Malacky	83	*D*		Servant	*D*	10th Decr 77	*D*	
442	Robt Guppy	8		*D*		*D*	10 Decr 77	*D*	
443	Charles Earls	49	*D*		Stroler	City Cork	14th Decr		*D*
444	Mary Moor	40		*D*	Redud Hkeeper	Dublin	14 Decr	*D*	
445	Diana Guppy	4		*D*		City Limk	27 Decr	*D*	
446	Cath Fowlow	14	*D*		Servant	City Cork	3 Jany 78		*D*
447	Mat Sullivan	80	R		R Housekeeper	County Kerry	6th Jany 78	*D*	
448	Mary Garlan	58	*D*		Servent	County Limk	13 Jany 78	*D*	
449	Morgan O'Brian	54	*D*		Stroler	County Clear	13 Jany 78		*D*
450	Dins Healy	64	*D*		Cordwinder	City Limk	15 Jany 78	*D*	
451	Margt Power	28	*D*		Servent	County Waterford	16th Jany 78		*D*
452	Cornls Culligan	52	*Do*		Boatman	County Clear	19th Janry 78	*Do*	
453	Geo Jackson	47		P	Weaver	City Limk	21 Jany 78	*D*	
454	Frans Barber	47		*D*	Rd Gentelwomn	County Limk	23rd Jany 78	*D*	
455	Richd Butler	76	*D*		Stroler	County Clear	28th Jany 78		*D*
456	Pat Buygo	27	*D*		Servant	City Dublen	28 *D* 78	*D*	

No. of bed	Condition when received Healthy	Sickly	Disease when received	How disposed of Discharged	Died	Eloped	Condition when discharged Healthy	Sickly	Observations
	D			*D*					
	D			*D*					
	D					27th Novr77			
	D			4th sepr 77			*D*		and gon to servis
	D			21st octr 77			*D*		and Gon to servis
	D		Lunatick			12th March 78			
			D	15th June 79					
		D		6th March 78					
	D			*Do*					
		D	Most Blind	7 Augst 78					without Fees
			Lame			14th Decr 77			
		D	Rheumatisam		7th octr 77				
			Lame	20th Sepr 77					By the mayor's order
						19th Sepr 77			
						D			
						D			
		D	Lunatick	25th Sepr 77					and sent to the City Bridewell By order of mayor
				23rd Sepr 77					On paying 1-11 by *D*
	D			9th 8ber 78					By order of a Committee
	D			9 8ber 78					*Do*
			Lame	2nd octr 77					By order of Mr Widenham and to go home to his own county
						10th Decr 77			and to go home to his own country
	D			8th Feby 78					
					16th June 79				
					14 Janry 78				
	D	*D*		6 March 78			*D*		By order a Comittee
	D					8th octr 77			
					12th Jany 78				
			Rheumatisam		26th Decr 77				
	D					8th Decr 78			
	D				24th April 78				
	D			25th August					Without Fees
	D				16th Augt 78				
	D			*Do*					
		D	Rheumatisam		9th Novr 77				
	D			1st Novr 77					
					31st May 78				
			Rheumatisam		11th Feby 78				
		D		11th Octr 83					By a Committee
	D					10th May 77			
				6 March 78					By order of a Committee
	D			11th Jany 78					
	D			on furlow					
	D			22 March 78					
	D				27 March 79				
				3d Jany 78					
				15th Jany 78					By order of a Committee
				13th Augt 80					By Henry Rose Esqr
						7th April 78			
	D			28th March 78					To Quit the Town
			Rheumatisam	8th Feby 78					
				26th Jany 78					By the mayor order and pg 4 1
					2nd Feby 78				
	D			18th Jany 78					By order of the Mayor and paying 1 1
			Fits Leam & Rupter			16th June 78			
				6th March 78					By order of a Comittee
		D				12th Feby 78			
				30 Jany 78					By order of the Mayor and paying 1 10
		D		7th Feby 78					

Current No.	Names	Age	Religion Roman Catholic	Protestant	Occupation	Late residence	Admitted	Voluntary	Compulsory
457	Jno Bourk	66	*D*		Sawier	City Limk	29th Jany 78		*D*
458	Wm Carmody	28	*D*		Fool	*D*	31 *D* 78	*D*	
459	Cath Light	18	*D*		Servant	*D*	6th Feby 78		*D*
460	Pat Barrey	50	*D*		Taylor	*D*	8 Feby 78		*D*
461	Saml Pecock	47		*D*		County Limk	9th Feby 78	*D*	
462	William Hayes	65	*D*			City Limk	13th Feby 78		*D*
463	Margt Light	55	*D*		Servant	*D*	13 Feby 78	*D*	
464	Jno McDermod	11		*D*		*D*	14 Feby 78	*D*	
465	Michl McDermod	6		*D*		*D*	14 Feby 78	*D*	
466	Danl Kerwickcan	56	*D*		Stroler	County Cork	19 Febry 78		*D*
467	Tim Keran	50	*D*		*D*	County Sligo	23 Feby 78		*D*
468	Cathr Shaughnessy	30	*D*		Servant	City Limk	23 Feby 78	*D*	
469	Edwd Godfree	80	*D*		*D*	County Limk	28 Feby 78	*D*	
470	Thoms Grady	70	*D*		Labr	City Limk	5 March 78	*D*	
471	Pat Ryan	69	*D*		*D*	County Limk	6 March 78	*D*	
472	Edmd Saymor	74		*D*	Waver	City Limk	9 March 78	*D*	
473	Dins Healy	60	*D*		*D*	County Clear	10 March 78	*D*	
474	Saml Johnston	45		*D*		County Limk	10 March 78	*D*	
475	Wm Trasy	39	*D*		Glover	City Limk	15 March 78	*D*	
476	Morgn Madden	70	*D*		Taylor	County kery	17 March 78	*D*	
477	Bridget Smith	80	*D*		Servant	County Clear	17 March 78	*D*	
478	Cath Murphy	35	*D*		Spinster	City Limk	19 d 78		*D*
479	Wm Murphy	6 months				*D D*	19 *D* 78		*D*
480	Elonr Dunn	43	*D*		Servant	*D D*	22 *D* 78		*D*
481	Dins Hayes	50	*D*		Waver	*D D*	22 *D* 78		*D*
482	Jno Gleeson	53	*D*		Sleater	County Limk	22 March 78		*D*
483	James Conner	77	*D*		Cordwinder	*D*	23 *D* 78	V	
484	Pat Morrison	50	*D*		*D*	*D*	26 *D* 78	*D*	
485	Darby Hayes	50	*D*		Delor	County Limk	27 *D* 78		*D*
486	Edwd Johnston	21		*D*	Servant	*D D*	28 *D* 78	*D*	
487	Lars Lahif	50	*D*		Cloather	City Limk	29 *D* 78	*D*	
488	Cath Murphy	35	*D*		Spinster	*D*	29 *D* 78		*D*
489	Wm Murphy	6 months				*D*	29 *D* 78		*D*
490	Edmd FzGibbon	29	*D*		Labourer	County Limk	30 *D* 78	*D*	
491	Maus Hinchy	60	*D*		Cooper	*D*	1s April 78		*D*
492	Sevel Parson	34		*D*	Sealor	Swedlan	2 April 78		*D*
493	Jeremia	1 Day					6 April 78	*D*	
494	Rogr Clanchy	70	*D*		Waver	City Limerick	10th *D* 78	*D*	
495	Cath Earcourt	14	*D*		Servant	*D*	13 *D* 78	*D*	
496	Pat Carrel	25	*D*		Fool	County Limk	16 *D* 78		*D*
497	Elenr Sanders	36		*D*	Ribonwaver	City Dublin	19th *D* 78	*D*	
498	Ales Sanders	15		*D*	*D*	*D*	*D*	*D*	
499	Robt Sanders	13		*D*	*D*	*D*	*D*	*D*	
500	Michl Sanders	6		*D*		*D*	*D*	*D*	
501	Geo Sanders	4		*D*		*D*	*D*	*D*	
502	Thoms Sanders	1		*D*		*D*	*D*	*D*	
503	Mor Mynehan	9	*D*			City Limk	25th April 78	*D*	
504	Mary Mynehan	6	*D*			*D*	*D*	*D*	
505	Jno Nail	70	*D*		Cooper	County Limk	26th April		*D*
506	Maus McDanel	86	*D*		Smith	*D*	29 Apr	*D*	
507	Mary Fahy	70	*D*		Spinster	*D*	2nd May	*D*	
508	Jno Gorman	9	*D*			City Limk	5th May	*D*	
509	Cat Ready	79	*D*		Servant	*D*	6 May	*D*	
510	Michl McEntier	60		*D*	Taylor	*D*	7th May	*D*	
511	Wm Conner	60	*D*		Mason	*D*	8 *D*	*D*	
512	Pat Ryan	61	*Do*		Garner	County Limk	15th May 78	*D*	
513	Wm Hayes	65	*Do*			*D*	*D*		*D*
514	Elenr Fennel	21	*Do*		Servant	County Clear	*D*		*D*
515	Elenr Shaughnesy	30	*D*		Spinster	City Limk	*D*	*D*	

No. of bed	Condition when received Healthy	Sickly	Disease when received	How disposed of Discharged	Died	Eloped	Condition when discharged Healthy	Sickly	Observations
				29th Jany 78					By paying 1s 4d by the Mayors orders
			Lunatick	21st Decr 78					By order of a committee see the Remark Book
			D			12th Feby 78			
				6th March 78					
			Mad			19th Feby 78			
				21st Decr 78					By order of a Committee see the Remark Book
				14 April 79					By order of committee. 12 Apr to go to Sarvis
				Do					
	D			6th March 78			*D*		By order of a Comittee
	D			6th March 78			*D*		By order of a Comittee
	D			6 March 78			*D*		By D
		Do			6th Feby 81				
		D			18th Der 79				
				Do					
				12 March 78					By paying 6
						11th April 79			
						7th June 78			
				17th March 78					By the mayor
					31st Jany 83				
					8th Novr 78				
				22 March 78					By the mayors order and paying 2 1
				D D D					
			Rheumatisam	10th June 80					By a Committee
			Blind	24th March 78					
			Criple		18th April 78				
			Rheumatisam		23d Octr 80				
	D					31st April 78			
						19th April 78			
		D		17th April 78					
			Sore Eyes	31st May 78					By the mayor and Dr Creagh
						9th April 78			
						9th April 78			
				11 April 78					By order of Thom Smith Es
				3rd April 78					By paying 1s 7
				3 *D* 78					Paying 1s 4d
					30th April 78				
		D				14th March 79	*D*		
				9th May 87					She haveing Gon to servis
				7 Augst 78					Without Fees
				17th June 78					By order of a Committee
				D					By order of a Committee
				D					By order of a Committee
				D					By order of a Committee
				D					By order of a Committee
					2nd June 78				
	D			*Do*					
	D								
				15th June 78					By paying 1s 1d
	D				10th May 78				
	D			30th March 78					By the Mayors orders
	D			26th Sepr 78					By order of a Committee
						18th Elopd			From Church with the Cloathing
			Asmetick		13th June 79				
	D			13th April					By order of a Comittee the 12 April with house Cloathing
						17th May 78			
			Most Blind	7th March 78					
	D			15th June 78					By order of a Comitee

Current No.	Names	Age	Religion Roman Catholic	Protestant	Occupation	Late residence	Admitted	Voluntary	Compulsory
516	Honr Shaughnesy	8	*D*			*D*	15th May 78	*D*	
517	Ann Shaughnesy	8	*D*			*D*	*D*	*D*	
518	Anstes Shaughy	2				*D*	*D*	*D*	
519	Geo Lloyd	24		*D*		County Limk	16 May 78		*D*
520	Edwd Fzgibbon	29	*D*		Labourer	*D*	17 May 78	*D*	
521	Mary Hartny	60	*D*		Servant	*D*	26 *D* 78	*D*	
522	Elezth Grady	34		*D*	*D*	England	27 *D* 78	*D*	
523	Charles Callens	64	*D*		Labourer	County Limk	*D* 78	*D*	
524	Jno Hasett	74	*D*		*D*	City Limk	28th 78	*D*	
525	Mary Sheehan	86	*D*		Servant	*D*	D 78		*D*
526	Bridget Dealy	9	*D*			*D*	30th 78	*D*	
527	Edwd Hayes	69	*D*		Butcher	County Limk	3 June 78	*D*	
528	John Wade	73		*D*	Waver	City Dublen	8 June 78	*D*	
529	Cather Barrey	12	*D*		Servant	City Limk	14 June 78	*D*	
530	Elenr Shaughnessy	30	*D*			*D*	16th June 78	*D*	
531	Honr Shaughnessy	8	*D*			*D*	*D*	*D*	
532	Ann Shaughnessy	8	*D*			*D*	*D*	*D*	
533	Anstes Shaughnessy	2				*D*	*D*	*D*	
534	Cath Stokes	62	*D*		Sarvant	County Clear	17 June 78		*Do*
535	Darby Linehan	26			Fool	County Limk	*D* 78		*D*
536	Morgn O'Brian	54	*D*		Stroler	*D*	22 June 78		*D*
537	Pat Brenon	64	*D*		S Weaver	City Dublen	23 *D* 78	*D*	
538	Corns Cullegan	52	*D*		Boatman	County Clear	24 June 78	*D*	
539	Jno Bourk	66	*D*		Sawer	City Limk	25 *D D*		*D*
540	Jams Ryan	31	*D*		Stoler	County Limk	25 *D D*		*D*
541	Simn Kennoo	60	*D*		Tinkerd	City Limk	25 *D D*		*D*
542	Eals Dunn	20	*D*		Servant	*D D*	25 *D D*		*D*
543	Ann Caughlan	13	*D*		*D*	Edenderey	25 *D D*		*D*
544	Jno Power	19	*D*		Servant	County Tipy	26th June 78		*D*
545	Mary Nugant	24	*D*		Stroler	County Waxford	*D D*		*D*
546	Easter Nugant	2			Child	*D*	*D*		*D*
547	Bridgt McMahon	19	*D*		Stroler	City Limk	*D*		*D*
548	Alexr McMahon	5			Child	*D*	*D*		*D*
549	Powel Boden	38	*D*		Sealor	France	*D*		*D*
550	Wm Hays	66	*D*		Stroler	City Limk	*D*		*D*
551	Tim Downs	76	*D*		Cooper	*D*	29 June 78	*D*	
552	Mary Manser	14		*D*	Servant	County Tipy	30 June 78	*D*	
553	Edmd Geal	27	*D*		Blindboy	City Limk	6 July 78	*D*	
554	Jno Tierny	36	*D*		Stroler	County Limk	8 July 78		*D*
555	Dins Deely	38	*D*		L Waver	*D*	10 July 78		*D*
556	Tim Canney	84	*D*		Labourer	County Clear	11th *D D*	*D*	
557	Lars Lahif	50	*D*		Cloather	City Limk	11th *D*	*D*	
558	Pat Pendergast	60	*D*		Labourer	County Tipy	20th *D*	*D*	
559	Maryan Fzgerald	24		*D*	Servant	County Meath	*D D*	*D*	
560	Ann McNail	20		*D*	*D*	City Limk	24 *D* 78	*D*	
561	Pat Hussey	66	*D*		Waver	*D*	*D D*	*D*	
562	Eals Mulouny	86	*D*		Servent	City Limk	25 *D*		*D*
563	Sisley Napper	58		*D*	*D*	Downpatrick	27 *D* 78		*D*
564	John Dun	74	*D*		Servant	County Limk	29 *D* 78	*D*	
565	Jery Hurley	75	*D*		*D*	County Cork	30 *D* 78	*D*	
566	Richd Brierly	58		*D*		Yorkshier	31 *D* 78	*D*	
567	John Salmon	12		*D*		County Limk	3 Augt 78	*D*	
568	Bridget Keef	14	*D*		Servant	City Limk	5 Augt 78	*D*	
569	Pat Hanrahan	75	*D*		Labourer	County Limk	13th *D* 78	*D*	
570	Thoms Hopkens	68		*D*	Waver	City Limk	15 *D* 78	*D*	
571	Ambs Hopkens	7		*D*		*D*	*D D* 78	*D*	
572	Charlot Adams	17	*D*		Servant	England	19 *D* 78	*D*	
573	Jone McCarty	67	*D*		Delar	City Limk	20 *D* 78	*D*	

No. of bed	Condition when received Healthy	Sickly	Disease when received	How disposed of Discharged	Died	Eloped	Condition when discharged Healthy	Sickly	Observations
	D			*D*					By order of a Comittee
	D			*D*					By order of a Comittee
	D			*D*					By order of a Comittee
				17th May 78					By the Mayor and pg 1s 1d
		D		12th July 78					and gon to the Informery
			Asmatick		23rd Octr 78				
		D		*Do*					
		D		27th June 78					
					21st March 81				
					9th Decr 78				
			Rheumatisam		18th Octr 78				
				30th July 78					By the Mayor
				18th July 78					By Mrs Massey
				2d Octr 78					By order of a Committee
				D					By order of a Committee
				D					By order of a Committee
					19th Augst				
					4th May 81				
				17th Augst 78					By order of Capn Hill on paying 1/1
				7 Augst 78					
				14th octr 78					And gon to work at his trade in Town
				Do					
				Do					
			Lame	14th July 78					By order of Mayor & Mrs Massy pay 1/1
				30th June 78					By order of the Mayor and Pg 2 4
				26th June 78					By order of a Comitee and pg 1 6
				26th Sepr 78					and gon to Mr Daffy to servis
			Lame	7 July 78					Without Fees
				27th June 78					By order of a Committee and pg 1/1
				D					
				D					By paying 1-1
				D					
				D					By paying 1-5
				24th Octr 78					By order of a Committee and not to be seen in the streets
				26th Sepr 78					By order of a Committee
				Do					
			Blind	19th Augt 82					by a committee
			Foolish	29th Sepr 78					By order of a Committee and to go to Bruff
				11th July 78					
				26 July 78					
			Most Blind	28 Augt 79					
			Most Blind			24th May 80			and Robb'd John Cain of a loose coat and Shirt
				Do July 11					
						2nd 8ber 78			
			Sore leg	14 Augt 78					and gon to the Informery
					29th Augt 78				
				28th July 78					Without fees
				7 Augst 78					*Do*
			Lame			Eloped 9 8ber 78			
					6 Augt 78				
				7th Augt 78					
		D		13 Augt 78					By order of Mr Phillip
				6th 8ber 78					By order of a Committee
			Lame	28th June 80					By order of Walter Widenham Esqr
				11th Octr 83					By a committee
				Turned out					By order of a Committe for being a Pergerure
				27 Jany 80					

Current No.	Names	Age	Religion		Occupation	Late residence	Admitted	Voluntary	Compulsory
			Roman Catholic	Protestant					
574	Owen Dealy	46	*D*		Cobler	County Clear	21 Augt 78	*D*	
575	Jno Lynch	80	*D*		Carpenter	City Limk	22 *D* 78	*D*	
576	Bridgt Dillon	9	*D*			*D*		*D*	
577	Margt Dillon	6	*D*			*D*		*D*	
578	Edmd Tierney	60	*D*		Labourer	*D*	25 *D* 78		
579	Ters Dannelon	78	*D*		Blacker	County Clear	28 *D* 78	*D*	
580	Bridget McKensey	71	*D*		Stroler	City Limk	3rd Sepr 78		*D*
581	Pat Houregan	8	*D*		Poor Boy	County Clear	6th Sepr 78	*D*	
582	Mary Fzgeral	2					7th78	Left at door	
583	Honr Farrel	70	*D*		Rd H keeper	City Limerick	8th *Do* 78		*D*
584	Edmd Shannehan	24	*D*			*D*	8th 78		*D*
585	Elezth Lindon	25	*D*		Rd H Keeper	kings County	8th *D* 78	*D*	
586	Mary Griffen	5				*D*	8th *D* 78	*D*	
587	Andw Griffen	18 month				*D*	8th *D* 78	*D*	
588	Ann Griffen	4 months				*D*	8th *D* 78	*D*	
589	Jno Heffernan	10		*D*	Idle Boy	County Limk	9 *D* 78		*D*
590	James Macowen	75		*Do*	Sarvant	King County	14 *Do* 78	*Do*	
591	Geo Asson	56		*D*	S Waver	City Dublin	15 *D* 78	*D*	
592	Elenr Russel	39	*D*		Servant	County Limk	15 *D* 78	*D*	
593	A Dum Woman sent in by Mr Grady					County Limk	19 Sepr 78	*D*	
594	Elenr Brian	27	*D*		Servant	County Limk	20 *D* 78	*D*	
595	Cors Brian	12	*D*			*D*	*D D D*	*D*	
596	Pat Brian	10	*D*			*D*	*D D D*	*D*	
597	Ann Brian	8	*D*			*D*	*D D D*	*D*	
598	Mat Brian	6				*D*	*D D D*	*D*	
599	Eliz Brian	2				*D*	*D D D*	*D*	
600	Cathr Cook	50	*D*		Servant	City Limk	21 Sepr 78		*D*
601	Honr Brown	3				County Limk	*D D D*	*D*	
602	Ann McNamara Kearney		80	*D*		Servant	City Limk	22 *D D*	*D*
603	Honr Dealy	38	*D*		*D*	*D*	29 *D D*	*D*	
604	Margt Harvey	40		*D*	*D*	*D*	30 *D*	*D*	
605	Luces Mullouny	30		*D*	Taylor	County Clear	30 *D*	*D*	
606	Bridget Spence	40	*D*		Servant	City Limk	3rd octr 78	*D*	
607	Bridget Spence	12			Child	*D*	*D*	*D*	
608	Andw Spence	4			*D*	*D*	*D*	*D*	
609	Alexr Spence	3			*D*	*D*	*D*	*D*	
610	James Conseden	2			*D*	*D*	*D*	*D*	
611	Geo Aston	56		*D*	Hoser	City Dublin	4 octr 78	*D*	
612	Eppr Pender	74		*D*	Cordwinder	County Tipy	7th *D* 78	*D*	
613	Jno Marrony	55	*D*		Taylor	County Limk	11th *D* 78	*D*	
614	Jno Kean	75	*D*		Tanner	City Limk	11 *D* 78	*D*	
615	Bridgt Shaughnessy	78	*D*		Servant	*D*	13 *D* 78		*D*
616	Jno Deegedan	6				*D*	13 *D* 78	*D*	
617	Honr Deegedan	14			Whore	*D*	13 *D* 78	*D*	
618	Aley Kelly	6				*D*	15 *D* 78	*D*	
619	Mary Fzgarald	70	*D*		Servant	County Limk	17th *D* 78	*D*	
620	Mathw Harthney	72	*Do*		Sarvt	County Clear	21 *Do* 78	*D*	
621	Sara Trueman	36		*Do*		Queen County	21 *Do* 78	*Do*	
622	Margt Caughlan	12	*D*			City Limk	27th Octr 78	*D*	
623	Alies Mynehan	35	*D*		Servant	*D*	30th *D* 78	*D*	
624	Alies Mynehan	2				*D*	30th *D* 78	*D*	
625	Tim Ryan	50	*D*		Waver	*D*	2 Novr 78	*D*	
626	Margt Morarty	18	*D*		Servant	*D*	2 Novr 78	*D*	

No. of bed	Condition when received Healthy	Sickly	Disease when received	How disposed of Discharged	Died	Eloped	Condition when discharged Healthy	Sickly	Observations
				23 Augt 78					By order and pg 1s 0d
			M Blind	*Do*					
				7th Decr					
				Do					
						27th June 80			
			Ripture		20th Sepr 78				
				26th Sepr 78					By order of a Comit [faded]
	D					10th Jany 81			went to Lady Harstronge and got a ticket to go to Charter School
				10 Jany					
			Lunitick		22d Novr 1778				
	D			9th Sepr 78					By order of Mr Ingram on paying 1s 1d
	D			12 Sepr 78					
	D			*D D D*					
	D			*D D D*					
	D			*D D D*					
						Eloped 13 Sepr 78			
	Do			27th Sepr 78					By order of a Committee and to go to his own country
			Most Blind & Lunitick	27th Sepr 78					By order of a Committee and to go to his own country
				28th *Do*					
					27th Octr 78				
	D			28 Novr 80					
	D				9th Decr 79				
	D				7th Decr 79				
	D				11th *Do*				
	D				13 Decr 79				
	D				7th Decr 79				
	D			26 Sepr 78					By order of a Committee and paying 1 1
	D					13th Sepr 79			
				Lame		6th Sepr 85			
			Dimness in her sight			26th June 80			
			Lunitick			27 sepr 79			
	D			17th May 79					By order of a Committee of the 8th May
	D			*Do*					
	D			*Do*					
	D			17th May 79					By order of a Committee the 8 May 79
	D				13th June 79				
		D	Lunitick		10th Novr 78				
			Rupture	18th Novr 78					And gon to his owne home
		D		23 Novr 78					By order
		D	Asmatick		22d Augt 82				
			Most blind	27th Decr					
	D			21st March 85		27th May 1784			By a Comm (all erased)
	D			15 Octr 78					By Mrs Mahon's order she promising not to beg
	D			4th Novr 81					by Capt Hill who bound her to a Dyer
	D				11th Octr 79				
		D			27 July 79				
	Do		Cripel	9 March 79					By order and to go to her owne Country
		D		10th Novr 78			*D*		By order of the Mayor to Capn Hill
	D			10th Jany 79			*D*		By order of Mr Phillips
	D			*D D D*			*D*		By order of Mr Phillips
		D	Astmatick	4th Novr 78			*D*		Dischd to go to the Infiermey
		D		10th Novr 78			*D*		By order of the Mayor to Cap Hill

Current No.	Names	Age	Religion Roman Catholic	Protestant	Occupation	Late residence	Admitted	Voluntary	Compulsory
627	Ann Brown	34		*D*	Balit Singer	City Dublin	5th Novr 78		*D*
628	Mary Clifford	26	*D*		Servt	County Limk	7 *D* 78	*D*	
629	Thomas McCormick	10	*D*			Couy Dublin	9th *D* 78	*D*	
630	Patrick Bourk	72	*D*		Millor	City Limk	18th *D* 78	*D*	
631	Michl Coleman	56	*D*		Baker	*D*	26th *D* 78	*D*	
632	Jams Bourk	11	*D*			County Limk	27th *D* 78	*D*	
633	Mat Mullouny	13	*D*		Tobaco Boy	County Clear	28 *D* 78	*D*	
634	Mat Speeran	55		*D*	Labour	Cy Limk	2d Decr 78	*D*	
634	Geo Fennel	78		*D*	Bucher	City Limk	*D D D*	*D*	
635	Edmd Fennel	4			Boy	*D*	*D D D*	*D*	
636	Davd Crehan	70	*D*		Labour	Cy Limk	4th *D D*	*D*	
637	Dins Twomey	79	*D*		*D*	County Clear	5th *D D*	*D*	
638	Mary Fennel	8		*D*	Child	City Limk	5 *D D*	*D*	
639	Michl Devine	54	*D*		Millor	C Clear	*D D*	*D*	
640	Thoms Grimes	55		*D*	pinter	City Limk	*D D*	*D*	
641	Danl Castelow	46	*D*		Labour	C Clear	11 *D*		*D*
642	Davd Herrod	60			Waver	City Limk	13 *D*	*D*	
643	Jos Anderson	80	*D*		S Dier	City Limk	19 *D*	*D*	
644	Davd Rawley	40	*D*			County Limk	25 *D*		*D*
645	Maus Barrey	55	*D*		Sealor	Waterford	28 *D*	*D*	
646	Jno Baldon	5				C Kerrey	*D D*	*D*	
647	Mary Baldon	8				*D D*	D *D*	*D*	
648	Cath Morisson	80	*D*			Servant [sic]	*D D*	*D*	
649	Mary Baldon	38	*D*		Patten	*D*	D *D*	*D*	
650	Morgn O'Brian	54	*D*		Pottermaker	C Clear	3 Jany 79	*D*	
651	Andw Stephisson	60		*D*	Sadler	C Anthrim	4 Jany 79	*D*	
652	Pat Hanrehan	80	*D*		Labourer	County Limk	7th *D* 79	*D*	
653	Pat Brenan	66		*D*	S Waver	Dublin	9 *D* 79	*D*	
654	Pat Callehan	84	*D*		Chairman	City Limk	9 *D* 79		*D*
655	Ann Gibbons	66	*D*		Servant	*D*	11th *D* 79	*D*	
656	Cath Shaughnessy	30	*D*		*D*	*D*	11 *D* 79	*D*	
657	Geo Bready	9				*D*	14 *D* 79	*D*	
658	Pat Bready	6				*D*	14 *D* 79	*D*	
659	Jno Mulqueeny	66	*D*		Laborar	County Limk	15 *D* 79	*D*	
660	Cath Conner	38	*D*		Servent	County Cork	17 *D* 79		*D*
661	Pat Kelly	78		*D*	Tobackens	City Limk	30 *D* 79	*D*	
662	Edmd Fennel	84		*D*	Cordwinder	*D*	*D D D*	*D*	
663	Ann Spence	33		*D*	Servent	*D*	3 Feby 79	*D*	
664	Ann Nevel	52	*D*		*D*	County Limk	5 *D* 79	*D*	
665	Dan Hogan	60		*D*			7 *D* 79		*D*
666	Mary Hartegan	77	*D*		Servent	City Limk	9 *D* 79		*D*
667	Honr Brown	56	*D*		*D*	*D*	11 *D* 79	*D*	
668	Mary Bourk	7				*D*	11 *D* 79	*D*	
669	Michl O'Hara	70	*D*		Begar	*D*	12 *D* 79		*D*
670	Phil Devitt	60			*D*	*D*	12 *D* 79		*D*
671	Richd Jackson	13		*D*		*D*	15th *D* 79	*D*	
672	Danl Clark	4				*D*	23 *D* 79	*D*	
673	Mary Clark	6				*D*	23 *D* 79	*D*	
674	Mary Creagh	2				*D*	24 *D* 79	*D*	
675	Mart Lynch	6				*D*	25	*D*	
676	Bridgt Lynch	5				*D*	25	*D*	
677	Mary FzGerald	60		*D*	Servant	C Tiparery	26		*D*
678	Jno Barron	56	*D*		Skiner	City Limk	March 2nd	*D*	
679	Honr Brian	40	*D*		R Housekeepr	*D*	7	*D*	
680	MartMorarty	20	*D*		Servant	City Limk	10 March 79	*D*	
681	Elenr Fzgerald	45	*D*		*D*	*D*	11 *D* 79	*D*	

No. of bed	Condition when received Healthy	Sickly	Disease when received	How disposed of Discharged	Died	Eloped	Condition when discharged Healthy	Sickly	Observations
		D		6th Novr 78			*D*		This woman Eloped and was found in her loding and made pay her fees 1s 1d
		D		17th Novr 78			*D*		for the Infermery
	D			17 Novr 78			*D*		and gon to Dublin
		D	Lame	*Do*					
		D		*Do*					
	D			3 Feby 79			*D*		By order of Capn Hill and at his mother's Request
	D			10th Decr 78			*D*		By order of Mr Ingram and paying 2s 9
		D	Fits			21 May 79			When he went to wash the Mop he being orderly
		D	Rheumatisam		14 Decr 78				
	D				12th Jany 79				By order of Mr Ingram
		D			30 Decr 78				
		D	Asmitick	11 Decr 78			*D*		To go to the Infermery
	D			11 Decr 78					
			Sore Leg	11 Decr 78			*D*		Gon to the Informery
	D	*D*				23 Feby 79	*D*		
		D	Dropsey			12th Decr 78	*D*		And Left 4s 0d
				1 Augt 79					
					1 Augt 79				
			Lame Hand			17th Jany 79			
			Lunatick	*Do* Augt 79					
		D		25 Feby 79			*D*		By order
		D		*D D D*			*D*		By order
		D		22 *D D*			*D*		By order
		D		25 *D D*					By order
		D	Sore Legg	11th Feby 79					At his own Request
		D	Rheumatisam	6th March 79					
		D	*D*			6th March 79			when at work in the Gardins
		D	Sore Leg			5th March			Took a woman with him to Dublin & the Cloathing
		D	Rheumatisam	13th Jany 79					By Mr Ingram orders and paying 1 10
		D		20 Jany 79					By order ofMr Heny Rose
	D			11th Octr 83					By a Committee
	D			24th Feby 80					
	D			4th May 80	4th May 80				By Capt Hill Esqr
		D		*Do*					
		D		6th Feby 79 (erased)	28 March 79	*D*			
			Ripture			5th Feby 79			When sent To work to Mr Duffey
		D	Asmatick	6 Feby 79					
	D			8 Feby 79					By order of a Committe the 12 April
		D		*Do*					
				Do					
				12th Feby 79					By order and paying 2 1
	D			4 March 79					By order
				21st Sepr 81					by order of Capt Hill
				16th Feby 79					By order of Capn Hill and paying 2 1
				14th Feby 79					By the Mayor order and paying 1 4
	D			23 *D* 79			*D*		By order
D [sic]				*Do*					
D [sic]				22d June 79					By Capn Hill and gon to her Parents
D [sic]				26 Feby 79					
	D			*Do*					
	D			*Do*					
	D			2d March 79					By order and pg 1s10d
		D		*Do*					
		D	Blind	9 March 79					By order of Capt Hill & to go to her Husband
		D		20th Apr 86					By a Committee
		D		*Do*					

Current No.	Names	Age	Religion Roman Catholic	Protestant	Occupation	Late residence	Admitted	Voluntary	Compulsory
682	Edmd Kean	56	*D*		Beggar	*D*	12 March 79		*D*
683	Mor Sullevan	64	*D*		R Housekeeper	*D*	15 *D* 79	*D*	
684	John McMahon	73	*D*		A Stroler	C Clear	16 *D* 79		*D*
685	John Sullevan	44	*D*		Cordwinder	City Limk	21 *D* 79	*D*	
686	Margt Killen	19	*D*		Servant	*D*	24 *D D*	*D*	
687	Ann Gibbons	67	*D*		*D*	*D*	*D D D*	*D*	
688	John Tierney	67	*D*		Tobacaniss	*D*	29 *D D*		*D*
689	Richd Butler	72	*D*		Stroler	County Tipy	*D D D*		*D*
690	Elenr Sheehan	62	*D*		Servant	City Limk	30th *D D*	*D*	
691	Ann Clohasey	31	*D*		*D*	C Clear	*D D D*		*D*
692	Elenr Sweeny	40	*D*		*D*	*D*	31 *D D*		*D*
693	Mat McNamara	28	*D*		Begger	County Limk	1st April 79		*D*
694	Mary Fzgerald	60		*D*	Servant	C Timpy	*D D D*		*D*
695	Tim Brian	41	*D*		Stroler	C Cork	2d *D D*		*D*
696	Lot Hinchey	46	*D*		Taylor	City Limk	5th *D D*	*D*	
697	Mary Kelly	60			Begger	*D*	6 *D D*		*D*
698	Mary Riordan	10				*D*	9 *D D*	*D*	
699	Margt Riordan	7				*D*	9 *D D*	*D*	
700	Thoms Downs	79	*D*		Waver	*D*	13 *D D*		*D*
701	Margt Stedman	23		*Do*	Servant	*D*	21st *D D*	*D*	
702	Elezth Bullen	47	*D*		R Housekeeper	Dublen	21st *D D*	*D*	
703	John Bourk	76	*D*		*D*	C Clear	29 *D D*	*D*	
704	Pat Murphy	60	*D*		Labourar	City Limk	*D D D*		*D*
705	Jams McAndrey	84		*D*	L Waver	C Derrey	30th *D*	*D*	
706	Mary Ginane	56	*D*		Servant	City Limk	May 1 79		*D*
707	Jone Ryan	25			Fool	*D*	*D D D*		*D*
708	Mary Hall	40	*D*		*D*	County Limk	*D D D*	*D*	
709	Wm Cornwell	44	*D*		Labourer	County Tipry	5 *D D*	*D*	
710	Mat Daw	88	*D*		Stroler	*D D*	*D D*		*D*
711	Ann Clanchy	30	*D*		Sarvent	County Limk	8th *D D*	*D*	
712	Jno Dealy	30	*D*		Stroler		9th *D D*		*D*
713	Wm Hayes	67	*D*		Madman	City Limk	10 *D D*		*D*
714	Mary Hogen	57	*D*		R Housekep	City Limerick	11th May 1779	*D*	
715	Mary FGerald	30	*D*		*D*	*D D*	*D D D*	*D*	
716	Mary FGerald	3				*D D*	*D D D*	*D*	
717	Aley FGerald	11				*D D*	*D D D*	*D*	
718	John FGerald	1				*D D*	*D D D*	*D*	
719	Dins Brian	4				County Limk	22 May 79	*D*	
720	Bridgt McKinzey	72	*D*		Stroler	City Limerick	*D D D*		*D*
729	John Fitzgerald	32	*Do*		Sailor	City Limk	26 May 79	Vol	
730	Thos Doherty	14		*D*	Stroler	County Roscommon	30 May 79	*Do*	
731	John Duhy	8	*Do*		*Do*	Cashel	28 May 79		*Do*
732	Mary Gallerey	70	*Do*		Begger	City Limk	June 1st 79		*Do*
733	Bridgt Brian	77	*D*		Sarvent	*D*	June 3 79	*D*	
734	Jno Brian	27	*D*		*D*	County Limk	June 7 79		*D*
735	Jno Steward				Stroler	North Britton	*D D D*		*D*
736	Gorden				Stroler	*D*	*D D D*		*D*
737	Danl Lues	34		*D*	Stroler	C Corke	9th June 79		*D*
738	Heny Casey	42	*D*		Servent	City Limk	12 D *D*	*D*	
739	Jno Murrey	40	*D*		Labr	County Clear	*D D D*	*D*	
740	Tim Noonan	56	*D*		Wheelwright	City Limk	14 *D D*	*D*	
741	Elenr Hynes	30	*D*		Servent	*D*	18 *D D*		*D*
742	Honr Scott	40	*D*		*D*	C Roscommon	19th *D D*		*D*
743	Jane Fox	46	*D*		a Dealer	City Limk	23d *D D*		*D*

No. of bed	Condition when received Healthy	Sickly	Disease when received	How disposed of Discharged	Died	Eloped	Condition when discharged Healthy	Sickly	Observations
		D		11th April 79					By order of Walter Windenham Esqr and paying 1 1
		D		13 June 79					13th By order of a Committee 10 June 79
		D	Asmatick		14 July 79				
		D		13th April 79					By order of a Comittee the 12th April
	D			21st May 80			Healthy		By order of a Committee
		D			Died 8th Jany 1791				The house bought her Coffin
		D		13th April 79					By order of a Comittee the 12 April on pay 3 5
	D			25th Augst 79					Discharged paying 16s 3d
	D			*Do*	18th June 87				
	D					24th Octr 79			Out of the Back Window of the Spining Hall
	D			16th April 79					By order of a Committee of the 12th April & pd 2 1
		D	Criple	11th april 79					By order of Wm Fzgerald Esq
		D	*D*		22d June 79				
	D			9 April 79					By order of Capn Hill and paying 2 10
		D							
		D		9th April 79					By order of Cap Hill & paying 1 11
	D			27th May 80					By order Capt Hill Esqr
	D			11th April 79					By order of Mr Phillips
				4th Jany 81					
	D					23d of April			
		D		22 April 79					By order of Mr Dawson
		D		8th May 79					By order of a Committee
				30th April 79					By order
		D			1st Sepr 79				
				8th May 79					By order of a Committee and paying 2 10
				Do					
	D			9th April (erased) 79					By order of a Committee
		D			8th May 79				
			a Broken aram	11th May 79					
			Sore aram	*Do*					
						May 27th			
		D							
	D			7th Augt 80					By a Committee
	D			*Do*					*Do*
	D			16th May 80					By Mr Phillips
		D		20th June 80					
					8 July 79				
				31 Jany 80					
		Do	Decay	11th June 79					
	Do			*Do*					
			His chin & chest tied together	28 May 79					By order of the Mayor
			Most Blind	24th Sepr 79					By order and paying 1 1
					18 sepr 79				
	D			10 June 79					on paying 1/10
				12 June 79					Carted
				12th June 79					Carted
	D			10 June 79					Without Fees
		D		11th Octr 83					By a Committee
		D	Foolish		6th Feby 82				Suddenly
		D	Blind	17th June 79					By order
		D	Dumb	22d June 79					By order of the Mayor to Quit the town
	D			23 *D* 79					By *D* D
	D			24th June 79					By order of the Mayor to Quit the town

Current No.	Names	Age	Religion Roman Catholic	Protestant	Occupation	Late residence	Admitted	Voluntary	Compulsory
744	Cath Morison	81	*D*		Servent	*D*	25th June 79		*D*
745	Pat Callehan	84	*D*		Chairman	City Limk	26th *D D*	*D*	
746	Danl Mullony	44	*D*		Labr	County Limk	1st July *D*	*D*	
748	Lars Braken	52	*D*		Stroling frenchman		2 *D D*		*D*
748	Hugh Hana	42		*D*	Cordwender	C Anthrim	4th *D D*		*D*
749	Richd Guie	46	*D*		Labr	City Limk	7 July *D*		*D*
750	Darby Kenely	84	*D*		*D*	*D*	11 July *D*	*D*	
751	James Clemons	74	*D*		Founder	*D*	16 July *D*	*D*	
752	Michl Bourk	5				City Limk	20 July *D*	*D*	
753	Mary Bourk	9				*D*	*D D D*	*D*	
754	Jno Cargen	61		*D*	R H Keeper	County Monehan	21 July *D*	*D*	
755	Geo Lloyd	25			Stroling fool	County Limk	24th July 79		*D*
756	Mary Ball	24		*D*	Servant	City Dublen	*D D D*	*D*	
757	Laus Flin	27	*D*		Stroling Bman	County Cavan	26 *D D*		*D*
758	Wm Corbit	60	*D*		Labourer	County Limk	30 *D D*	*D*	
759	Margt Ready	21	*D*		Servant	City Limk	30 *D D*	*D*	
760	Ann Minchion	24	*D*		*D*	County Limk	4 Augt		*D*
761	Thoms Fox	8				City Limk	13 Augt	*D*	
762	Jams Fox	6				*Do*	13 *Do*	*D*	
763	Judy Kelly	40	*D*		Ballitsing	Galway	15 *D*		*D*
764	Sibey Tulley	60	*D*		*D*	*D*	*D*		*D*
765	Domnick Fzgerald				Child		17 *D*	*D*	
766	Elezth Fzgerald	44	*D*		Servent	City Limk	*D D*	*D*	
767	Mary Fzgerald	7	*D*			*D*	*D D*	*D*	
768	John Carey	60	*D*		Labourer	County Limk	18 *D*	*D*	
769	Mary Montgomery	44		*D*	Servant	C Kilcenny	20 *D*	*D*	
770	Elezth Barrey	32		*D*	*D*	C Cork	23 *D*	*D*	
771	Jery Hurley	76	*D*		Servant	*D*	24 *D*	*D*	
772	Elezth Conery	20	*D*		Criple	City Limk	1 Sepr 79	*D*	
773	Michl Holmes	8				*D*	5 *D D*	*D*	
774	Mary Holmes	10	*D*			*D*	5 *D D*	*D*	
775	Andw Stepenson	61		*D*	Sadler	C Anthrim	7 *D*	*D*	
776	Jno Halleran	3 months				City Limk	9 *D*	*D*	
777	Elenr Sweeny	40	*D*		Servant	City Limk	9 *D*	*D*	
778	Jams Conner	54			Smith	*D*	10 *D*	*D*	
779	Margt Donehow	56	*D*		Stroler	*D*	10 *D*		*D*
780	Danl Healy	60	*D*		Stone Cuter	County Cork	14 *D*		*D*
781	Teresa Bassett	46		*D*	City Dublin Servant	City Dublin	18 *D* 79	V	
782	Mary Mollony	40	*D*		Servant	City Limk	22 Sepr 79	*D*	
783	Pat Pendergast	61	*D*		Prockter	County Galway	25 *D*		*D*
784	Michl Mulvehil	60	*D*		A Stroler	City Limk	30 Sepr		*D*
785	Tim Hartegon	74	*D*		Labourer	County Limk	2d Octr	*D*	
786	Laus Lahif	54	*D*		Waver	City Limk	4 *D*	*D*	
787	Michl Mulvehil	60	*D*		Stroler	City Limk	10 *D*		*D*
788	Richd Moor	56		*D*	*D*	County Limk	15 *D*		*D*
789	Elenr Butterfild	48	*D*				17 *D*		*D*
790	Michl Butterfild	12	*D*				*D*		*D*
791	Cors Flanegan	73	*D*		Waver	C Clear	23d Octr 79	*D*	
792	Robt French	80		*D*	*D*	City Limk	26th *D D*	*D*	
793	Thoms Doharty	16	*D*		S Vagibone	C Roscomon	1 Novr 79		*D*
794	Reb.a Folensby	67		*D*	Servant	City Limk	4 *D D*	*D*	
795	Thoms Sweeny					*D D*	6 *D D*	*D*	
796	Saley Sweeny					*D D*	6 *D D*	*D*	
797	Elenr White	35	*D*		Servant	*D D*	19th *D D*	*D*	
798	Jone Ahern	30	*D*		Servant	*D D*	19th *D D*	*D*	
799	Mary Ahern	7	*D*			*D D*	19 *D D*	*D*	
800	Bridgt Ahern	5				*D D*	19 *D D*	*D*	
801	Thoms Ahern	1				*D D*	19 *D D*	*D*	
802	Thoms Deegan	40	*D*		Shuemaker	*D D*	21 *D D*		*D*

No. of bed	Condition when received Healthy	Sickly	Disease when received	How disposed of Discharged	Died	Eloped	Condition when discharged Healthy	Sickly	Observations
		D			30th July 79				
		D	Rheamatisom	3d July 79					By order of a Committee and pd 1 10
		D	Scurbatick		19th Decr 79				
	D			*Do*					
	D			6th July 79					By the Mayors order to Mr Clark
	D					17 July 79			When at work
				Do					
		D	Cripel	*Do*					
	D								
	D					22d Sepr 83			carried away petticoat
				16th Augt 79					
	D			2d Augt 79					By order of a Committe
	D								*Do* without fees
	D		Blind	25 Augt 79					discharged Without fees
	D			*Do*					
				Do					
				25th Augt 79					Without fees
	D			11th Octr 83					By a committee
	D					14th Sepr 81			he was a good Boy
				25th Augt 79					Without fees
				25 Augt 79					
	D			*Do*					
	D			*Do*					
	D			*Do*					
				25 Augst 79					Without fees
						13th May 80			with the House Cloathes
				25 Augt 79					without fees
				29th May 82					By a Committee
				15th Jany 83					By a Committee
				Do					
		D		20th July 1784					
				13th Sepr 79					By order the having Disorders not fit to be kept in the house
				13 Sepr 79					
		D							
	D			18th sepr 79					By order of a Committee & paying 2/2
				D D 79					By order without fees
					23d Novr 80				
				Do					
			nigh Sighted			24th May 80			
		D	Scorbutick			3d Octr 79			
		D	Sore Legg	*Do*					
			Blind	*Do*					
			Scurbutick	*Do*					
	D			23 Decr 79					By order of a Comittee
				Do					
				Do					
		D	Scurbutick			14th Decr 79			this man Went to Berey his wife and did not Return but sent back the Clasas
						26th June 80			
	H					17 Decr 79			
				7th Novr 79					By order of the Mayor
				Do					
				Do					
	D			5th Jany 81					By order of the Gentlemen to go to service, at her own request
	D			*Do*					
		D		27th May					By order of Capt Hill
	D			*Do*					
	D			*Do*					
	D			22 Novr 79					By order of the Mayor and paying 1 4

Current No.	Names	Age	Religion Roman Catholic	Protestant	Occupation	Late residence	Admitted	Voluntary	Compulsory
803	John Dealy	31	*D*		Stroler	County Limk	9 Decr 79		*D*
804	Jone Mulvhil	100	*D*		R Housekeeper	City Limk	14 *D D*		*D*
805	A Dum Boy	10					15th *D*		*D*
806	Rose McCollough	9		*D*		County Anthrim	21	*D*	
807	Cath McCollough	13		*D*		*D*	*D D*	*D*	
808	Mary McCollough	41			R House Keepr	*D*	*D D*	*D*	
809	Marg McCollough	6				*D*	*D D*	*D*	
810	Alex McCollough	8				*D*	*D D*	*D*	
811	Pat McManis	12	*D*			County Down	22 Decr *D*	*D*	
812	Jams McManis	7				*D D*	*D D D*	*D*	
813	Maryan McCollough	18		*D*	Servent	C Anthrim	29 *D D*	*D*	
814	Iseble Mathes	50			Stroler		Jany 1st 1780		*D*
815	Faney Coningham	70	*D*		R Housekeeper	Dublen	5 *D*	*D*	
816	Tim Twomey	23		*D*	Bre Maker	City Limk	*D D*	*D*	
817	Edmd Conner	60		*D*	Cooper	*D*	7 *D D*	*D*	
818	Thoms Doherty	16		*D*	Stroler		10 *D D*		*D*
819	Ann Devlin	5					13 *D D*	*D*	
820	Mary Devlin	36	*D*		Servant		13 *D D*	*D*	
821	Jno Devlin	6					13 *D D*	*D*	
822	John Buckley	60		*Do*	Servant	C Limerick	22d	*D*	
823	Eliz Curry	60	*D*		Servt	C Tipperary	30th	*D*	
824	James Dea	60	*D*		Farmer	C Limerick	1st Feby	*D*	
825	Hannah Fahey	35	*D*		House Keeper	C Clare	5th Feby	*D*	
826	David Evans	6	Catho			City Limk	8th Feby	Volun	
827	Jane Evans	8	Catho			City Limk	8th Feby	Volun	
828	Mary Creighton	60	Catholic		House-keeper	City of Limerick	25th of Feby 80		Com
829	Mary Lynch	40		Protes	Servant	County Clare	27th Feby 80	Volun	
830	Timothy Sullivan	64	Catholic		Porter	City of Limk	15th Feby		
831	Mary Howe	5	Catholic			City of Limk	22d Feby	Volun	
832	Patt Ryan	63	Catholic		Gardener	County Clare	21st of *Do*	Volun	
833	John Howe	10	Catho			City Limk	22d *Do*	Volun	
834	Morgan Brien	60	Catholic		Patten Maker	Killaloe	24th of *Do*	Volun	
835	Michl Lynch	3		Protes	Child		27th of *Do*		
836	John Onsurlow	40	Catholic		Frenchman	Paris	4th of Feby		
837	Sone Totego	18	*D*		Fren'chman	Bourdeaux	4th of Feby	Volun	
838	Mary Cahill	50	Catholic		Reduc'd H Keeper	City Limerick	3d of March		Com
839	James Ryan	60	Cath		Farmer	County of Limk	14th Feby	Volun	
840	Willm Minehan	60	Catholic		Porter	County Limk	22d of March	Volun	
841	John Flinn	59	Catholic		Slater	County Limk	23d of March	Volun	
842	Michl Digman	11	Catholic			City Limk	23d	Volun	
843	Danl Healy	59	Catho		Stone Cutter	City Limk	24th		Com
844	Ellinor Carmody	61	Catholic		Reduc'd H Keeper	City Limk	30th	Volun	
845	Molly Forsayth	33		Protest	Traveller	Manchester	31st	Volun	
846	Nancy Brien	19		Protest	Quill Winder	City Limerick	April 1st		Com
847	Bridgt Lowe	72	Catholic		Reduc'd H Keep	City Limerick	6th	Volun	
848	James Lynch	7		Protes	Child	County Clare	27th Feby	Volun	
849	Danl Doyle	6	Catho			City Limk	8th April	Volun	
850	John Doyle	8	Catho			City of Limk	8	Volun	
851	Charlotte Adams	19		Protest	Servant	England	15th	Volun	
852	Bridgt Bourk	20	Cath		Servant	Galway	10th	Volu	
853	Ellinor Brien	38	Catho		Servt	Killaloe	11th	Volun	
854	Mary Brien	52		Protest	Actress	County Galway	22d	Volu	
855	Patt Kelly	46		Protest	Tobacconist	County Limk	18	Volun	
856	David Welsh	61	Catholic		Farmer	County Clare	19	Volun	
856	Thos Davernor	8			Orphan	Co Limk	10th Apr 80		
857	Sarah Hardy	13	Catholic		Actress	Galway	22d April	Volun	
858	Willm Griffith	43		Protest	Sailor	England	20	Volun	
859	John Farrell	50	Catho		Labourer	County Clare	21st	Volun	
860	Robt Murray	61		Protest	Labourer	County Clare	7th May	Volun	
861	Winfred McMahon	70	Catho		Beggar	City Limerick	6th		Com
862	Thoms John Downs	54	Catho		Sports Man		13th	Volun	

No. of bed	Condition when received Healthy	Sickly	Disease when received	How disposed of Discharged	Died	Eloped	Condition when discharged Healthy	Sickly	Observations
			Sore aram			Elopd 17th Decr 79			
		D		22 Novr 79					By order of a Committee & pd 1 1
	D			*Do*					
	D			dis 21st June 1780					Dischargd by Capt Hill Esqr
	D			*Do*					by *Do*
	D			*Do*					by *Do*
	D			*Do*					by *Do*
	D			*Do*					by *Do*
	D			Jany 80					
	D			*Do*					
	D			*Do*					
				Do					
				Do					
		D		*Do*					
		D		8th Jany 80					By Mr Phillips
				Do					
				9th Augt 81					By 3 Governors
				9th Augt					By *Do*
				9th *Do*					By 3 Governors
		D	Head-ach	26th to the Infirmary					By Col Smyth Esqr
		D	pain in the leg	15 March 80					By a Committee
		D	Rupture	31st May					By a Committee
		D	Decay	12 June					By Capt Hill Esqr
	Healthy			15th Feby					By a Comittee
	Healthy			15th Feby					By Capt Hill Esqr
		Infirm		26th Feby				Infirm	By three of the Governors
	Health			20th May 80					
					8th Decr 82				
				7th July			*Do*		By a Comittee
			Cough	20th May					By Capt Hill Esqr and other Governors
				11th Octr 1783					By a Committee
			Sore Legs	10th June					By three of the Governors
	Healthy			30th May					By Capt Hill Esqr
	Healthy			8th May					By the Collector he pd for their diet
	Healthy			8th May					By the Collector
			Infirm	7th March					By 3 of the Governors
			Sore Leg		Died 25th May 80				
		Sickly	Sore Leg	21st of April				Sickly	By a Comittee
	Healthy		broken Leg	30th May			Healthy		By a Comittee
		Blind	Stone Blind	28th March					By Capt Hill Esqr
			Infirm			run'd away			
		Sickly	Asthma		Died 28th April 86				
	Heathy			5th May			Healthy		By Capt Hill Esqr
	Heathy			25 July 80					By Capt Hill Esqr
					28th Feb 86				
	Healthy				Died 19th April 81				
	Healthy			27th May 80					By a Commitee
	Healthy			27th					By a Comittee
	Healthy		Healthy			25th Octr			
	Healthy			discharg'd 28 June 80					By Capt Hill Esqr
	Healthy			15th Augt 80			Healthy		By a committee
		Sickly	Sickly		Died 3d May 81				
			sickly	27th May					by a comittee
			a pain in the Heart		died 29th June 80		Healthy		
			Fool		Died 4th March 85				
	Healthy			16th Feby 81					By Alderman Widenham
		Sickly	Bloody Flux	7th July					By a Comitee
	Healthy			22d April			Healthy		By Capt Hill Esqr
		Sickly	Foolish		20th May 80				
		Sickly	Infirm	10th May					By Walter Widenham Es
			Swell'd Knee	14th Apr 82					(Dennis got a furlow and did not return inserted above)

Current No.	Names	Age	Religion Roman Catholic	Protestant	Occupation	Late residence	Admitted	Voluntary	Compulsory
863	Ellinor Dunn	36	Catho		Beggar	County Clare	15th May 80		Com
864	Mary Murphy	45	Catholic		Gloveress	County Dublin	16		Com
865	Mary Shinnors	4*	Catho			County Clare	15th		Com
866	Margt Leary	7	Catho			City Limk	16	Volun	
867	Ann Lynch	61	Catho		Servant	City Limk	16	Volun	
868	Cornelius Maher	54	Catho		Farmer	City Limk	28th	Volun	
869	Mortough Kerly	72	Catho		Beggar	City Limk	29th		Com
870	Andrew Devitt	21		Protest	Crier of News	Ennis	31st	Volun	
871	Henry Ferguson	19	Catho		Serge Weaver	City Limk	3 Jun	Volun	
872	Cath Molony	22	Catho		Reducd	County Tipperary	3 Jun	Volun	
873	Owen Daly	56	Catho		Broguemaker	County Clare	7th	Volun	
874	Jerimiah Ahern	62		Protes	Sailor	England	7		In
875	Mary Hill	59	Catho		Beggar	City Limerick	17th June		C
876	Bridg Gleeson	72	Catho		Beggar	City Limerick	22d		C
877	Moria Thomkins	20		Protest	Reduc'd H K	City Limerick	24th		
878	Timothy Ryan	64	Catho		Labourer	City Limk	6th July	Volun	
879	Maurice Fitzgerald	65	Catho		Reduc'd H K	County Kerry	9th	Volun	
880	Hannah Freeman	50	Catho		Reduc'd H K	City Limk	9th	Volun	
881	Tho Tobin	12	Cath		Beggar	County Clare	11th	Volun	
882	Patt Baldwin	50	Catho		Beggar (erased) Steward	County Kerry	14th	Volun	
883	Bridgt Magrath	32	Catho		Spinner	City Limk	14th	Volun	
884	Connor Casey	61	Catho		Labourer	West County Clare	15	Volun	
885	Nicholas Dobbin	54		Protest	Sieve Maker	City Limerick	19th	Volun	
886	John Pendergast	61	Catho		Farmer	Ballingarry	21st		
887	Biddy Fitzgerald	28	Cath		bad Girl	City Limerick	17th	Volun	
888	Hannah Holloran	30	Catho		Reduc'd	City Limerick	24th	Volun	
889	Cath Bradshaw	6	Catho		a Child			Volun	
~~879~~	~~Nancy~~ Daly	5					~~20th~~		
890	Bridget Higgins	58	Catho		Soldier's Wife	County Limk	1 Augt 1780		
891	Patrick FGerald	49	Catho		Sailor	Cork	10th	Volun	
892	Mary FGerald	50	Catho		School Mistress	Cork	10th	Volun	
893	Richd Mulloye	60	Catho		Sailor	Cork	18th	Volun	
894	Robt Mitchell	62	Catho		Cabinet maker	England	19th		Com
895	Catharine Frize	49		Protest	Soldier's Wife	America	22d	Volun	
896	John Sixpence	60	Catho		Labourer	C L Cahirconlish	26th	Volun	
897	Bridgt Morrison	50	Catho		House keeper	City Limerick	31st	Volun	
898	Terence McMahon	11			Poor boy	City Limk	6th Sepr	Volun	
899	Michl Qinlevan	60	Catho		Chairman	City Limk	10	Volun	
900	Susy Waistcott	12		Protes	Let out with the thread	maker	City Limk	4th	Volun
901	Mary Shaughnessy	50	Catho		H Keeper	City Limk	10	Volun	
902	Willm Minehan	62	Catho		Porter	City Limk	12		
903	John McMahon	56	Catho		Beggar	City Limk	17th		Com
904	Emd Fitzgerald	62	Catho		Joiner	Tipperary	12	Volun	
905	John Macantire	54		Protest	Taylor	City Limerick	25th	Volun	
906	Elizabeth Marrah	29	Catho		Servant	County Limek	25th	Volun	
907	John Minehan	7	Catho		a poor Child	City Limk	26th	Volun	
908	Garrett Cavanagh	58		Pro	thread maker		3d Octr	Volun	
909	Patt Norris	60	Catho		Ideot	County Limk	3d Octr	Volun	
910	Joseph Birmingham	13		Pro	a poor Boy	County Clare	11th Octr	Volun	
911	Mary Downs	64	Cath		a Meal womn	City Limerick	11th	Volun	
912	Willm Gearon	20		Protes	a Linen Weaver	County Clare	15th		Com
913	Margt Barre	4		Protes			17th Octr	Volun	
914	Jane Ahern	44	Catho		a poor, house keeper	City Limk	22d	Volun	
915	Bridg Ahern	6	Catho			City Limk	22d	Volun	
916	Thos Ahern	1 1/2 yr				City Limk	22d	Volun	
917	Hannah Hartigan	34	Catho		Harlot	City Limk	22d	Volun	
918	Elizabeth Campbell	16		Protes	poor Woman	County Clare	Octr 26th 80	Volun	
919	Elizabeth Connor	her 6 months	Catho			*Do*	*Do*	Volun	
920	Joseph Hiffernon	9 yrs	Catho		poor boy	County Kerry	11th Octr	Volun	
921	Roger Clancy	76	Catho		Weaver	City Limk	26th 1780	Volun	
922	Geo Shank	9		Pro	poor boy	City Limk	26	Volun	

No. of bed	Condition when received: Healthy	Sickly	Disease when received	How disposed of: Discharged	Died	Eloped	Condition when discharged: Healthy	Sickly	Observations
	Healthy					24th May			
	Healthy			17th					pd 1s 1d her fees
	Healthy					24th May			
				Do					
	Healthy					20th			
	Healthy			29th of May 80					By Capt Hill Esqr
	Healthy		Mad (erased)		6th March 83				
			a pain in the Back	8th July			healthy		By a Committee
			Mad	5th June 1780					
			Big with Child	15th Decr					By Capt Hill Esqr
				20th July					By the Mayor after paying 1s 6d
	Healthy			10th June					By the Mayor, paying 1s 1d
			Blind	4th Jany 1781					By paying 1s 1d a Comittee
				28th June					By order of Capt Hill on paying 2s 4d
				17th May 83					
			Old age, Infirmity	5th Octr 86					
			Old age	10th Sepr					By Capt Hill Esqr
			Blind	21st Sepr					By Capt Hill Esqr
			Sore Legs			Elop'd 18th July 82			carried 1s 1d from Bassett
				20th Augt	20th Augt 1780				By Capt Hill Esqr
	Healthy		Bad disorder	18 July					by the Revd Jaques Ingram
			Sore legs	Octr 28th					By order of a Comittee
	Heathy			28th octr					By order of a comittee
			Mad	1st Sepr					
			a bad Disorder			25th July			
			a pain in the legs	13th			Healthy		By Capt Hill Esqr
	Healthy			13th			Healthy		By Capt Hill Esqr
					~~20th May 80~~				
			Dead palsy		8th Augt 1780				
			Stone Blind	9th Augt 81	9th Augt 81				By 3 Governors
			Big with Child	9th Augt 81	9th Augt 81				By 3 Governors
	Healthy			26th Jany 81					By a Committee
	Healthy			28th octr					By order of A Comittee
	Healthy			*Do*	15th Jany 1790				The house bough her coffin
			Sore Leg		30th Novr 81				
			Foolish	28th Octr					By order of a Comittee
	Healthy					6th Jany 81			took the House Cloaths
	Healthy			*Do*					
	Healthy			26th Octr					
			Stark Mad	21st July 1784	24th Augt 86				
			Sore Legs	22d June 81					By a Committee
	Healthy			18th Sepr					By order of Sheriff Harrison and paying 1 4
			Deaf	4th Octr					By order of Capt Hill Esqr
Healthy					10th Jany 81				took the House Scissars
			a Fever		15th Octr 80				
Healthy			*Do*						
						12th Decr 80			
						11th Novr 80			
						24th Octr 80			
			Broken bones		3d Octr 80				
			Mad	28th Octr					By order of A comittee
	Health			23d May					By a note Signed by Capt Hill Esqr and Mr Ferar
				30th Augt					By 3 Governors
				30th Augt					By *Do*
				30th Augt					By *Do*
			full of Whiskey	Octr 28 80					By order of a Comitee
				28th Octr					By order of a Comittee
				Do					*Do*
	Healthy					24th			
			Sore Eyes	March 19th 1781			Healthy		By order of a Committee
	He			13th Sepr 81					By a Commitee of 3

Current No.	Names	Age	Religion Roman Catholic	Protestant	Occupation	Late residence	Admitted	Voluntary	Compulsory
923	Danl Brein	58	Cath		Chairman	City Limk	29th Octr 80	Volun	
924	Bridgt Cobbraith	21		P	Cord-maker	City Limk	30th Octr 1780		C
925	John Flinn	60	Cath		Slater	Co Limk	Novr 3d 80	V	
926	Garrett Donne	54		P	Servt	Co Kerry	3d	V	
927	Mary Murphy	30	Cath		Harlot	Bridewell	8th		C
928	Nell Fitzgerald	50	Cath		Idler	City Limk	11	V	
929	Mary Cain	36	Cath		House keepr	City Limk	11	V	
930	Hannah Hartig	40	Cath		Harlot	City Limk	18	Volun	
931	Bridgt Daly	39	Cath		poor woman	City Limk	21		C
932	Michl Daly, her Child	5	Catho		Child	*Do*	*Do*		C
933	Mary Cain Sheehan	42	Catho		Idler	City Limk	22	Volu	
934	Ellinor Sheehan	8	Cath		Child	*Do*	22d	Volun	
935	Mary Fitzgerald	1 day	Catho		Born in the House of	Industry	24th		
936	George Humphries	60	Catho		Servant	County Limerick	29	Volu	
937	Leddy Fletcher	46	Cath		Servant	City Limerick	*Do*	Volu	
938	Bell Fletcher	15	Catho		Servant	City Limerick	*Do*	Volu	
939	Joan Meehan	30	Catho		a poor Girl	City Limk	3d Decr	Volu	
940	Cath Dwyer	36	Catho		a foolish Womn	County Limk	29th Novr		C
941	Mary Graddy	30	Cath		a Servant	City Limk	5th Decr	Volu	
942	Henry Leacock	43	Catho	P	Sailor	Co Longford	6th Decr	Volu	
943	Thady McNemara	2 son to Alley Brown			child	City Limk	8	Volun	
944	Mary Gradey	42	Catho		poor Womm	County Limk	5th	Volun	
945	Ellinor Connors	30	Catho		Harlot	County Clare	10th	Vo	
946	Ally Brown	32	Cath		poor Womn	Parteen	8th	Volu	
947	Phillip Hardiman	60	Catho		Farmer	County Clare	16	Volu	
948	Bridgt Daly	12	Catho		Orphan	City Limk	12	Volu	
949	John Cosgerry	70	Catho		Labourer	City Limk	23	Volun	
950	Thomas McMahon	12	Catho		Orphan	City Limk	30	Volun	
951	Margt Haley	49	Catho		Soldier's Wife	City Limk	30th	Volun	
952	James Haley	2yrs son to Margt Haley							
953	Michl Murphy	4			Orphan	City Limk	1st Jany 81		Vo [sic]
954	Margt Murphy	3			Orphan	City Limk	1st *Do*		Vo [sic]
955	John McNemara	61	Catho		Porter	City Limk	2 *Do*		Vo [sic]
956	Cath Evans	49	Catho		R Housekeep	City Limk	4th *Do*		Vo [sic]
957	Mary Evans	14	Catho				4th *Do*		Vo [sic]
958	David Evans	8	Catho				4 *Do*		Vo [sic]
959	Henry Brien	11	Catho		poor boy	City Limk	3d *Do*		Vo [sic]
960	John Cahill	59	Catho		Turf porter	City Limk	4 *Do*		Vo [sic]
961	Mary Carthy	15	Catho		Harlot	Rathkeale	2d *Do*		
962	Margt Dillon	13	Catho		Whore	Dublin	10th		
963	Edm Seymour	62		P	Clothier	City Limk	11th	*Do*	V [sic]
964	Mary White Kennedy	20	Cath		Kenry poor Girl	Kenry	11	*Do*	
965	Mary White	42	Catho		R Housek	County Tipy	12		Co
966	Jane White	9	Cath		a Child		12th		Com
967	Margt ,Crooke	70	Cath		a Beggar	City Limk	15		Com
968	Elizabeth Evans	14		P		City Limk	15	Vo	
969	Dan Shea	54	C		Porter	City Limk	20	V	
970	Thos Downs	72	C		Saucy fellow	City Limk	22		C
971	Mary Hardy	15		P	Harlot	City Galway	24	V	
972	Thos Downs	70	C		Weaver	Clothier [sic]	22 Jany		C
973	Mary Ahern	9	C			City Limk	24th	V	
974	Cornelius Donnellan	70	C		Labourer	Co Limk	25th	V	
975	Thom Doherty	20	Ca		Vagabond	Co Galway	29th		C

No. of bed	Condition when received Healthy	Sickly	Disease when received	How disposed of Discharged	Died	Eloped	Condition when discharged Healthy	Sickly	Observations
	Health			*Do*					
	Healthy			31st Decr			In bad Health		By Cap Hill Esq at the Committees
			Lame	*Do*					
	Healthy			25th June 81					By a Committee 18th June
	Healthy		Bad Disorder	29th Decr 80					By the Revd Jaques Ingram
			Sore Eyes			25th July			carried away the house Cloaths
			Baddisorder	20th May 81					
	Healthy		givento Drink	21st May 81					By giving Security that she woud quit Limerick
	Healthy					20th Sepr			She was on the Orderly, for washing &c
						26th Augt 82			
			Bad Disorder	16th Jany 81					By a Comittee
				16th Jany					By *Do*
			Bloody Flux		21st Decr 80		*Do*		By a Committee (all erased)
			Pox & Clap	10th Apr 81					By a Commitee
	Do			10th *Do*					By a Committee
			Insane			11th March			By breaking the Cell
	Healthy			Elop'd, by throwing herself over the Garden Wall and cutt with the Glass which is in the Wall					
		Sickly		30th Augt 82					by a committee of 3 Governors
			Subject to fits	4th Jany 81					by a Committee
	Healthy			*Do*					
		Sickly		*Do*					
			Bad disord			6th Apr 81			after being curd of the bad disorder
	Healthy			*Do*					
			Lame, of both legs	4th Jany 81					
	Healthy			*Do*					
			in a Fever		31st Decr 80				
	Healthy			July 19th 84					
			baddisorder	11th July					By a Committee
					20th May 81				of the bad disorder
	Healthy			5th Jany 81					By Order of Capt Hill Es
	Healthy			5th Jany 81					By Order of Capt Hill Esqr
			a pain in the head			5th Jany 81			carryd nothing away
	Heal			27th Octr 82					By 3 Governors - a bad tongue she had - see the report
	He			21st July 1784					
	Do			11th Octr 83					By a committee
	Do								
	Do			17th March 81					By a comittee
			bad disorder	17th March					having curd her here
			bad disorder	17th Jany					She wasturnd out on having the bad disorder
		Health [sic]				17th Jany 1781			
		Do	bad Disorder			20th Jany 81			
		Do				Elop'd 17			By Breaking the Window and taking out her Child
		Do				Elop'd 17			
			Blind of one Eye	18th Jany 81					By paying 1s 1d
	Do			21st July 1784					
	Do			19th March			*Do*		By a Committee
		Do		18th Apr 83					
	Do					6th Apr 81			and robbd a child of a new shift, and shoes
		Do	Raging Fever	25th Jany 81					By Capt Hill Esqr
		Do		30 Augt 81					By 3 Governors
			a raging fever		28th Feby 81				
	Do					14th Feby 81			By breaking the Cell

Current No.	Names	Age	Religion Roman Catholic	Protestant	Occupation	Late residence	Admitted	Voluntary	Compulsory
976	Sheelah Pendergast	49	Ca		R Housekeep	City Limk	30th Jany 81	Volu	
977	Thom Pendergast	8 son to Sheelah				*Do*	*Do*	V	
978	Peggy Pendergast	4	Daugh to *Do*			*Do*	*Do*	V	
979	John Cloon	44	Ca		Mountebank	CoTyrone	Feby 1st 81		C
980	Jane Holloran	44	Catho		Huckster	City Limk	5th Feby 81	Vo	
981	Willm Burnam	70		P	Smith	City Limk	7th	Vo	
982	Margt Ryan	27	Catho		Servant	Co Waterford	11th Feby 81	Vo	
983	Cath Ryan	1 1/2	Cath		a Child		*Do*	Vo	
984	Mary Kennedy	20	Cath		Harlot	Kenry Co Lim	13th	Vo	
985	Tim Hagahan	54	C		Shuler	Rathkeale	14th		C
986	Will Walcott	39	C		Beggar	Roscommon	18th		C
987	Nancy Smyth	14		Pro	deluded from her parents	Queen's County	17th	Vo	
988	Molly Lacy	50	C		Bawdy R D house keepr	Abbey	18th	Vo	
989	Norry Lacy	10	C		a Girl	*Do*	18th	Vo	
990	Thoms Lacy	12	C		a Boy	*Do*	18th	Vo	
991	Nelly Murphy	22	C		Harlot	County Clare	19th		C
992	Nelly Lowry	23	C		Silk-Winder	City of Dublin	19th	Vo	
993	Biddy Lowry	1 1/4					19th	Vo	
994	Eliza Madget	50	C		R H Keepr	City Limk	22d	Vo	
995	Thos Downs	74	C		Clothier	City Limk	March 1st		C
996	James Meehan	65	Cath		Clothier	City Limerick	17th Feby	Vo	
997	Mary Ivers	12	P [sic]			City Limk	March 5	Vo	
998	John Ivers	5	P [sic]			*Do*	*Do*		
999	Thom Ivers	3	P [sic]			*Do*	*Do*		
1000	Thom Boland	70		C [sic]	Taylor	*Do*	*Do*		
1001	Tim Towmey	26		C [sic]	Brogue Maker	Co Limk	10th	Vo	
1002	Joan Meehan	20		C [sic]	Harlot	City Limerick	11		C
1003	John McMahon	65		C [sic]	Skinner Clothier	City Limerick	12	Vo	
1004	Mary White	61	P [sic]		R housekeepr		13	Vo	
1005	Nelly Connors	9	P [sic]		a Child		13	Vo	
1006	Norry Connors	6	P [sic]		a Child		13	Vo	
1007	Eliza Ashbee	20		C [sic]	Spinner	City of Limk	13	Vo	
1008	Patrick Gardiner	49	C		Labourer	County Limk	13th March 1781	Vo	
1009	John Daley	48	C		Beggar	Co Clare	14th		Co
1010	Jane Holloran	44	C		Huckster	City Limk	16		Co
1011	Martin Gibson	28		P	Baker	City Limk	16		C
1012	Garret Cavanagh	68	C		Threadmaker	City Cork	16th	Vo	
1013	Dennis Brien	60	C		Butcher	City Limk	17th		Co
1014	Martin Heher	58	C		Beggar	City Limk	18th		Co
1015	Ann Goss	15	C		poor Girl	City Limk	20	Vo	
1016	Elizabeth Ivers	46	C		R housekeeper	City Limk	20	Vo	
1017	Ellinor Ivers	2	C			*Do*	20	Vo	
1018	Michl Dempsy	8	C			*Do*	26	Vo	
1019	Mary Dempsy	6	C			*Do*	*Do*	Vo	
1020	Patrick Brien	60	C		Skinner	*Do*	27	Vo	
1021	Anstice Kennedy	70	C		Quill Winder	*Do*	27	Vo	
1022	Diana Guppy	6	C		poor Child	*Do*	27th	Vo	
1023	Michl Kearney	59	C		Gardener	Co Clare	24	Vo	
1024	David Gilmore	10		P	poor boy	City of Limk	April 2d		
1025	Honor Blackhall	36	C		Thief	Co Limerick	3d		C
1026	Judith Oakly	50	C		Thief	City Limk	3d		C
1027	Bridgt Flanagan	20	C		Harlot	Ennis Co Clare	3d		C
1028	John Mulloy	70	C		Stone Cutter	City Limk	7th	Vo	
1029	John Cahill	60	C		Porter	City Limk	9th	Vo	
1030	Murto Sullivan	72	C		Labourer	City of Limk	10th	Vo	
1031	Moll Carrold	18	C		poor Girl	City Limk	11th	Vo	
1032	Michl Riordan	8	C			City Limk	12		

No. of bed	Condition when received: Healthy	Sickly	Disease when received	How disposed of: Discharged	Died	Eloped	Condition when discharged: Healthy	Sickly	Observations
		Do	Dropsy	13th Feby					by Order of the Doctor
			Scald Head	13th *Do*					by *Do*
				13th					by *Do*
			Will eat nothing	7th Apr					By a committee, and on paying 6 1/2d
	Do		Loves Liquor	11th March					By Mrs Massey
	Do			11th March					By Mrs Massey
	Do			12th Ap 81			*Do*		By a committee
				12th			*Do*		By a committee
	Do		dressd in boys Cloths			28th Feby			By breaking her Bolts
			Lame	22d Feby					by Alderman Widenham Esqr
				7th Apr 81					By a Committee
	Do			11th July 81					By a Committee held the 18th June 1781
				4th April 92					by Mr Andw Watson
				5th May 87					Shee haveing gon to servis
				22d June 81					By a Committee the 18 June
			Bad disorder			6th Augt 81			She was a maid in the kitchen, and went out
	Do			19th May 81			*Do*		By a Committee
	Do			19th			*Do*		By a Committee
		Sickly	Dropsy		14th March 81				
					18th Apr 83				
			Old Age	12th June 82					
				7th Octr 81					by 3 Governors
				Do					*Do*
				Do					*Do*
	Do			11th March					By Mrs Massey
		Sickly	Evil	5th July					By a Committee
			Insane			26th Apr 81			broke her Irons
		Sickly			June 21st 81				of Old Age
					13 Feby 83				
				14th Sepr					by Walter Widenham Esqr
				Do					
			big with Child	3d Apr					dischard by the Stewd she being in Labour
		Sickly	Fits	22d Jany 82					
			Sore hands	22d March 1781					By paying 3s 1d Enlisted and dischargd by a Comittee
			Drunk	16th March					By a Comittee
			Drunk Mad	1st Apr 81					By order of Revd Mr Ingram
	Healthy		Insane	14 July 81					he having got the bad Disorder, by lying with a fool
			Lame	*Do*	2d Novr 84				
	Do			19th March					By paying 1s 1d
			Ptisick	21st May 81					by Lady Hartstrong, and gave her a Wheel by her order
	Do			7 Octr 81					By 3 Governors
	Do			*Do*					By *Do*
	Do			30th Apr					By Revd Mr Ingram
	Do			30th Apr					By Revd Mr Ingram
				3d May 81					By the Mayor
					11th Octr 81				
						28th March			
					2d March 83				
						Sepr 81 ~~Elop'd 10th Apr~~			over the Kitchen Wall
	Do					Elop'd 10th of April			thro' the Garden
	Do			4 June 81					
			Bad disorder	18th Apr 81					By a Committee
			a pain in the back		11th Augt 81				
					10th Jany 83				
			Infirm	22d June 81					By a Committee
	Do			9 April 82					By a Committee

Current No.	Names	Age	Religion Roman Catholic	Protestant	Occupation	Late residence	Admitted	Voluntary	Compulsory
1033	Patt Kinsly	30		P	America [sic]		16th April 1781		C
1034	John Craig	32	C		America [sic]		16th		C
1035	Charles Donne	45	C			America	18		C
1036	John Molony	80	C		Lime-Burner	City Limk	20th	Vo	
1037	Alex McColough	9		P	poor Child	City Limk	21st	Vo	
1038	Rose McColough	8		P	poor Child	*Do*	21st	Vo	
1039	Cath McColough	10		P	poor Child	*Do*	21st	Vo	
1040	Danl Linehan	58	C		Shagg Weaver	City Limk	30	Vo	
1041	Mary Bourk	60	Catho		R D house keepr	City Limerick	May 1st 81	Vo	
1042	Fanny Whelan	20		P	Soldier's Wife	Corke	2d	Vo	
1043	Mary Murphy	12	C		Servts Child	City Limk	2	Vo	
1044	Biddy Murphy	11	C		*Do*	*Do*	*Do*	*Do*	
1045	Peg Moloney	70	C		House keepr	City Lim	1st	*Do*	
1046	Cath Dondon worth	34	C		was in Gaol, House keep	City Limk	6th	*Do*	
1047	Margt Amboy	7	C		Orphan	City Limk	10th	*Do*	
1048	Jams Holloran	60	C		Labourer	City Limk	13th	*Do*	
1049	Mary Fitzgerald	32	C		Pedlar	Co Waterford	15th June		Co
1050	Mary Carthy	50	C		Servant	Co Clare	15th		Co
1051	Cato Downs	20	C		Harlot	Kings Co Birr	15th	Vo	
1052	Jams Donevan	8	C		poor boy	Co Limk	15th	Vo	
1053	Polly Spellesey	17	C		Harlot	Kilrush	15th	Vo	
1054	Jane Coppinger	52		P	Mantua Maker	Newcastle	20th	Vo	
1055	Mary Connors	64	C		Beggar	Co Limk	21st		Co
1056	Marg Hogan, alias Pagan	25	C		R House keepr	City Limk	21		Co
1057	Bridget Clancy	15	C		Disobedient Girl	Park Co Limk	21st		Co
1058	Bridget Butler	40	C		Publican	City Limk	22	Vo	
1059	Ellinor Walsh	36	C		R house keepr	Nenagh	23d	Vo	
1060	Peg Walsh	8	C				23d	Vo	
1061	Mary Walsh	3	C				23d	Vo	
1062	James Walsh	9 months	C				23d	Vo	
1063	Eliza Bullen	48	C		Spinster	Dublin	23d	Vo	
1064	Patt Ryan	60	C		Gardiner	Co Clare	27th	Vo	
1065	Norry Connors	17	C		a poor Child	City Limk	28th	Vo	
1066	Judith Connors	11	C		*Do*	*Do*	28th	Vo	
1067	Patt English	39	C		Servant	Tipperary	30th	Vo	
1068	Ellinor Walsh	36			R house keepr	Nenagh	3d June	Vo	
1069	Peg Walsh	8			a Child	*Do*	*Do*		
1070	Mary Walsh	3 yrs					June 3d	Vo	
1071	James Walsh	9 months					June 3	Vo	
1072	Ned Collopy	8 yrs	C		Butcher's Son	City Limk	June 4	Vo	
1073	Nancy Brien	15	C		Harlot	City Limk	June 4	Vo	
1074	Nancy Gradey	20	C		Servt	City Limk	June 4	Vo	
1075	Ann Lardd	36	C		Servt	Dublin	June 5th	Vo	
[107]6	Jane Foorde	90	C		Beggar	Dublin	9th	Vo	
[107]7	Willm Field	54		Pro	Linen Weavr	North	11th	Vo	
[107]8	Honor Fitzgerald	26	C		poor Womn	Bruff	15		C
[107]9	John Kannah	79	C		Labourer	City Limerick	16th	Vo	
1080	Susannah Gorman	18	C		Mantua Maker	City Limk	16	Vo	
[108]1	Mick Keaton	2	C		Child	*Do*	*Do*		
[108]2	Jams Ryan	60	C		Servant	City Limk	18th	Vo	
[108]3	Mary Sarah Burns Gore	58	C		Tripe Womn	City Limk	18th		C
[108]4	Sam Burns Gore (inserted above)	8	C		poor boy	*Do*	*Do*		C
1085	Mary Gore	6	C		Child	*Do*	*Do*		C
[108]6	Thoms Boland	59	C		Taylor	Co Limk	*Do* 21st	Vo	
[108]7	Tim Hartigan	66	C		Labourer	Co Limk	20th	Vo	

No. of bed	Condition when received		Disease when received	How disposed of			Condition when discharged		Observations
	Healthy	Sickly		Discharged	Died	Eloped	Healthy	Sickly	
			Asthma			14th June			over the necessary House
			Broken Back			10th June			broke 1 pain of Glass and got out
	Do					10th May 81			By going into the Necessary house and climbing over the Wall
	Do				11th Augt 81				
				30th Apr 81					By Capt Hill Esqr
				Do					By *Do*
				Do					By *Do*
			Sore Legs	11 June					By the Doctor, he being cur'd
			Infirm	20th Octr 81					by a Committee
	Healthy			9th Apr 82					by a Committee
				5th May 81					By Mrs Massey
				5th May 81					By Mrs Massey
		Sickly		19th					By a Committee
		Sickly		29 May 82					By a Committee
	Do			15th Jany 83					By a Committee
		Sickly			29th May 81				he was past Recovery when he come in
	Do		Asthmah	22d June					By a Committee
	Do			18th May					By Capt Hill Esqr on paying 2s 2d
			Bad disorder	13th July 81					She having the bad disorder
	Do			18th May					By Lady Harststonge
	Do			6th Novr					By a Committee
	Do			20th June					By a Committee on paying 1s 1d
		Do		22d					By a Committee on paying 1s 1d
		Do	Lunatick			8th Sepr 81			supposed to be let out of the cells by one of the mason's
	Healthy			22d June					by a Committee
		Do	a pain in the Heart	24th May (erased)		24th May			Slipt out of the Door
	Do			30th					By Lady Hartstronge
				Do					By *Do*
				Do					By *Do*
				Do					By *Do*
		Do	Nervous disorder	6th June		6th June			got leave to go out by a Visiting Lady
				7th Novr 81					By a Committee
				11th Feby					by a Committee
				19th Apr 82					By a Committee
		Sickly	Headach			4th June			he had nothing belonging to the House
				24th Augt					by 3 Governors
				Do					
	Hea			24th Augt					
	Healthy			24th Augt 81					with his Mother by a comittee
	Healthy			17th Decr 82		27th July			by a Committee ~~going into the Water~~
		Sickly	her Jaws tis lock'd with the bad disorder		6th Apr				carried the flannel Shift
	Do					29th Decr 81			She was washing in the Kitchen, and Elop'd
	Do					30th June			took nothing
	Do		a Cripple		29th June 83				
		Do	Rheumatism	11th Octr 83					By a Committee
				22d June 81					By a Committee
					Died the 12th May 1791				the house bougt his Coffin
		Sick		22d June					By a Committee
	Do			22d June					By *Do*
				22 June Discharg'd					By a Committee
		Sickly		13th Sepr 81					By Henry Rose Esqr
		Sickly				10th Octr			by a ticket on the file
				29th July					by Revd Mr Ingram
	Healthy				3d Feby 83				he having come in of his own accord
						16th July			by getting leave go out, from Revd Mr Ingram

Current No.	Names	Age	Religion Roman Catholic	Protestant	Occupation	Late residence	Admitted	Voluntary	Compulsory
[108]8	Michl Houragan	58	C		Labourer	City Limk	22d June 81	Vo	
[108]9	Corneluis Maher	64	C		Labourer	Co Clare	23d	Vo	
1090	Nancy Daley	4			Orphan	City Limk	21st	Vo	
[109]1	Cath Honor Dunfort Markahan	75	C		Beggar	Co Clare	3d July		C
[109]2	Mary Burns	90	C		Beggar	Co Clare	24th June	Vo	
[109]3	Hanah Regan	80	C		Beggar	Co Clare	26th *Do*	Vo	
[109]4	Thos Parker	64		P	Taylor	City Limk	July 1st	Vo	
1095	Connor Sullivan	18	C		Pedlar	Co Limk	3		C
[109]6	Danl Cooney	49	C		Labourer	Co Cork	5	Vo	
[109]7	Nance Green	15	C		poor Girl	City Limk	7	Vo	
[109]8	Cath Green	3	C		a Child	City Limk	7	Vo	
1099	Mary Torphy	18	C		had a Child by a Mr Lynch	Co Limk	July 9th		C
1100	Mary Ahern	22	C		H keepr	City Limk	11th July	Vo	
[110]1	Corns Ahern	4	C			*Do*	*Do*		
[110]2	James Ahern	2	C			*Do*	*Do*		
[110]3	Mary Ahern	4 months	C			*Do*	*Do*		
[110]4	Lot Hinchy	60	C		Taylor, Elop'd and now came in		16th	Vo	
1105	Garret Cavanagh	72	C		thread maker		16th July		
[110]6	Murto Sullivan	64	C		Labourer		16th	Vo	
[110]7	Mary Smyth	42	C		Soldier's Wife	City Limk	19th	Vo	
[110]8	Mary Kean	26	C		Harlot	Co Clare	21st	Vo	
[110]9	Jams Walsh	11	C		Orphan	City Limk	24	Vo	
1110	Poll Walsh	9	C		*Do*	*Do*	*Do*	Vo	
[111]1	Honor Fitzgerald	41	C		bad disorder	Co Clare	23d	Vo	
[111]2	Edmond Ryan	70	C		Labourer	City Limk	27th	Vo	C
[111]3	Pierce Kelly	9	C		poor boy	Ennis	28th	Vo	
[111]4	Thoms Buttimar	10			poor boy	City Limk	28th	Vo	
1115	Willm Clark	50		P	Linen Weaver	Co Tipperary	31st	Vo	
1116	Mary Fitzpatrick	59	C		Servant	City Limk	3 Augt		
[111]7	Patrick Molony	14	C			Co Clare	6th	Vo	
[111]8	Honor Fitzgerald	42	C		Bad disorder	Co Clare	5th Augt	Vo	
[111]9	Mary Ivers	11	C		poor Child	Co Clare	4th	Vo	
1120	Cath Brien	50	C		R houseke	Co Limk	10th	Vo	
[112]1	Dennis Kennelly	60		P	poor man	City Cork	11th	Vo	
[112]2	Nanny Nihill	37	C		Shuler	Ct Limk	8		Co
[112]3	Michl Molony	7	C		Orphan	City Limk	10th	Vo	
[112]4	Dennis Molony	5	C		Orphan	City Limk	10th	Vo	
1125	Michl Kennelly Nihill	60	C		Clothier	Killaloe	13th	Vo	
[112]6	Molly Ryan	27	C		Harlot	City Limk	17th		C
[112]7	Mary McDonnell	50	C		R house keepr	City Limk	13th	Vo	
[112]8	Ellinor Jackson	70		P	R house	Co Clare	17th	Vo	
1129	Cath Fitzgerald	22	Catho		R housekeepr	Co Clare	17th Augt	Vo	
1130	Nancy Fitzgerald	1	C		Child to the above				
[113]1	Thoms Hopkins	74		P	Clothier	City Limk	17	Vo	
[113]2	Edwd Foster	52		Pro	Turner	City Limk	22		C
[113]3	Thoms Holloran	60	C		Beggar	City Limk	22		C

No. of bed	Condition when received Healthy	Sickly	Disease when received	How disposed of Discharged	Died	Eloped	Condition when discharged Healthy	Sickly	Observations
					16th Decr 81				an Asthma
			Dumb		29th May 82				
			Sore Eyes	8th July 81					on paying 3s 0d
		Sickly	Cripple		21st Augt 81				
			Decay	1st July					By Doctor Creagh
			Shaking Ague	6th		23d Augt			on paying 1s 1d
			Shaking Ague	6th July					on paying 1s 1d
	Healthy			22d March 83					he being a Cork man
						15 July			They took nothing
						Do			
			Insane						
	H		came in drunk	14th Sep					by the Mayor
	H					13th Sep			they were stole over the wall, by the Mother
	H					13th Sep			
	H			14th Sepr					by the Mayor broke a pain of glass 1st Sepr 81
			Infected with a bad disorder	27th July					he was in the bad disorder turnd out by the Doctor
				10th Jany 83	10th Jany 83				
				22d Sepr					by Henry Rose Esqr to go servt to Mr Basset
	H		bad disorder	27th July					Turned out by being dirty by Revd Ingram
				7th Novr 81					by a Commitee
		S	bad disorder	24th 7th Novr 81					She having the bad disorder By a Committee
			bad disorder	24th July					She having the bad disorder by Rev Mr Ingram
			Costive		12th Augt 81				
	Healthy		Naked			9th Augt 81			by being left to wash himself, he stole away
	Do			14th Sepr					
		Sickly	Ague			23d			by going out, he having leave to go out, from the Doctor
		Sickly	Asthma	7th Augt 81					By Order of the Mayor on paying 1 71/2
	Healthy		hump back'd			12th Augt			by the Means of Joiners who were working in the Garden
		Sick		8th Augt					by Mrs Hill, on her being dirty
	Healthy					7th May 1784			
	Healthy				17th Decr 81				by drinking Whiskey Excess-by Acct she drank 29ts of it, an died
					15th Decr 81				Old Age
		Sickly	Insane						
	Healthy			13th Sepr 81					
	Healthy			13th Sepr 81					
	Do			15th Jany 1783					By a Committee
			dead Drunk			20th Augt			by putting on a Strange cloak, escaped the Door keeper
			Astmah	5th Sepr 81					By Capt Hill Esqr
	Healthy					27th Augt			Stript of the House Shift and went out naked
		Sickly	Sore Leg		27 June 1783	*Do*			
					27-Jun-81				his Coffin was bougt by his own
		Sickly	Decay	27th Augt 82	Died Sepr 1st 81				
			Sore hand	23d Augt					found on him 4 4 returned to him 3 3 before Lady Hartstrong

Current No.	Names	Age	Religion Roman Catholic	Protestant	Occupation	Late residence	Admitted	Voluntary	Compulsory
[113]4	John Mulqueeny	81	C		Labourer	Co Limk	24 Augt 81	Vo	
1135	Joan Foster	32	C		R housekeepr	Co Kerry	28	Vo	
[113]6	Eliza Foster	11		P		City Limk	28		
[113]7	Mary Foster	9		P		*Do*	*Do*		
[113]8	Sally Foster	4		P		*Do*	*Do*		
[113]9	Fanny Foster	2		P		*Do*	*Do*		
1140	John Foster	14		P		*Do*	*Do*		
[114]1	Ned Foster	6		P		*Do*	*Do*		
[114]2	Ellinor Walsh	37	C		R housekeepr	Nenagh	29th	Vo	
[114]3	James Walsh	1 yr	C		Child		29th	Vo	
[114]4	Mary McCarthy	60	C		Beggar	Charleville	31st		C
1145	Rebecca Freeman	3		P		Reading In Berkshire	3d Sepr	Vo	
[114]6	Charles Earls	56	C		Sailor	Co Cork	3d Sepr		C
[114]7	Connor Gorman	10	C		poor boy	Co Kerry	4th Sepr		
[114]8	Hannah Hartigan	41	C		a common Harlot	City Limk	4th		C
[114]9	Eliza Leary	40	C		Insane	City Limk	4th	Vo	
1150	Mary Collins	60	C		R House keepr	City Limk	5th	Vo	
[115]1	Connor Biddy Gorman Butler	42	C		poor boy drunkard	City Limerick	6th		C
[115]2	Peg Connell	19	C		poor Girl	City Limerick	6th	Vo	
[115]3	Patt Kelly	60	C		Tobacconist	City Limk	10th	Vo	
[115]4	Willm Conway	4	C		Orphan	City Limk	22d	Vo	
1155	Ellinor Hawksford	21	C		Whore	Co Dublin	24th	Vo	
[115]6	Mary Kelly	70	C		Beggar	Co Limk	26th		C
[115]7	Jams Rahilly	64	C		poor Man	Co Limk	26		
[115]8	Eliza Fletcherraser	17		P	Mantua maker	Co Galway	6th Octr	Vo	
1159	Jane Fletcher	50	C		poor Woman	Co Limk	6th		C
1160	John Fahey	23	Papist		poor lad	City Limk	9th Octr	Vo	
[116]1	Biddy Butler	43	*Do*		pox'd	City Limk	8 *Do*		Co
[116]2	Dorcas Shea	21	*Do*		Whore	Co Dublin	9th		Co
[116]3	Judy Donevan	23	*Do*		a poor Girl	City Limk	9th	Vo	
[116]4	Thom Donevan	1yr	*Do*		Son the above	in the Abbey	9th	Vo	
1165	Poll Sheehan	24	*Do*		a bad Girl	Co Dublin	20th	Vo	
[116]6	Thom Ivers	2		P	poor Children	Carlow	21st	Vo	
[116]7	John Ivers	3		P	*Do*	*Do*	*Do*		
[116]8	Julia Hassett	80	C		R house keepr	City Limk	22 Octr 81		
[116]9	Mary Ivers	11		P	*Do*	*Do*	*Do*		
1170	Andrew Rye	43		P	Marine	Mayo	26th Oct		C
[117]1	Willm Coffee	60	*Do*		Smyth		27th	Vo	
[117]2	Ann Conner	39	*Do*		R House Keepr	Cork	Novr 1st		
[117]3	Ursula Connor	11	*Do*				*Do*		
[117]4	Eliza Conner	8	*Do*				*Do*		
[117]5	James Connor	5	*Do*				*Do*		
1176	Biddy Hurly	12	*Do*		poor Girl		*Do*		
[117]7	Eliza Barry	40		Pro	Sempstress	Co Limk	Novr 4th	Vo	
[117]8	Jams Shea	18	*Do*		Thread maker	Co Limk	5th	Vo	
[117]9	Biddy Butler	40	*Do*		Drunkard	City Limk	8th		C
1180	Francis Moore	36	*Do*		Tread maker	Co Dublin	10th		C
[118]1	Penny Bennett	80	*Do*		poor Woman	City Limk	18th	Vo	
[118]2	Poll Hinchy	18	*Do*		Whore	Queen's Co	18		C
[118]3	Sarah Fee	75	*Do*		poor Womn	Co Limk	18		C
[118]4	Edwd Collopy	10	*Do*		Bastard	Co Limk	17th	Vo	
[118]5	Martin Kennedy	12	*Do*		Orphan	Kilkenny	22d	Vo	
1186	John Conner	11 son to Ann	*Do*		poor Child	Cork	26th	Vo	
1187	Patt Brien	62	*Do*		Skinner	City Limk	29th	Vo	
1188	Roger Clancy	73	*Do*		Linen Weaver	City Limk	29th	Vo	
1189	Patt Gardiner	34	*Do*		Labourer	Co Clare	29th		
1190	Ellinor Daly	42	*Do*		Hatter	City Cork	10th Decr	Vo	

No. of bed	Condition when received		Disease when received	How disposed of			Condition when discharged		Observations
	Healthy	Sickly		Discharged	Died	Eloped	Healthy	Sickly	
		Sickly	desperate Sore Leg		3d Octr 81				
	Heal			6th Sepr 81					after burying her husbd
	Do			9th Sepr					by LantHill Esq
	Do			*Do*					
	Do			*Do*					
	Do			*Do*					
	Do			6th Sepr					
	Do			*Do*					
	Do		dead Drunk	25th Decr 81					She came in drunk, and was turned out, being in Labour
	Do			*Do*					
			a pain in the heart	2d Sepr 81					by the Mayor, on paying 1s 1d
					25th Jany 83				
				7th Novr 81					By a Committee
				7th Novr 81		27th Feby 82			putting in Turf by a Committee
				12th March 83					
			Insane	8th Sepr	8th Sepr				By Order LantHill Esqr
			Imposthume	28th Sepr 81					By the Doctor
			Drunkard			6th Octr 81			thro' the Garden
				6th Novr 81 (erased)	6th Novr 81				by a committee a Ladder
			a pain in the back	11th Octr 83					By a Committee
			Fool		10th Apr 82				He was a fool and died with fits
				28th Sepr 81					By the Doctor, She being rotten with the pox
	Do			2d Octr 81					on paying 1s 1d and 1s 6d for her diet
				7th Novr 81					by a Committee
		Sickly	Bad disorder	7th Octr 81					discharged by Henry Rose Esqr
	Health			29th Decr 81					on paying 1s 1d
			Lame of 2 legs	10th Apr 82					By a Committee
			dead drunk	16th Octr					being rotten with the Venerl and paying 1 1
			big with Child			14th Octr 81			thro the street door at night fall
	Do			9th Novr 81					by a Committee
	Do			9th *Do*					by *Do*
	Do					6th Novr 81			Over the Necessary house
				7th Novr 81					by a Committee
				7 *Do*					by *Do*
				10th Apr 82					by a Committee
				7th					by *Do*
			the loss of an Hand	7th					by *Do*
			lame of 2 legs		6th Feby 82				
		Sickly	Consumption		17th March 82				after a tedious illness
				20th March 82					by 3 Governors
				20th 82					by *Do*
				20th 82					by *Do*
		Do				9th Novr 81			
			Rheumatic	22 June 82					By a Committee & never to be admittd
		Do		19th Jany					
			Drunk	22d Decr Novr					by a Committee
	Do			14th Novr					by a Committee
		Do	Bed Ridden		2d Jany 82				
			Just brought to bed	22d Novr 81					By a Committee
	Do			20th Augt 82					
	Do			9th Decr					
						9th Sepr 82			over the necessary house
		Do		20th March 82					By 3 Governors
		Do	a pain in the back		4th July 83				
			loss of Sight	10th Apr 82					by a Committee
			Fits	*Do*					
			Running Evil	29th Decr 81					By the Doctor and apothecary

Current No.	Names	Age	Religion Roman Catholic	Protestant	Occupation	Late residence	Admitted	Voluntary	Compulsory
[119]1	Thoms Cahill	59	*Do*		Porter	City Limk	12th Decr 81		
[119]2	Jams Cahill	16			Porter	City Limk	12th		
[119]3	Danl Donevan	67	*Do*		Taylor	*Do*	13th		
1194	Edmd Hayes	55	*Do*		Taylor	*Do*	29th		
1195	Eliza Lock	28		P	Soldier's Wife	City Limk	26th Decr 81	Vo	
[119]6	Sieve Marshall	14	C		poor Girl	City Limk	24th 81	Vo	
1197	Thoms Lock	6		P	Son to Eliza Lock		26th	Vo	
1198	Matthew Loragan	70	C		School Mastr	City Limk	29th	Vo	
1199	John Davernor	13	C		poor boy	City Limk	29	Vo	
1200	Nell Hennessy	29	C		Sawyer's Wife	Nenagh	9th Jany 82	Vo	
[120]1	Biddy Hogan	26	C		Taylor's Wife	City Limk	9th	Vo	
[120]2	Thoms Flanagan	18		P	Servant	Co Carlow	15th	Vo	C
[120]3	Cath Ready	64	C		Beggar	City Limerick	16th		C
[120]4	Judy Hennessy	4 months			a Child to Nell Hennessy		21st	Vo	
[120]5	Dennis Molony	50	C		Labourer	Co Limk	21	Vo	
[120]6	Matthew Holoran	60	C		Boatman	Co Limk	22d	Vo	
1207	Patt Regan	75	C		Butter Broker	City Limk	*Do*	Vo	
[120]8	Norry Lynch	17	C		Lace Maker	City limk	*Do*	Vo	
[120]9	Jane Ahern	32	C		R house keep	City Limk	23d	Vo	
1210	Mary Ahern	9			Child	*Do*	*Do*	*Do*	
1211	Biddy Ahern	8			*Do*	*Do*	*Do*	*Do*	
[121]2	Thom Ahern	3			*Do*	*Do*	*Do*	*Do*	
[121]3	Michl Marra	76	C		Baker	City Limk	24th	Vo	
[121]4	Mary Hall	50	C		Fool	Co Limk	28th	Vo	
[121]5	Judy Henessy	1 month			Child	City Limk	21st	Vo	
1216	Patt Mead	53			Piper	Co Limk	28	Vo	
1217	Jams Bourk	58	C		R house keepr	Co Limk	29th	Vo	
[121]8	Andw Stephenson	60		P	Sadler	North	29th	Vo	
1219	John Dinnison			P	S Weaver	Dublin	29		
1220	Michl Houragan	70	C		Stone Cutter	City Limk	Feby 4th	Vo	
[122]1	Michl Molony	7			GrandSon to the above		4th	Vo	
[122]2	Eliza Shanahan	24	C		Harlot	Cork	7th	Vo	
[122]3	Danl Gordan	13	C		poor boy	Co Limk	2d	Vo	
[122]4	Cath Murphy	19	C		Harlot	Cork	7th	Vo	
[122]5	Norry Bourk	21	C		bad Girl	City Limk	7th	Vo	
[122]6	John Bourk	2			Child to the above		7th	Vo	
1226	Nell Bourk	1			*Do* to the above		7th	Vo	
1227	Honor Haly	19	C		Harlot	City Limk	8th	Vo	
[122]8	Mary Doran	3			Child to the above		8	Vo	
[122]9	Nancy Doran	2			Child to the above		8	Vo	
1230	Thos Dalton	74	C		Butcher	City Limk	18th	Vo	
[123]1	Poll Kennedy	10	C		Orphan	City Limk	18th	Vo	
[123]2	Peg Kennedy	6	C		Orphan	City Limk	18th	Vo	
[123]3	Mary Durgan	29		Pro	Drunkard	City Limk	19th		C
[123]4	Eliza Marra	19	C		Button maker	City Limk	20th	Vo	
[123]5	Sally Hardy	15		P	Tumbling Girl	Galway	23d	Vo	
1236	Thady McNemara	62	C		Porter	Limk	22d		C
1236	Mary Nihill	25	C		Orphan	Co Limk	25th	Vo	
[123]7	John Brown	50	C		Porter	Limk	27th	Vo	
[123]8	Mary Fitzgerald	40	C		Servant	Limk	March 1st	Vo	
[123]9	Francis Keefe	36		P	Barber	Limk	22d Feby		
1240	Sarah Hill	25		P	Mad this 11yr	Co Limk	8th March	Vo	
[124]1	John Lindon	43	C		Sawyer	City Limk	4th	Vo	
[124]2	Moll Ryan	29	C		Tripe Womn	City Limk	13th		C
[124]3	Cate Hurley	18	C		poor Girl	Adare	26th	Vo	
[124]4	Nance Hurley	14	C		poor Girl	*Do*	*Do*	Vo	
1245	Honor Doran	19	C		R house kepr	Limk	25th	Vo	
1246	Michl Bourk	70yrs	C		Comber	City Limk	24th March	Vo	
1247	Mary Doran	3				City Limk	25th March 82	Vo	
[124]8	Nancy Doran	2				City Limk	25th March	Vo	

No. of bed	Condition when received Healthy	Sickly	Disease when received	How disposed of Discharged	Died	Eloped	Condition when discharged Healthy	Sickly	Observations
				11th Octr 83					By a Committee
				20th Apr 82					by a Committee
			loss of Sight		10th Feby 82				
			Ague	20th Jany 82					by Capt Hill Esqr
	Healthy			16th Feby 82					by Henry Rose Esqr and the Doctr
	Do			17th Sepr 82					
			Itch	16th Feby 82					By Henry Rose & Doctr
			Subject to Fits	2d May 82					by a Committee
				9th Octr 83					by a Committee
			came in Drunk	10th Apr 82					By a Committee
				16th Feby					being a Tief and Drunkard by H Rose Esqr & Doctr Creagh
						19 Jany 82			Out of the Necessary
				7th Feby 82					on paying 1s 1d
				10th Apr 82					By a Committee
		Mad	Insane			16th Feby			after being cur'd by the Doctr
			Rheumatism			16th Feby 82			
			Rupture	11th Sepr 82					
				7th Feby 82					having the bad disorder
				11th Octr 83					By a Committee
				27th Augt 1789					By A Committee
				11th Octr 83					
			Insane			13th Augt			Out of the Cell
				10th Apr 1782					By a Committee
			Lame of 2 Legs	12th March 83					By a Committee
	Do			6th Feby 82					by Henry Rose Esqr
	Do			26th Feby 82					by Mr Phillips
	Do			10th Apr 82					By a Committee
		Sickly	Asthma		16th Feby 82				of the Asthma
				18th Feby 83					
		Do	Bad disorder	22d Feby 82					By Henry Rose & Doctr
	H			5th Feby					Bound to a Linen Weaver by H Rose and Doctor
		Do	Bad disorder	*Do*					
				17th March					By Revd Mr Ingram being a Nuisance
				17th					
				15th					
		Sickly	Inveterate Pox	13th March					by the Doctr on her having the Clap
				17th					these were Children belonging to the above Doran
				13th					
		Sickly	Rheumatism		11th Sepr 82				
	Hea			May 1st 83					
	Healthy			*Do*					
	Healthy		Inebriated	26th Apr 82					By a Committee
	Healthy			26th Apr 82					By a Committee
				12th march 83					By a Committee
			Drunk	8th March 1782					By Henry Rose Esqr and the Doctr
	healthy			3 May 82					by a Committee
			Insane	*Do* [sic] 11th Octr 83					
		Sickly	Scurvy	22d june 82					By a Committee
		Sick	Cancer	8th March 82					turned out, being Incurable
			Insane	12th Augt 82					by 3 Governors
			Broken Leg	23d March 82					being cur'd By Henry Rose Esqr
		Do	dead drunk			20th March			by the fault of the Door-keeper
	Do					26th novr 82			went to wash at the River
	Do			5th Octr 82					by a Committee
	Do			10th Apr 82					By a Committee
			old Age		3d Apr 82				he was very ill when recd
	Do			10th Apr 82					By a Committee
	Do			10th Apr 82					By a Committee

Current No.	Names	Age	Religion Roman Catholic	Protestant	Occupation	Late residence	Admitted	Voluntary	Compulsory
[124]9	Thoms Donegan	60	Pap		Labourer	*Do*	March 28th 82	Vo	
1250	Cate Jams Hurley Bourk	21	Catho		Cripple	Ennis	29th	Vo	
1251	Moll Cleary	30	C		R house keepr	Co Limk	30th	Vo	
1252	James Cleary	60	C		poor Man	*Do*	*Do*	Vo	
[125]3	Kitty Cleary	2	C			*Do*	*Do*	*Do*	
[125]4	Thoms Cleary	1	C			*Do*	*Do*	*Do*	
[125]5	John McDermott	13	C		Servt to Thos Smyth Esqr	City Limk	Apr 1		C
[125]6	Cath Fitzgerald	19	C		Mad Girl	City Limk	2		C
1257	John McMahon	54	C		Serge Weaver	City Limk	3d		
[125]8	Mary Cleary	4	C		poor Child	Co Limk	6th	Vo	
[125]9	Joan Fitzgerald	80	C		R House-keepr	City Limk	8	Vo	
1260	Patt Cannaw	47	C		Spinner	North	10th	Vo	
[126]1	Geo Dundon	8	C		poor boy	Co Tipperary	9th	Vo	
[126]2	Arthur Athlenic	10	C		poor boy	Dublin	12th	Vo	
[126]3	Willm O'Brien	80	C		Linen Weaver	City Limk	14th	Vo	
[126]4	Biddy McNemara	26	C		Beggar		14th	Vo	
[126]5	Mary McNemara	8	C		a poor Child		14th	Vo	
[126]6	Thoms Doherty	16			a Rogue	Co Galway	16	Vo	
1267	Murto Murphy	60	C		Labourer	Co Limk	19th	Vo	
[126]8	Hannah Supple	60	C		Beggar	Co Limk	19th		C
[126]9	Mary Ryan	30	C		bad Woman	Co Clare	19th		
1270	Richd Marra	2	C		Child to No 2 [entry 1269 Mary Ryan]		19th		
[127]1	Thos Moll Doherty Ryan	23	C		Stroler	City Limk	21th Apr 1782		C
[127]2	Nell Fitzgerald	36	C		bad Woman	City Limk	24th	Vo	
[127]3	Margt Hudson	63	*Do*		Cook	*Do*	29th	Vo	
[127]4	Jams Macantire	13		P	Poor Scholar	Dublin	6th May	Vo	
[127]5	Willm Gorman	62	C		Taylor	City Limk	8	Vo	
[127]6	Agnes Gorman	53	C		Wife to the above	*Do*	*Do*	*Do*	
1277	Norry Lynch	19	C		Harlot	*Do*	*Do*	*Do*	
[127]8	Jane Leary	22	C		Soldier's Wife	North	*Do*	*Do*	
[127]9	Will Leary	1	C			*Do*	*Do*	*Do*	
1280	Mary Kirwigan	18	C		Common Stroler	Limk	9th		Co
[128]1	Mary McNemara	58	C		Beggar	Limk	11		C
[128]2	Nell Dunn	43	C		Beggar	Limk	11		C
[128]3	Julia Hassett	70	C		house Keeper	Limk	11th	Vo	
[128]3	Darby Nunan	61	C		Cobler	Limk	12	*Do*	
[128]4	Dens Molony	54	C		Sawyer	Co Limk	13	*Do*	
[128]5	Cath Robinson	50	C		R house keep	Limk	14	*Do*	
[128]6	Thoms Hartigan	70	C		Beggar	Limk	16		C
1287	Matt Loragan	69	C		Beggar	Limk	13		C
[128]8	Mary Barry	45	C		Beggar	Limk	17		C
[128]9	Mau Barry	2	C		Child	*Do*	*Do*		
1290	Willm Sallinger	60	C		Stroller	Tipperary	17		C
[129]1	Danl Leslie	48		P	Stroller	C Meath	17th		C
[129]2	Johanna Joyce	19	C		Thief	Charleville	20th		C
[129]3	Biddy Daley	39	C		bad Woman	City Limk	21		
[129]4	Eliza Ivers	42		P	R house keepr	North	22d		
[129]5	Mary Ivers	13		P					
[129]6	Willm Burnam	70		P	Smyth	City Limk	23		
[129]7	Ann Ivers	2							
1298	Ann McDermott	39	C		R H keepr	Co Limk	19th	Vo	
[129]9	Cath Hogan	50	C		Beggar	Co Tipperary	19		C
1300	Peg Kirwagan	18	C		Strumpet	Limk	2d June		C
1302	John Cloone	26 yrs	C		toll Gatherer	City Limk	4th June	Vo	
[130]3	Margt Fitzgerald	46	C		R House Keepr	Co Limk	3d		C
[130]4	Joan Fitzgerald	5	C		Child	*Do*	*Do*		Co
[130]5	John Dennessy	70		P	Clothier	Limk	18	Vo	
[130]6	Mary Creagh	5	C		Orphan	Limk	17th	Vo	

No. of bed	Condition when received Healthy	Sickly	Disease when received	How disposed of Discharged	Died	Eloped	Condition when discharged Healthy	Sickly	Observations
	Do		Lax	9th Apr 1782					By a Committee
			Lame of his legs	11th Octr					By a Committee
				27th May 83					
				1st Decr 83					went to Ballingary
				27th May 83					
					20th May 83				
						12th Sepr 82			Over the Necessary House
				11th May 83					By a Committee
			a Fever		5th Apr 82				
					15th March 83				
					2d Octr 82				
			Insane	19th May 82					By a Committee
						6th May 83			
				14th May 82		14th May 82			over the Back Wall
					2d Jany 85				
				12th May 82					got a tickett from Capt Hill, to the Infirmary
				12th May 82					daughter to the above
	Do					14th May			thro' the back yard
	Do			2d May 82					By a Committee
						24th July 82			at night over the Gardn
		Sicly	bad disorder	26th Apr 82					By a Committee
		Sick		26th Apr 82					By a Committee
			Dead drunk	19th May					on paying 4s 4d
			Sore Eyes			8th Feby 83			she was a big thief
	Do				2d March 83				
	H				3d Decr 85	11th May 82			Over the Back Wall
		Sickly		24th May 82					
	Do			24th May 82					By a Committee
				17th Augt 82					by a Committee
				22d June					By a Committee, & never to be admittd
				22d *Do*					
				19th May					by a Committee
				12th May 82					on paying 1 1 and 3d to the Carr. by the Mayor
				19th May					by a Committee on paying 1 4 by Lant Hill Esq
				26th July					
	Do			19th Augt 82					by a Committee
				11th Octr 1783					By a Committee
				22d June 82					By a Committee
			a Cripple		3d Feby 83				
				6th Jany	6 Jany 83				
				24th May 82					By a Committee
				24th 82					By a Committee
			his Nose Eat off	19th May 82					By a Committee
			Dead drunk	19 May 82					By a Committee
	Healthy			24th May 82					By a Committee
				6th June					By a Committee
				6th *Do* [sic] June					by *Do* a Committee
				6 June					By a Committee
				22d June 82					By a Committee
				6 *Do*					by *Do*
			a Sore Leg	29th May 82					by the Doctor, she having the pox
				29th June					on paying 1 1
				19th Augt 82					by a Committee on paying 2s 2d
		Sickly	Blind	12th Novr 82					by Dean Creagh
			with Child	22d June 82					By a Committee
	Healthy			22d *Do*					By a Committee
		Sick	Bloody Flux		26th June 82				
				26th Sepr 82					by the Doctor

Current No.	Names	Age	Religion Roman Catholic	Protestant	Occupation	Late residence	Admitted	Voluntary	Compulsory
[130]7	Nell Behawn	40	C		Widow	Limk	18th June 1782	Vo	
[130]8	Biddy Behawn	2	C			*Do*	*Do*	Vo	
1309	Mary Smyth	72	C		Widow	Co Limk	*Do*	Vo	
1310	Moll White	30	C		Spinster	Limk	*Do*	Vo	
1311	Biddy Durick	24	C		Dealer	Limk	20th	Vo	
[131]2	Jane Bowes	42	C		Widow	Ennis	20th	Vo	
[131]3	Darby Shaughnessy	60	C		Beggar	Limerick	22d		C
[131]4	Willm Minehan	50	C		Cripple	Limk	24th	Vo	
[131]5	Denis Molony	49	C		Clothier	Co Limk	27th	Vo	
[131]6	Mary Brown	34	C		Beggar	Co Limk	26		
[131]7	Peg Little	19	C		Beggar		26		C
[131]8	Thoms Cambell	20	C		Servant	Dublin	28th		
1319	Mary Connors	80	C		Beggar	City Limk	4th July		
[132]0	Cate Cain, alias Rurk	19	C		Beggar	City Limk	5th		C
1321	Mary Rourk	2	C						
[132]2	Michl Rourk	3	C						
[132]3	Jams Dea	68	C		Servt		7th	Vo	
[132]4	Willm Brien	50	C		Broguemaker		6th	Vo	
[132]5	Patt Kelly Hurly	42	C		Beggar		10th		C
[132]6	Jery Fool	28	C		Fool		12th		C
[132]7	Nell Donohue	36	C		Stroller		12th		C
[132]8	Danl Lucy	30	C		Labourer		13th	Vo	
1329	Corns Sarsfield	36			Cobler		16	Vo	
1330	Red Moll alias Ryan	23			Whore		16		
1331	Bulls Eye Stapleton (alias Mary)	19			Whore		16		
1332	Mary Hackett	50		P	Semstress	City Limk	20 July		C
1333	Mary Reddin	9	C		Stroller	City Limk	18		C
1334	Mary Keogh	17	C		Orphan	*Do*	22d Henry Rose		
[133]5	James Tracy	19	C		Linen Weaver	*Do*	23d by L Hill		C
[133]6	Moll Fitzgerald	30	C		Spinster	Co Limk	23d L Hill	Vo	
[133]7	Mary Foorde	23		P	Sempstress	Co Limk	25th	Vo	
[133]8	Alice Enwright	33	C		Servant	Co Limk	28th	Vo	
1339	Mary Howe	7			Child	*Do*	*Do*	Vo	
1340	Mary Gibbons	1			Child	*Do*	*Do*	Vo	
[134]1	Mary Carr	19		P	Servant	City Limk	29		
1342	Ann Hayes	30	C		Servant	Co Limk	30th	Vo	
[134]3	Jams Hayes	10	C		Boy	*Do*	*Do*		
1344	Garrett Donne	59			Servt	*Do*	*Do*		
[134]5	Paddy Hayes	5				*Do*	*Do*		
[134]6	Eliza Hayes	2							
[134]7	John Hayes	1 yr 9 Months							
[134]8	Patt Mulvehill	14			poor boy	City Limk	1 Augt 82		
[134]9	Willm Shortel	70		P	Servant	England	5th	Vo	
1350	Ally Brown	28	C		bad woman	Co Limk	6th	Vo	
[135]1	Thady McNemara	3				*Do*	*Do*		
1352	Mick McNemara	1				*Do*	*Do*	Vo	
1353	Tim McNemara	54	C		Drunkard	City Limk	7th		
[135]4	Mary Houragan	30	C		Stroller	Co Limk	23d		C
[135]5	Eliza Houragan	3 months				*Do*	*Do*		C
[135]6	Tim Houragan	6 yrs				*Do*	*Do*		
[135]7	Biddy Durick	24	C		house keepr	*Do*	26th		
[135]8	Sarah Green	40	C		house keepr	Co Limk	2d Sepr	Vo	
[135]9	Dennis Montgomery Green	5							
1360	Thos Green	10 weeks							
[136]1	Eliza Montgomery	17				Dublin	2d	Vo	
[136]2	Cath Dundon	30				Co Limk	4th	Vo	

No. of bed	Condition when received Healthy	Sickly	Disease when received	How disposed of Discharged	Died	Eloped	Condition when discharged Healthy	Sickly	Observations
					22d March				
				29th June 82					by a Committee
			Mad	13th Augt 82					by 3 Governors
			Mad	*Do*					
	Health			22d June 82					by a Committee
	Health			23d Novr					by a Committee on paying 1s 1d
				17th Augt 82					by a Committee
			Blind	furlow					
				8th Sepr 82					By 3 Governors
			Fool		4th Decr 1795				the house bougt her Coffin
			Cripple	5th Octr 82					he Enlisted
		Sick			20th Apr 83				
				20th July 82					On paying 1s 1d
				Do					
				Do					
		Sick			Died 31st Octr 82				
			nigh sighted	3d Augt 82					by Capt Hill
				12th July 1782					By 3 Governors
			Insane		11th Augt 82				
				19th Augt 82					a great Tief
		Sick		5th Octr 82					he being Enlisted
			Insane		23d Octr 82				
				17th					on paying 1s 4
				17th Augt 82					on quitting the town
			Drunk	30th July 82					by 3 Governors on paying 1s 1 by 3 Govs
			found Stealing	30th 82					by the Mayor on paying 1 1 by the Mayor
		Health				14th Sepr 82			thro' the back Yard
			Foolish	17th Augt 82					By 3 Governors
						9th Octr 82			but returned again, and was discharged 23 Octr 82
		ealth		18th Jany 83					by a Committee
				27th Apr 83					By the Doctor
				18th Jany 83					by a Committee
			Insane	21st Febuy 1785					
				20th Feby 83					
						8th Sepr 83			over the Wall
				19th Augt 83					by a committee
				25 Augt 83					By the Doctr
					14th Feby 83				
					29th May 83				
			Insane			Augt 3d 82			over the Gard Wall
				19th Augt 82					by a Committee
	H			12th March 83					By a Committee
				Do					*Do*
					16th Jany 83				
			dead drunk	17th Augt					on paying 1s 4d
				24th Novr 82					By a Committee
				24th *Do*					*Do*
				24th *Do*					*Do*
			Insane	2d Octr					by Revd Dean Hoare being Recovered
				17th May 83					by a committee
				17 *Do*					by *Do*
					4th Novr 82				
			Sick			9th Octr 82			
			Lax	14th Sepr					by the Doctr

Current No.	Names	Age	Religion Roman Catholic	Religion Protestant	Occupation	Late residence	Admitted	Voluntary	Compulsory
1362	Nance Houragan	20	C		Stroller	Co Cork	6th Sepr 82		C
[136]3	Hugh Tuhahy	70	C		poor man	Co Limk	6	Vo	
[136]4	Andw Stephenson	60		P	Sadler	North	6	Vo	
[136]5	Mary Brein	63	C		Beggar	City Limk	11th		C
[136]6	Biddy McGrath	24	C		Whore	City Limk	11		C
[136]7	Bridgt Bryan	56	C		Beggar	*Do*	13th		C
[136]8	Mary Brown	61	C		poor Woman	*Do*	13	Vo	
1369	Patt Linsey	31	C		Linen Weaver	Galway	16th		C
1370	Cate Light	50	C		Smuggler	City Limk	16	Vo	
[137]1	Mad Hayes	46	C		Stroller	*Do*	23		C
1372	Darby Nunan	58	C		Cobler	*Do*	23d	Vo	
[137]3	John Maguire	76	C		Stay maker	*Do*	25th	Vo	
[137]4	Eliza Heden	34		Pro	Semstress	Co Tipperary	26	Vo	
[137]5	John Heheden	5							
[137]6	Edwd Headen								
[137]7	Roger Clanchy	72	C		Linen Weaver	City of Limerick	27th	Vo	
[137]8	Ann Lord	50		P	Sempstress	*Do*	28th	Vo	
1379	Grace Kelly	70	C		Cook	City Limk	29th	Vo	
1380	Mary Murphy	36	C			*Do*	2d Octr	Vo	
[138]1	Ellinor Gradey	30	C		R H keepr	Co Limk	4th	Vo	
1382	Molly Gradey	11	C				*Do*	*Do*	
[138]3	Jams Gradey	2 1/2	C				*Do*	*Do*	
[138]4	Bridget Gavin	40	C		Sempstress	City Limk	5th	*Do*	
[138]5	Ellinor Gavin	12				*Do*	5	Vo	
[138]6	Mary Nihill	20	C		poor Girl	Killaloe	8th	Vo	
[138]7	Fanny Jones	18	C		bad Girl	Dublin	12	Vo	
[138]8	Chars Rickards	42	C		Nailer	Limk	15th Compelld		
1389	Poll Murphy	10	C		Orphan	Co Clare	*Do*	Vo	
1390	Dens Kennedy	20	C		Servant	Co Cork	20th	Vo	
1391	Cate Freeman	19	C		Sempstress	City Limk	24	C [sic]	
1392	Hannah Goggin	37		P	Servt	Yorkshire	25th Octr		
1393	Robt Lemmon	6		P	Orphan	City Limk	31st Octr 82	Vo	
1394	Margt Lemmon	4		P	Orphan	*Do*	*Do*	Vo	
1395	John Hogan	39	C		Pedlar	*Do*	Novr 1st	Co [sic]	
1396	Cath Rourk	19	C		House keepr	*Do*	Novr 1st	Vo	
1397	Mary Rourk	2				*Do*	*Do*	Vo	
1398	Michl Rourk	3				*Do*	*Do*	Vo	
1399	Ann Donevan	36	C			Co Limk	4th	Vo	
1400	Jams Donevan	8				*Do*	*Do*		
1401	Willm Donevan	4				*Do*	*Do*		
1402	Mary Creagh	9			Orphan	City Limk	7th	Vo	
1403	Jams Meehan	80	C		Serge Weaver	*Do*	9	Vo	
1404	Jery Molony [written above is 'hony' to imply 'Mohony']	58	C		*Do*	*Do*	9		
1405	Margt Hickson	59	C		R House keepr	*Do*	9		
1406	Mary Hickson	20	C		*Do*	*Do*	9		
1407	Christian Lynch	18	C		Sempstress	City Limk	11th	Vo	
1408	Mick Murphy	10			Orphan	*Do*	*Do*		
1409	Terence Meskill	5	C		*Do*	*Do*	*Do*	Vo	
1410	Peg Murphy	6	C		*Do*	*Do*	*Do*	Vo	
1411	Margt Hudson	29	C		Servt	*Do*	13th	Vo	
1412	Peg Enright	31			daughter to the above		*Do*	Vo	
1413	Jane Hunter	39	C		Soldiers Wife	*Do*	13th	Vo	
1414	Catharine Arthur	17	C		poor Girl		11th	Vo	

No. of bed	Condition when received Healthy	Sickly	Disease when received	How disposed of Discharged	Died	Eloped	Condition when discharged Healthy	Sickly	Observations
	Healthy					13th Sepr 82			thro' the Gardn
		Sick			13th Sepr 82				
			Lax	6th Octr 82					
				5th Octr 82					by a Committee on paying 1s 1
				15th March 83					by a committee
				5th Octr 82					
				5th Octr 82					by a Committee
			Scurvey		29th May 83				after a tedious Illness
					10th Novr 82				
			Mad			23d Octr			drew the Hinge of the Cell, and carried away a Blanket & Sheet
	Healthy				11th July 82				died about 12 O Clock Morning Suddenly
				20th July 83					
	Healthy			28th Decr					by the Doctor, she having the bad disorder
	Do			*Do*					
	Do			*Do*					
	Healthy				24th Decr 84				
					18th Jany 83				
	Healthy			24 Jany 83					
				15th Jany 83					by a Committee
				15th March 83					By a Committee
				Do					*Do*
				Do					*Do*
				15th March 83					*Do*
				Do					*Do* but admitt'd again and discharged 4th Augt 1783
	Do			19th Feby 83					
	Do			19th Octr 82					By a Committee
			Mad	21st Novr					by 3 Governors
				21st Novr 82					by 3 Governors
						4th Novr 82			Enlisted
	Healthy					9th			late at night
	Healthy			14th Novr 82					By a Committee
	Healthy			14th June					By a Committee
	Do			*Do*					By *Do*
			Insane	6th Novr 82					being Recovered
				15th Decr 82					
				18th Decr 82					By a Committee
				Do					*Do*
				Do					*Do*
				16th					*Do*
				Do					By the Doctr
				Do		Elopd 1st Jany 83			came in 1 day, was now discharged with her 2 Children 15th March 1783 [sic- this probably refers to entry 1399 Ann Donavan]
			Old and Sick	15th Jany 83					
				Do 3d Jany 83					having Enlisted
				3rd Jany 83	17th May 85				having Enlisted
			15th March 83		27 Augt 86				by a Committee
				15th March 83					
				15th March 83					By Dean Creagh
				14th Jany 83					By Dean Creagh
					18th Jany 83 [sic]	12th Octr 85			the doorkeeper Let her Out
					2d March 83				
				2d March 83					
				11th Decr 82					his Worship gave her 4s 10 wch was allowd on the Book
				15t Apr 83					

Current No.	Names	Age	Religion Roman Catholic	Protestant	Occupation	Late residence	Admitted	Voluntary	Compulsory
1415	Margt Brien	60	C		R House keepr	*Do*	15th Octr 82	Vo	
1416	Willm Chamber	49		P	Shuler		18	C [sic]	
1417	Jams Gill	60 yrs	C		Paver	City Limk	18th Novr	Vo	
1418	Lucy Barton	50			H Keepr	*Do*	22d Novr	Vo	
1419	Ann Lemmon	30		Protest	Soldier's Wife	Dublin	23d	Vo	
1420	Frances Lemmon	4	C		Child	*Do*	*Do*	Vo	
1421	Mary Houragan	30			Stroller		27th Novr	Vo	
1422	Eliza Houragan	4 months							
1423	Tim Houragan	6 yrs							
[142]4	Moll Houragan	8							
[142]5	Patk Green	13	Cath		poor boy		30th	Vo	
[142]6	Ann Nickson	19			Stroller	Dublin	28th	*Do*	
[142]7	Mau Minehan	13	C		Rogue	Limk	2d Decr	*Do*	
[142]8	Mary Coleman	20			Stroller		3d	*Do*	
[142]9	Peg Coleman	6 month					3d	*Do*	
1430	Mary Kennedy	9			Orphan	Cork	3	*Do*	
1431	Peg Kennedy	5			*Do*	*Do*	3	*Do*	
1432	Loughlin Brien [Carmody written above]	60			Labourer	Co Limk	8th	*Do*	
1433	Francis Donevan	70			*Do*	Co Clare	9th	*Do*	
1434	John Massey	64			Labourer	Co Limk	10	*Do*	
[143]5	Willm Brien	40			Cobler	*Do*	15th	*Do*	
[143]6	Catharine Shaughy	40	C		Millers Wife	Co Limk	17th	*Do*	
[143]7	Nance Shaughy	11					*Do*		
[143]8	Mich Shaughy	9					*Do*		
[143]9	Mary Shaughnessy	6					*Do*		
1440	Eliza Shaughnessy	5					*Do*		
1441	Den Shaughy	3					*Do*		
[144]2	Peg Shaughnessy	9 month					*Do*		
[144]3	Jams Woods	64	C		Clothier	City Limk	20th		
1444	Margt Flanagan	20	C		R HKeeper	City Limk	*Do*		
1444	John Flanagan	9 yrs	C			City Limk	20th Decr 82	Vo	
[144]5	Tery Flanagan	2	C			*Do*	*Do*	*Do*	
[144]6	Poll Flanagan	5	C						
[144]7	Patt Flanagan	4	C						
[144]8	Ben Bradshaw	60		P	Butcher	City Limk	29th	Vo	
1449	Ben Hide	62	C		Nailer	*Do*	30th	Vo	
1450	Mary Haley	21	C		R Hkeeper	City Limk	23	Vo	
1451	Jams Haley	3	C				*Do*		
1452	John Haley	6 months	C				*Do*		
1453	Eliza Ivers	43		P			*Do*		
[145]4	Mary Ivers	14					3d Jany 83		
[145]5	Ann Ivers	3					*Do*		
[145]6	Eliza Ivers	2 months					*Do*		
[145]7	John Farrell	40			Stroller		6th		C
[145]8	Ellinor Doyle	74			*Do*		6th		C
1459	John Courtney	60			Co Cork [sic]	Glover [sic]	7th	Vo	
1460	Eliza Hall	24			Stroller			Vo	
1461	Sally Cooney	3 mths			Orphan	Soldier's Child	8th	Vo	
[146]2	Edmd Bourk	30			Stone Cutter	City Limk	9th		C
[146]3	Mick Gradey	12			poor boy	*Do*	9		
[146]4	Cath Evans	40			Soldier's Wife	*Do*	12th	Vo	
[146]5	Jams Flinn	60			Labourer	*Do*	18	Vo	
[146]6	Mary Dea	33	C		Joe Phair's Wife	*Do*	20	th [sic]	
1466	Dens Brien	60	C		Clothier	City Limk	25th Jany 1783	Vo	
[146]7	Mary Daley	26	C				29th		
1468	Robt French	89		P	Clothier	*Do*	28		
1469	Ned Foster	9		P	Orphan		30th	Vo	
1470	Sally Foster	5			*Do*		*Do*		

No. of bed	Condition when received Healthy	Sickly	Disease when received	How disposed of Discharged	Died	Eloped	Condition when discharged Healthy	Sickly	Observations
			30th Novr 82	30th Novr 83					By a Committee
			Lame of one hand	29th Novr 82					By a Committee
	H								
			Insane		12th Decr 82				found dead in the Cells
				10th June					By a Committee
				Do					By *Do*
	H			2d March 83					By a Committee
	Do			2d March 83					By a Committee
	Do			8th Apr					
	Do			8th Apr					
	Do			9th Jany 1783					by Capt Hill
				7th Apr 83					by a Committee
						9th Decr 82			
				16th Jany 83					By the Doctor
				Do					*Do*
				1st May 83					By the Doctr
				Do					
				11th Octr 83					By the Committee
				1st May 82					
	Do					16th Decr 82			
			Nigh Sighted			12th March 83			By a Committee
	Do								
	Do								
					18th May 83				
						7th Feby 83			took nothing
	Healthy					4th Jany 83			By 3 Governors
				4th Jany 83					By 3 Governors
				Do					*Do*
				Do					*Do*
				Do					*Do*
				24th Jany 83					By a Committee
					22d Jany 83				
				17th May 83					by a Committee
					13th March 83				
					18th March 83				
				13th Feby 83					By a Committee
				16th Jany 83					by the Doctr as she got a Service abroad
				Do 13 Feby					By a Committee
				Do					
			a pearl on his Eye		11th Jany 83				found on him 1s 10d gave him his Money
			Lame 1 hand	21st Augt 83					By the Doctr
			want of Sight	14th Jany 83					By a Committee
				15th Jany 83					By a Committee
				12th Jany 83					By H Rose Esqr
			Insane			29th March 83			broke 3 Cells with his Nails and got out
				17th Jany 83					
				17th May 83					she was a noted disturber and a bad woman
						20th Jany 83			
				25th Jany 83					By a Committee
	He			11th Octr 83					
			Insane	17th May 83					By a Committee
	H			1st of March 83					By a Committee
				11th Octr 83					By a Committee
				25th May 85					By Lant Hill Esqr

Current No.	Names	Age	Religion		Occupation	Late residence	Admitted	Voluntary	Compulsory
			Roman Catholic	Protestant					
[147]1	Fanny Foster [Peg written above]	3			*Do*		30th Jany 17983	Vo	
[147]2	John Molony	50			Servt	NewCastle	5th Feby	Vo	
[147]3	Willm Kennelly	13		P	Beggar	England	14		C
[147]4	Ellinor Brien	30	C		Servt	Tipperary	14	Vo	
[147]5	John Brien	1					*Do*		
[147]6	Eliza Lock	33	C		Soldier's Wife	Co Limk	15th	Vo	
[147]7	Thoms Lock	4					*Do*		
1478	Jams Lock	1					*Do*		
1479	John Flinn	60			Labourer	City Limk	18th	Vo	
1480	Thos Carthy	58			Clothier	*Do*	*Do*		
[148]1	Cate Carthy	9					*Do*	Vo	
[148]2	John Toohy	60	C		Brogue maker	City Limk	*Do*	Vo	
[148]3	Jams Coughran	22		P	Pedlar	North	19	Vo	
[148]4	Poll Hardy	17	C		Whore	Galway	21st		C
[148]5	Mary Devitt	28	C		House keepr	City Limk	21st	Vo	
[148]6	Henry Devitt	2					*Do*	*Do*	
[148]7	Margt Devitt	6						*Do*	
1488	Ben Bradshaw	62		P	Butcher	City Limk	22d	*Do*	
[148]9	Jane Evans	12				City Limk	26th	Vo	
1490	Elizabeth Ricardson	20			Idler	*Do*	5th March	Vo	
[149]1	John Richardson	1 yr					*Do*		
1492	Kitty Stewd	40			Soldier's Wife	North	8th		C
1493	Sarah Brien	32		P	Hosier	City Limk	8th March	Vo	
1494	Mary Brien	11			*Do*	*Do*	*Do*		
1495	John Brien	3					*Do*		C
[149]6	Willm Brien	4 months							
[149]7	Morgan Brien	60			Patten maker	Co Clare			C
1498	Willm Webb	70			Schoolmaster	Co Limk			
1499	Honor Downs	26			Beggar	City Limk	28th	Vo	
1500	Thos Downs	2					*Do*		
1501	Peg Downs	3 weeks					*Do*		
1502	Eliza Headen	35		P	Semstress	Tipperary	31st	Vo	
1503	John Headen	5							
1504	Edwd Headen	1							
[150]5	Edmd Finahy	20	C		Beggar	Limk	3 Apr	Vo	
[150]6	Margt Johnston	80		P	Soldier's Wife	North	*Do*	Vo	
[150]7	John Kirwig	60	C		poor man	Co Limk	19	Vo	
1508	Richd Parker	20			bad boy	City Limk	20	Com [sic]	
1509	Richd Brien	50	C		Butcher	*Do*	22d	Com [sic]	
1510	John Bowdy	60	C		Merchant	*Do*	25	Vo	
1511	John Brien	60			Servt	Co Limk	8th May 83	Vo	
1512	Willm Bourk	72			Chairman	City Limk	12		
[151]3	Honor Blackhall	40	C		bad woman	Co Limk	12th June	Vo	
[151]4	Jane Evans	12	C			City Limk	12th	Vo	
[151]5	Ellinor Shaughnessy	14			Servt	Co Limk	27th May		
1516	Jams Kennellydy	80	C		Shoe maker	City Limk	12 June	Vo	
1517	Patt McNemara	70	C		Labourer	*Do*	21st		
[151]8	Eliza Hopkins	40		P	R HKeepr	*Do*	4 July	Vo	
[151]9	Moll King	50	C		Beggar	*Do*	5th July		C
[152]0	Watt Parker	23		P	Rogue	*Do*	8th		C
1521	Mick Malone	20	C		Servt		10th		C
[152]2	Mary Moore	44	C		Servant	Co Limk	12 July	Vo	
[152]3	Jams Brown	7	C		Orphan	*Do*	12th	Vo	
1524	James Hayes	60	C		Stroller		23d		C
1525	Thoms Coffee	36	C		Fool	Co Limk	16th		C
1526	John Tate	50		P	Joiner	*Do*	31st	Vo	
1527	Willm Morony	70	C		Servant	*Do*	1st Augt	Vo	
1528	Jane Loughlin	24		P	wife to Mr Bouchier	City Lim	2		C
1529	Mary Brodey	36	C		poorman	*Do*	7th	Vo	
1530	Cath Kennedy	16		P	Soldier's Wife	*Do*	10th	Vo	

No. of bed	Condition when received Healthy	Sickly	Disease when received	How disposed of Discharged	Died	Eloped	Condition when discharged Healthy	Sickly	Observations
				25th *Do* 85					
					3d Feby 84				
						11th March 83			out of the Cells
				12th March 83					by a Committee
				Do					by *Do*
				3d Sepr 83					by the Doctor
					18th May 83				
				3d Sepr 83					By the Doctr
				22d Feby	22 Feby 83				By the Doctor
			Cripple		20th Augt 85				
				13th Sepr 85					By Capt Hill Esqr
			dead at one side		23d March 84				
			Evil	16th Apr					By a Committee
						26th Feby 83			
				27th May 83					By a Committee
				Same day					
				Same day					
				1st March 83					by a Committee
				17th May 83					by a Committee
				27th May 83					
					20th May 83				Small pox
			Sore legs	12th March 83					By a Committee
	H			25th Augt 83					By the Doctr
	Do			8th Sepr 83					*Do*
				8th Sepr 83					*Do*
					8th June 80 [sic]				
			Lame 1 leg	11th July 83					by Geo Smyth Esqr Mayr
				18th March 83					By the Doctor
				4th April 83					
				Same day					
				Same day					
			Healthy	29th Apr 82					she got a month to stay and Sir Harry was to pay for it
			Do	*Do*					
			Do	Same day					
			Blind, and decrepid	19th July					By a Committee
			yellow Jaundice		13th Apr 83				
			puking blood	5th June 1784					By a Committee
			blind 1 Eye			3d May 83			
			Insane		10th Augt 83	29th Apr 83			
				29th Apr 83 (erased)		29th Apr 83			got leave to go out
	Do			17th May 83					By a Committee
			Asthma	31st 83					By a Committee
			puking blood			29th June 83			over the Wall
				11th Octr 83					By a Committee
				10th July 83					by the Doctr
			Sore Eyes		8th of May 86				
			Scurvey		12th July 83				his wife Bout a Coffin
			Sick,sore Breast	15th July 83					by 3 Governors
			Canker	15th July 83					on paying 1s 1d
			Subject to fits		13th July 83				Suddenly
			Insane			4th Augt 83			carried the hand cuffs and broke the Cell in piecs
		fits	blind 1 Eye	10th of Augt 1783					By the Doctor
			subject to Worms	*Do*					By *Do*
		Insane	blind 1 Eye	26th July					by a Committee
			Insane	21st Augt 83					By Capt Hill
			lame 1 Leg		9th Augt 1783				went to air himself and died suddenly
			Cripple		July 5th 1784				
				9th Augt					by a Committee
					9th Augt				was almost dead when Recd
		Healthy [sic]		11th Octr 83					

Current No.	Names	Age	Religion Roman Catholic	Protestant	Occupation	Late residence	Admitted	Voluntary	Compulsory
1531	Matthew Wild	40	C		Farmer	Co Limk	14th Augt 83		C
1532	Jams Carmody	40	C		Priest	City Limk	17th		C
1533	Ellinor Lynch	13	C		Orphan	*Do*	17th	Vo	
1534	Morgan Donovan	64	C		Labourer	Co Limk	20th	Vo	
1535	Dorathy Ponsonby	40		P	Huckster	City Limk	20	Vo	
1536	Thos Ponsonby	12		*Do*		*Do*			
1537	Mary Ponsonby	10				*Do*			
1538	Fany Ponsonby	6				*Do*			
1539	Nick McMahan	12			poor man	*Do*	19th	Vo	
1540	Jams Hayes	60			Stroller	*Do*	21		C
1541	John Brien	12			Orphan	*Do*	25th	Vo	
1542	Edwd Shea	62			Servt	*Do*	2d Sepr	Vo	
1543	John Hogan	40	C		Pedlar	*Do*	3		C
1544	Willm Cleary	19			Apprentice	*Do*	4		C
1545	Winifred Maddin	42	C			Co Limk	5 Sepr 83		C
1546	Garrett Gibbons	60	C		Porter	City Limk	7th 83	Vo	
1547	John Gearon	50		P	Weaver	Co Clare	16th		C
1548	Alice McCarthy	40	C		House Keepr	City Limk	17		
1549	Joan Condon	7			Orphan	*Do*	19th		
1550	Peg Hallinan	50			house keepr	*Do*	19th		
1551	John McNemara	60			Stroller	*Do*	19th	C [sic]	
1552	Honor Doran	40			house keepr	*Do*	22d	Vo	
1553	Eliza Clifford	24			*Do*	*Do*	22d		
1554	Mary Clifford	6 months				*Do*	22d		
1555	Dennis Keogh	14	C		Beggar		26	Vo	
1556	Jery Mahony	40			Clothier	*Do*	28th	C [sic]	
1557	Jams Beauhon						29th		
1558	Eliza Smyth	60	C		Shuler	*Do*	30	C [sic]	
1559	Mary Hurley	30	C		Shuler	*Do*	30th		
1560	Thoms Eagan	50	C		Beggar		5	C [sic]	
1561	Joe Borman	48	C		*Do*		5th	C [sic]	
1562	John Kerby	50	C		poor man	City Limk	6th Octr	Vo	
1563	Susannah Cooper	30		P	Servt		7th	Vo	
1564	Frances Cooper	4					*Do*	Vo	
1565	Hester Cooper	5 months					*Do*	Vo	
1566	Nell Fitzgerald	20			Tief		*Do*	Com [sic]	
1567	Patt Sullivan	40	C		Cooper	Co Limk	25	V	
1568	Ann Flavan	9		P			31	Vo	
1569	Dennis Molony	55	*Do*		Sawyer	Co Limk	Novr 1st	Vo	
1570	Molly Lacy	60	*Do*		Semstress	City Limk	3d	Vo	
1571	Danl McNemara	72	P		Baker	*Do*	15th	Vo	
1572	Michl Collins	21	C		Labourer	Co Limk	26th	Vo	
1573	Grace Cambpill	30		P	Semstress	City Limk	9 Decr	Vo	
1574	Patt Bryan	19	P		Labourer	Kings County	13 Jany 84	Vo	
1575	Corns Maddin	15			poor boy		1st Feby		C
1576	Thoms Parsons	12		Pro	*Do*	Newport	5th		C
1577	Nell Power	60	C		Beggar		7th		C
1578	Tim Power	12							C
1579	Thom Power	10							C
1580	Walter Magrath	60	C		Tutor	City Limk	15		
1581	Mary Peacock	18			Beggar	New York	17th	Vo	
1582	Michl Dineen	70	C		Schoolmaster	Co Limk	2d March	Vo	
1583	Thos Galvin	12			poor boy	Limk	14		
1584	John Johnston	20			Servt	Limk	6th Apr	Vo	
1585	Peg Richardson	30			poor Woman	City Cork	15th May	Com [sic	
1586	Joan Finucane	13			Orphan	Limk	21st	Vo	
1587	Joan Fahy	60			Servant	Limk	22d	C [sic]	
1588	Biddy Allen	60			poor Woman	Limk	23		
1589	Ellinor Eagan	79	P		poor Woman	County Limerik	8th July	V	

No. of bed	Condition when received Healthy	Sickly	Disease when received	How disposed of Discharged	Died	Eloped	Condition when discharged Healthy	Sickly	Observations
			Insane	20th Decr 83					
			Insane	2-Jun-84					By a Board
				11th Octr 1783					By a Committee
				11th Octr 83					*Do*
	Do			13th Apr 84					By the Doctr
				11th Octr 83					By a Committee
				22d Jany 84					sent to the Charter School
				Do					*Do*
			Scurvy						
			Insane	11th Octr 83					By a Committee
			Sore Chin	*Do*					
			Loss of sight		Died 28th Decr 1791				the house bougt his Coffin
			Insane	8th Sepr					by J Howley
				5th Sepr 83					By the Mayor
			Insane		26th Jany 1784				
						26th June 1789			Went Over the gardin wall
			Insane	12th Sepr 83					By a Committee
			Lame 1 Leg		1st Sept 1785				
	H			11th Octr 83					By a Committee
			Insane	Dischd Octr 4th					
			dead drunk	12th Sepr 83					By a Committee
			Sore leg	11th Octr 83					By a Committee
				Do					
				Do					
			Blind	9th Octr 83					By a Committee
				Do					*Do*
				Do					*Do*
				Do					*Do*
				Do					*Do*
				Do					*Do*
				Do					*Do*
			Fever		23d Octr 83				
				11th Octr 83					By a Committee
				Do					*Do*
				Do					*Do*
						27th Octr 83			Over the Wall
			Loss of his feet	10 Jany 84	By a Committe [sic]				Recd - 15 days diet a 2 1/2d
			Loss of 1 hand	5th Octr 85					By the Doctor
			Lame step		21st Novr 86				
	Healthy								
			Rheumatism	10th Jany 84					By a Commitee
			Sore leg	12th Decr 83					By the Doctr
			Violent Itch	16 Apr 84					by LntHill & Mr Huson
			Insane			13th Feby 1784			broke the Cells, and carried away the handcuffs, returnd
						20th 1784			over the Wall
				20th Feby 84					by P[?] son Seymour &c found on her 4s 4 1/2
				Do					found on her 4 4
				Do					
			Insane		6th March				Mesor Husen & Hill
	Healthy			16 Apl					
			Asthma	15th Apr	15th Apr 84				by the Doctor
			Insane		30th Octor 85				his Mother bougt A Coffin
			Sore leg	16 Apl					Mesrs Huson & Hill
			Insane	5th June 84					By a Committee
			Insane			26th April 85			Went Out Eloptd
			Sick & weak		26th May 1784				
			Insane		7th of Feby 1785				
			Sick & weak		3d of May 85				

Current No.	Names	Age	Religion Roman Catholic	Protestant	Occupation	Late residence	Admitted	Voluntary	Compulsory
1590	Catrin Welsh	20	Papist		Out of her senses	City Limerk	29th Augt 84	V	
1591	James White	75		Pro	Wiver	City Limk	15th Sept	V	
1592	Mary McDonnold	70	P		School mistress	City Cork	8th October	Vo	
1593	Bengemine Cane	60	P		Weaver	City Limk	Octor 22d	Vo	
1594	John Hogan	40	P		Pedler	County Limk	Novr 15th		Com
1595	Ann Farguson	19	P		Servant	City Limk	23d Novr 84	V	
1596	Mary Goss	17	Pa		poor Girl	City Limk	13th Decr 84	V	
1597	John Fitzgrald	50	P		Labourer	County Limk	16th Decr 84	V	
1598	Willm Kennedy	53	P		Weaver	City Limk	24th Decr 84	V	
1599	Catrin Gibbons	40	P		A poor Woman	County Limk	28th *Do*		
1600	Bridgt Daly	13	P		A poor Girl	City Limk	9th Jany 1785	V	
1601	John Heher	70	P		A Farmer	County Limk	18th Jany	V	
1602	John Dealy	40	P		A Stroller	County Limk	23d Jany 85		Co
1603	John Neckelson	22		P	Sealour	England	30th Jany 85		C
1604	Mary Keevin	70	P		Poor Woman	County Limk	18th Feby 85		
1605	John Fahy	45	P		A Barbour	City Limerick	28th Febuy	V	
1606	Margt Molowney	27	P		Poor Woman	County Clear	4th March	V	
1607	Ann Devis	50		Pr	A Quiltor	City Dublin	20th March	V	
1608	Ann Evritt	60	P		A poor Woman	City Limk	1st April	V	
1609	Timethy Hartagan	75	P		A Beggar	County Limk	7th April	V	
1610	Micl Brien	60	P		Labourer	County Clear	12th April	V	
1611	John Roch	82	P		A Carpentor	County Clear	28th April	V	
1612	John Karney	50	P		A Carpentor	City Cashel	8th May		
1613	Patrick Hussey	65	P		Weaver	City Limk	14th May 85	V	
1614	Amby Hopkins	12		P	Poor Boy	City Limk	26th *D*	V	
1615	Moria Tomkins	23		P	Poor Girel	City Limk	23d *D*	V	
1616	Eliza Hopkins	47		P	House keepr	City Limk	27th *Do*	V	
1617	Mary Ringrose	30	P		poor Woman	County Limk	27th *Do*		C
1618	Jams Creagh	23	Pap		Fool	County Limk	2d of June 85		C
1619	Danl Dincen	13	P		Orphan	County Limk	3d *D* 85	V	
1620	Margt Bourk	70			House Keeper	City Limk	4th *D*	V	
1621	John Cuishen	21	P		poor Boy	City Limk	15th *D*	V	
1622	John Shortill	70		Pro	Servant	County Limk	27th *Do*	V	
1623	Patrick Mulconery	25	Pap		poor Man	City Limk	28th *Do*	V	
1624	Margt Brandon	27	Pat		Servt	City Limk	28th *D*		C
1625	Patrick Ryan	70	P		Gardnor	County Limk	9th July	V	
1626	Eliza McBenn	21		Pro	Semstress	City Dublin	13th *D*	V	
1627	Mary Heden	26	P		Servant	County Limk	5th Augt		
1628	Margt Brandon	27	P		Servt	City Limk	8th *Do*		
1629	John Nealon	21	P		Carpentor	County Limk	15th Augt		
1630	Mary Hickey	19	P		A Harlot	City Limk	10th *D*		C
1631	Ellinor Leo	26	P			County Limk	20th Septr 85		
1632	Mary Laulour	12	P		poor Girl	County Limk	23d *Do*	V	
1633	Ann Laulour	6	P			County Limk	23d *Do*	V	
1634	Devid Lenehan	60	P		Maulster	City Limk	28 *D*	V	
1635	John Heaphey	60	P		Farmer	County Limk	5th October	V	
1636	Catn Fitzgrald	26	P		A Harlot	City Limk	21st *D*		C
1637	Ann Lillbern	5	P			City London	*D*		
1638	Johana Bourk	36	P		Stroller	City Limk	27th *D*		C
1639	Ellinor McNemara	40	*D*		*D*	*D*	*D*		
1640	Mary Bray	46			*D*	*D*	*D*		
1641	Mary Feenick	46			*D*				
1642	Mary Hoggoston	3			*D*				
1643	Mary Leary	36		Pro	*D*				
1644	Catrn Mara	62	P		*D*				

No. of bed	Condition when received Healthy	Sickly	Disease when received	How disposed of Discharged	Died	Eloped	Condition when discharged Healthy	Sickly	Observations
			Insane	18th Febuy 1785					
			Sickly		5thof Jany 1785				
			Sick & weak		31st Decr 1788				
			Sickly		2d March 1785				
			Insane	23d Novr 84					By the Mayor he haveing Come to his senses
			Insane			the 30th March			She having come to her senses, Elopt, by Lady Hartstonge
	Healthy		lost the use of her arm (all erased) Sickly	25th June 87		19 Decr 84 (erased)			by Lady Hartstonge Went Out by Order of the Doctor Eloptd
			Lame 1 Arm			Eloptd 19 Decr 84			
			A most Blind			10th July 85			Went Out Eloptd
			Insane		21st Feby 86				
	Healthy		Healthy	3d June 85					By Lant Hill Esqr
			Sickly	26th May 85					By Lant Hill Esqr
			A Sore Arm	31st Januy 85					By Order of the Mayor and Mr Phillips
			Insane	18th Januy					By Order of Cap Hill Esqr he haveing come to his senses
			Insane		20th Febuy 1785				Died Mad in the Cells
			Blind 1 Eye			20th July 86			
			Dropcy	23d April 85					By Capt Hill Esqr
		Sickly							
			A Cripple		Died 29th April 85				
			A Cripple						
			Sickly and Weak		Died 19th April 85				Was almost Dead when, Recd
			Infirm		5th March 86				
			Insane		23d Novr 85				in the Cells
	Healthy				27th Decr 1788				
				8th Feby 1788					bound Aprintis
						6th Augt 86			Went Out for Water Eloptd
				7th June 1791					by Ordr of Mr Andw watson
			Insane	9th July 85					By the Mayor She haveing Come to her senses
			Insane		Septr 25 85				Died mad in the Cells
			Insane		15th Feby 1789				Died in the Cells
			Insane		25th Decr 85				
		Sickly			18th Septr 85				
				25th July 85					By Order of the Mayor
		Sickly							
			Insane	11 July 85					By the Mayor she haveing come to her senses
		Sickly		12th *Do*					By the Revd Mr Seymour
	H			1st May 86					By Order of Capt Hill Esqr
			Insane		16th Augt 85				her Husband bougt A Coffin
			Insane			6th April			Went Out for Water Elopd
			Blind	14th May 86					By Capt Hill Esqr
		Sickly		25th Decr 85					by Mr Phillips She being Coured of the bad Disorder
			Insane	3d Sept 86					By Capt Hill Esqr
	H			27th July 86					By Capt Hill Esqr
	H								
		Sickly			15th Octor 85				
						11th Octobr 1785			Went Out Eloptd
	H					30th *D*			Went out the Street door at night fall
						30th of *D*			
						19th Jany 86			Went Out the street door, Elopd
				30th Octr 85					By Order of the Mayor
				28th *D*					By the Mayor
				28th *D*					By the Mayor
				28th *D*					By the Mayor
						1st Novr 86			Over the Wall
									By *D*

Current No.	Names	Age	Religion Roman Catholic	Protestant	Occupation	Late residence	Admitted	Voluntary	Compulsory
1645	Jaine Brown	36		Pro	*D*	North	27th October 85		
1646	John Leary	11		*D*					
1647	Ellinor Shine	6	P		Child	City Limk	27th Octor 85		C
1648	John Shine	6				*D*	*D*		
1649	Patrick Sheehon	72	*Do*		Butcher	City Limk	*D*		C
1650	Danl Brien	65			Chair Man	County Clare	29 *D*		
1651	Ann Boyl	21	*D*		Cripple	County Clare	29th *D*		
1652	Ann Keeff	20			Harlot	City Limk	31st *Do*		
1653	Josep Craffort	17		Pro	Stroulour	County Limk	31st *D*		
1654	Margt Craffort	20		*D*	*D*	County Limk	*D*		
1655	Mary Leary	13	*D*			City Limk			
1656	Thoms Stubbins	25		Pro	Shoe Boy	England	5th Novr		C
1657	Cornes Shea	22	*Do*		Stroulour	City Cork	7th *D*		C
1658	Mary Ryan	30	*D*		Harlot	City Limk	7th *D*		C
1659	Cathrin Brien	22	*D*		Harlot	City Limk	7th *D*		C
1660	Sara Bourk	21	*D*		*Do*	City Limk	*Do*		C
1661	Mary Jackson	19	*D*		*D*	City Limk	*D*		C
1662	John McNemara	60	*D*		Labourer	County Clare	15th *D*	V	
1663	Mary Shaughnessy	1			Child				
1664	Bridgt Hurrly	19	*D*		Harlot	City Limk	17th *D*		C
1665	Honor Conoway	30	*D*		Cripple	City Limk	*D*		C
1666	Kitty Smyth	32	*D*		A Spinnor	North	25th *D*		
1667	Mary Murphy	25	*Do*		*Do*	City Dublin	*D*		
1668	Bridgt Camble	25	*D*		Hkeeper	City Limk	26th *Do*		
1669	Rose Camble	3	*D*			*D*	*D*		
1670	Patt McInnerny	14	*D*		Servant	City Limk	27th *D*		
1671	Thoms Fitzgrald	36	*D*		A Porter	City Limk	2d Decr		
1672	Joan Brown	40	*D*		A Servant	City Limk	2d *Do*		
1673	Jams Hinchey	60	*D*		A Labourer	County Clare	13th *D*		
1674	Honor Noughton	7			Orphan	City Limk	15th		
1675	Joan Carroll	25	*D*			City Limk	19th *D*		
1676	Thoms Gannon	30	*D*		Servant	City Dublin	26th *D*		
1677	Eliner Murphy	40	*D*		Servant	County Limk	6th Jany 86		
1678	Mary Carr	30		*Do*	*D*	City Limk	14 Jany 86		
1679	Mary Dorhorty	31	*D*		*D*	County Clare	19th *D* 86		
1680	Danl Fool	16				County Limk	23d *D*		
1681	Mary Daly	21	Roman		Servant	City Limk	27th Jany 86		C
1682	Richard Welsh	17		Pro	Cabnetmaker	City Limk	30th *Do*		
1683	Darby King	60	*D*		Labourer	*Do*	14th Feb 86		
1684	Timethy McNemara	60	*D*		Strolour	County Clear	14th Feb 86		
1685	Johana Bourk	50	*D*		*D*	City Limk	16th *D*		
1686	Mary Bourk	20	*D*		Harlot	City Limk	16th *D*		
1687	Mary Collins	50		Pro	HouseKeeper	City Limk	22d *D*		
1688	Margt Flimmon	25	*Do*		Harlor [sic]	County Limk	8th March 86		C
1689	John Davornor	30	*D*		A fool	City Limk	9th March		
1690	Jams McMenous	14	*D*		Orphan	City Limk	9th *D*		
1691	Thoms Thomson	70	*D*		A Maulstor	County Limk	11th *D*		
1692	Joane Laffin	30	*D*			County Limk	16th *D*		
1693	Dins Lynch	40	*D*		Stroulour begar	County Limk	19th *Do*		
1694	Brian Sweenny	60	*D*		Shoemaker	County Clear	27th *D*		
1695	Micl Mara	70	*Do*		Baker	City Limk	2d Apr		
1696	Dins Brien	75	*D*		Comber	City Limk	*D*		
1697	Patrick Terney	60	*D*		Strolour begar	County Limk	*D*		C
1698	Mary Cane	60	*D*		Strolour begar	City Limk	*D*		C
1699	Ellinor Fennell	60		Pro	HKeeper	City Limk	3d *D*		
1700	Patrick Toohy	65	*D*		A Tannar	County Tipperary	6d *D*		C
1701	Miss Hannah Rudd	21		Pro		City Limk	10th *D*		C
1702	Mary Ryan	40	*D*		Strolour begar	City Limk	11th *D*		C
1703	Cathn Mara	60	*Do*		Strolour begar	City Limk	11th *D*		C
1704	Martin Shea	50	*D*		*D*	County Kerry	11th *D*		C
1705	Patt Shea	18	*D*		*D*	*Do*	11th *D*		C

No. of bed	Condition when received Healthy	Sickly	Disease when received	How disposed of Discharged	Died	Eloped	Condition when discharged Healthy	Sickly	Observations
				16th May 1792					by Order of Mr Andw watson
				[1]st Sept 1789					By order of A Committee
				[1]st Sept 1789					By Order of A Committee
				[1]st Sept 1789					By Order of A Committee
			Lame 1 Arm			25th Decr 85			Went Out to Mass Eloptd
			Lame of her Legs						
						18th Jany 86			Over the Garden Wall
						23d *D* 86			
				1st Novr 85					By the Mayor
			Blind	1st Novr 85					By *D*
				[1]st Sept 1789					By Order of A Committee
	H			14th Feby 86					
						8th Novr 85			Over the back yard Wall
				27th Novr 85					By the Mayor
						7th of May 86			Over the Wall
						11th Decr 85			Over the Garden Wall
						8th Jany 86			Over the Garden Wall
			Lame of one Arm	9th July 86					by Order of Mr Phillips
				27th Novr 85					By the Mayor
C [sic]						12th Janury 86			Over the Garden Wall
			Sickly		20th Novr 85				
				22d June 86					By Order of the Mayor
						30th Jany 86			
			Lame of 1 Leg	28th Feb 86					by Lady Hartstongue
					22d Decr 85				
				2d Decr 85					By Colonel Liffroy
			Sickly	2d Feby 86					
			Sickly			21st Decr 87			Went Out the Street door
			Blind	25th July 87					By Order of the Mayor
			Sickly			18th Jany 86			
						4th April			Broke the lock of the Garding door Eloptd
			Sickly		18th Jany 86				Her frinds bougt a Coffin
			Insane						
			Sickly	27th Feb 86					by Order of Mr Phillips
			Insane						
			Insane			5th Feb 86			She haveing Come to her Senses
			Insane			14th Feb 86			
						11th [Novr 86 altered to] Sept 88			Went Out the Street door
						11th April 86			Went Over the Garden Wall Eloptd
						31st May 86			Went Over the Wall
						28th feb 86			Eloptd Over the Garden Wall
			Insane						
						7th of May			Went Over the Wall
			Blind 1 Eye						
						12th March 86			Went Out to prayers Eloptd
						14th Augt 86			Went Out the door
			Insane		14th Augt 88				Died Mad in the Cell
			Criple	28th March					By Order of the Mayor
			Infirm	10th Decr 87					By Alderman Fitzgerald
				24th Decr 86					By Order of the Mayor
				20th Novr 86					by Order of the Mayor
				14th April 86					by Order of the Mayor
				11th April 86					By Order of the Mayor
				8th April 86					By Order of the Mayor
			Insane	19th June 86					By the Revd Mr Seymour
				12th April 86					By Order of the Mayor
				15th April					By Order of the Mayor
				18th April					By Order of the Mayor
						14th April 86			Elopt Over the Garden Wall

Current No.	Names	Age	Religion Roman Catholic	Protestant	Occupation	Late residence	Admitted	Voluntary	Compulsory
1706	John Gahagan	17*	*D*		*D*	County Limk	11th Apr 86		C
1707	Richard Bourk	45	*D*		*Do*	County Limk	11th *D*		C
1708	Mattw Shaughnessy	70	*D*		*D*	City Limk	11th *D*		C
1709	Elinor Coffy	50	*D*		*D*	City Limk	14th *D*		C
1710	Margt Reedy	36	*D*		*D*	City Limk	14th *D*		C
1711	Charlas Crosby	23	*D*		*D*	County Derry	14th *D*		C
1712	Edward Burns	33	*D*		*D*	City Limk	14th *D*		
1713	Elinor McNemara	50	Roman		Begar	City Limk	13th April		C
1714	Farguson Crowly	17	*D*		Orphan	City Limk	11th *D*		C
1715	Patt Fogarty	56	*D*		Stroler	County Tipperry	14th *D*		C
1716	Patt McGee	64	*D*		Stroler	County Limk	14th *D*		C
1717	Patt Emorson	3	*D*			City Limk	14th *D*		
1718	Hana Crow	70	*D*		H Keeper	City Limk	21st *D*	V	
1719	Ann Brien	20	*D*		poor Girl	City Limk	21st *D*	V	
1720	Thoms Heaphey	85	*D*		piper	City Limk	26th *D*		C
1721	Terence McMahon	80	*D*		taylor	City Limk	30th *D*	V	
1722	John Kenny	70	*D*		Brougmaker	City Limk	1st of May		
1723	Eliza McBenn	21		P	Spinner	City Dublin	6th *D*		
1724	Edward Cane	70	*Do*		Begar	City Limk	12th *D*		
1725	Margt Sexton	69	*D*		HousKeeper	City Limk	17th *D*		
1726	Elizebth Morgan	33	*D*		A poor Woman	County Limk	31st May		
1727	Jams Grady	2	*D*		A Child	*D*	31 *D*		
1728	Patrick Kelly	70		P	Begar	City Limk	3d June		
1729	Patt McGee	60	*D*		*D*	County Limk	4th *D*		
1730	Richard Welsh	18		P	Cabnetmaker	City Limk	3d *D*	*Do*	
1731	John Kenny	60	*D*		Brougmaker	City Limk	9th *D*		
1732	John O'Dea	60	*D*			County Limk	13th *D*		
1733	Timethy Kelly	60	*D*		Strouler	County Limk	17th *D*		C
1734	Mary Coleburn	[50, altered to] 38		P		England	22d	V	
1735	Edward Fitzgrald	11	*D*		A poor boy	City Limk	22d	V	
1736	John Nealon	23	*D*		Carpenter	County Clar	27th *D*		
1737	Mary Ahern	12	*D*			County Limk	28th *D*		
1738	Mary Hickey	20	*D*		A Harlot	City Limk	27th *D*		
1739	Willm Brien	60	*D*		A Beggar	County Limk	5th July 86		
1740	Eliza Bolond	40	*Do*		H Keeper	City Limk	11th *D*		
1741	Mary Bolond	12	*Do*			City Limk	11th *D*		
1742	Micl Craty	60	*D*		Beggar	County Limk	14th *D*		
1743	Bridgt Brien	60	*D*		H Keeper	City Limk	18th *D*		
1744	John Daly	42	*D*		A Strouler	County Limk	23d *D*		C
1745	Patt Shea	15	*D*		*D*	*D*	23d		
1746	Mary Ryan	50	*D*		*D*	*D*	23d		
1747	Mary Dohorty	25	Roman		Harlot	County Clar	31st July 86		C
1748	Ann Keeff	24	*D*		Harlot	City Limk	31s *D*		
1749	Mary Barry	40	*Do*		Stroler	County Cork	31st *D*		
1750	John Daly	30	*D*		Stroler	County Limk	1st Augt		
1751	Martain Hayes	70	*D*		Beggar	City Limk	1st *D*		
1752	Thoms Cahill	60	*D*		*D*	City Limk	1st *D*		
1753	Cathr Gorman	22	*D*			City Limk	4th *D*		
1754	Jams Bourk	23	*D*		Beggar	County Clar	11th *D*		
1755	Mary Keton	22	*D*		Harlot	County Limk	17th *D*		
1756	John McQueston	60		Pro	Mason	North	2d *D*	V	
1757	Mary Connors	20	*D*		Poor Girl	Nenough	24th *Do*	V	
1758	Jams Nicholson	19		Quaker		North	28th *D*		C
1759	Mary Barry	40	*D*		Stroler	County Cork	28th *D*		C
1760	Richard Welsh	22		Pro	Cabnetmaker	City Limk	1st Septemr		
1761	Eliza McNeal	50		Pro	Servant	North	2d *D*	V	
1762	John Farrell	60	*D*	Pro	Servant	Kings County	3d *D*		
1763	John Finchby	40		Pro	Beggar	America	4th *D*		
1764	Patrick McNemara	74	*D*		A Comber	County Clar	4th *D*		
1765	Micl Daly	7	*D*						

No. of bed	Condition when received		Disease when received	How disposed of			Condition when discharged		Observations
	Healthy	Sickly		Discharged	Died	Eloped	Healthy	Sickly	
				17th April 86					By Order of the Mayor
				19th April 86					By Order of the Mayor
				13th April 86					By Order of the Mayor
				15th April					By Order of the Mayor
				15th April 86					By Order of the Mayor
				16th April 86					By Order of the Mayor
				31st May 86					By Order of the Mayor
	H			15th April 86					By Order of the Mayor
			Insane			19th May 86			Went Out the street door
				31st May 86					By Capt Hill Esqr
				15th April 86					By Order of the Mayor
					28th July 86				
				5th June 86					By Order of the Mayor
				1st May					By Order of the Mayor
						7th of May			Got Leve to Go out by Alderman Shergant Eloptd
						7th of May			Went Out the Street door
				15th Augt 86					By Order of Capt Hill Esqr
			Infirm						
			Infirm		12th Jany 88				
				3d Octr 86					by Order of Capt Hill
				3 *D*					by Order of Capt Hill
			Blind 1 Eye	3d May 1790					by A Committee
			Infirm	13th Octr 86					by the Revd Mr Ingram
			Insane			2d Augt 86			Broke the Cell door
			Infirm			2d Augt 86			
			Insane						
					11th July 86				Died in the Cells
						17th July 86			Went Out the Street door
						1st Decr 86			Went Out the Kitchen window
			Blind						
						11th Augt 86			Went Out the Street door
						29th July 86			Brokc thc Cell door
			Blind	3d Octr 86					by Order of Capt Hill
						12th Novr 86			Went Out the door
						14th Augt 86			Went Out the door
				18th Octr 86					by Order of Mr Ingram
						2d Augt 86			Broke the Cell door
						27th July 86			Went Over the Wall
				24th July 86					By Order of the Mayor
	H					2d Augt 86			Wen Over the Wall
						2d Augt 86			Went Over the Wall
				13th Augt					By Order of the Mayor
			Insane			10th Octr 86			Elopt Out of the Garden
						6th Augt 86			Broke the Cell door
						7th Octr 86			Eloptd Out of the Garden
			Insane			11th Augt 86			Broke the Cell & Carred Away the Hand Cuffs
			Criple	12th March 87					by Order of the Revd Mr Ingram
			Sickly			16th Jany 87			
			Sickly		11th Octr 86				
			D		11th Octr 86				
					21st Novr 86				
				26th Octr 86					by Order of the Mayor
			Insane	13th Sept 86					by Order of Mr Ingram
				30th Novr 86					Shee haveing gon to servis
			Sickly		10th of Sepr 86				Was almost ded wen Recd
			1 Leg	10th Octr 86					By Order of the Mayor
				10th Octr 86					by Doctor Creagh

Current No.	Names	Age	Religion Roman Catholic	Protestant	Occupation	Late residence	Admitted	Voluntary	Compulsory
1766	Elinor Enright	40	*D*		Servant	County Limk	9th Septemr 86		
1767	Thoms Fitzgrald	43	*D*		Beggar	City Limk	16th *D*		
1768	Timethy McNemara	60	*D*		Beggar	County Clar	16th *D*		
1769	Alias Vaughan	60	*D*		Servant	City Limk	16th		
Returned so far to the Grand Jurys 19 Septr 1786/1,833 persons there being a mistake in the numbering some of the forgoing ones									
1833	Judy Barronton	21	*D*		A Harlot	County Clar	18th *D*		
1834	Cornelous Sulivan	60	*D*		Beggar	County Limk			
1835	Timethy Hartagan	60	*D*		Beggar	County Limk	26th		
1836	Patrick Mulconery	38	*D*		City Limerick Beggar	City Limk	28th		
1837	Mary Ryen	38	*D*		Bad Girl	City Limk	27th		
1838	Margt Shaughenessey	2	*D*		A Child		27th		
1839	Ann Hallaran	56	*Do*			County Llar [sic]	10th of Octr		
1840	Elinor Mealy	40	*D*		Servant		12th *D*		
1841	Martha Barton	11	R		Poor Girl	Lity [sic] Limk	16th Octr 86	V	
1842	Mary Barton	7			*D*	C	*D*	V	
1843	Danl Barton	6			*D*	*D*	*D*	V	
1844	Ellinor Carrol	50	*D*		H Keeper	City Limk	19th *D*	V	
1845	Ellinor Daly	50	*D*		*D*	City Limk	20th *D*	V	
1846	John Elms	12		Pro	Poor Boy	City Limk	23d *D*		
1847	John Fahy	40	*D*		Barbor	City Limk	24th *D*	V	
1848	Bridgt Pursil	22	*D*		Servant	City Limk	24th *D*		
1849	Luscy Barry				Infant		24th		
1850	Margt Carrol	18	*D*		Poor Girl	City Limk	24th		
1851	Ann Ryen	20	*D*		Harlot	Queens County	28th *D*		
1852	Ann Keff	22	*D*		Harlot	City Limk	30th Octr		
1853	Jams Rilly	60	*D*		Weavor	City Lity [sic]	3d Novr		
1854	Jaine Mellsup	30		Pro		City Limk	4th *D*		
1855	Ann Leary	40		Pro	Beggar	City Limk	11th *D*		
1856	Judy Connell	25	*D*		a Rogue	County [Llar, altered to] Clar	16th *D*		C
1857	Mary Barry	40	Roman		A Rogue	County Cork	20th *D*		
1858	John Fahy	41	*D*		A Barbor	City Limk	28th *D*		
1859	Margt Neal	32	*Do*		A bad Girl	County Cork	29th		C
1860	Joan Bagwill	50	*D*			County Limk	26th *D*		
1861	Stephen Mullons	8			A Poor Child	City Limk	5th Decr		
1862	Mary Bourk	17	*D*		A bad Girl	City Limk	21st *D*		
1863	Nell Sweeny	40			*D*	*D*	21st *D*		
1864	Margt Fitzgibons	30	*D*		A poor woman	County Limk	22d *D*		
1865	Ned Fitzgrald	2			A Child	*D*	22d *D*		
1866	Joane Consider	40	*D*			County Limk	20th *D*		
1867	Mary Neal	40	*D*		Servant	County Limk	29th *D*		
1868	Mary Neal	7				Child [sic]	29th *D*		
1869	Ann Neal		Rom		Child	City Limk	29th Decr 1786		
1870	Timethy Neal	11		Pro	*Do*	City Limk	29th		
1871	Signor Latore	40		Pro	Danceing Master	Italan	29th Decr		
1872	John McMahon	21	Rom		taylor	City Limk	5th Jany 1787		
1873	Bridgt Brien	50	*D*		A Spinnor	County Limk	7th *D*		
1874	Mary Brien	33	*D*		*D*	City Limk	9th *D*		
1875	Bridgt Hurly	20	*D*		Harlot	City Limk	16th *D*		
1876	Patt Hallaran	60	*D*		A Brewer	City Limk	16th *D*		
1877	Patrick Henery	50	*D*		Wevor	City Limk	19th *D*		
1878	Ann Donohoe	10	*D*			City Limk	23d Jany 87		
1879	Mary Ahern	11	*D*			City Limk	10 Feby		
1880	Jerry Scanlan	60	*D*		Wevor	City Limk	11 March		
1881	Danl Shaughnessey	70	*D*		Laborer	City Limk	11 March		
1882	Micl Mara	70	*D*		Baker	City Limk	21st March		
1883	John Nealon	28	*Do*		Carpentor	County Clar	21st *D*		
1884	Mary Peircy	60			A poor H Keepr	City Limk	24th *D*		
1885	Margt Michell	60	*D*		A poor H Keepr	City Limk	26th *D*		
1886	Mary Murphy	18	*D*		A Spinnor	County Cork	30th *D*		
1887	Jams Conney	40	*D*		A Shoemaker	England	31st *D*		
1888	Danl Keanan	40	*D*		A Schoolmaster	County Clar	1st April		
1889	Eliza Lock	43	*D*		House,Keeper	City Limk	3d *D*		
1890	Micl McEnnerny	80	*D*		taylor	County [Llar, altered to] Cimrk [recete - Limk]	7th *D*		

No. of bed	Condition when received Healthy	Sickly	Disease when received	How disposed of Discharged	Died	Eloped	Condition when discharged Healthy	Sickly	Observations
			Sore brest	13th Sept 86					by Order of Capt Hill Esqr
			Sickly	6th Octr 86					By Order of the Mayor
			Sore Leg						
			Infirm	18th Sept					By Order of the Mayor
						6th April 1787			Went Out the Street door
			Sickly		2d April 1787				
			Sore Legs			12th October 86			Went Out of the Garden
					26th Decr 86				
				12th Octr 86		23d June 87 (erased)			by Order of the Mayor
				12th *D*					by Order of the Mayor
			Insane			23-Jun-87			Shee haveing Com to her senses
			Sickly						
	Health					11th Augt 88			Went Out the Street door
	D			27th Augt 1789					By A Committee
	D			27th Augt 1789					By A Committee
			Infirm	27th Octr 86					by Order of the Mayor
			Infirm	27th Octr	died 27th Novr 86				by Order of the Mayor
	D					28th Novr 86			Went Out the Street door
			Infirm	28th Octr	24th Decr 87				by Dctor Hassett
	D			12th Jany 87					by Order of the Mayor
					4th Jany 87				the House paid 1s 1d for a Coffin
	D					20th Novr 86			Went Out the Street door
			Infirm			30th Octr 86			Went Out the Street door
			in the bad Disorder			21st Decr 86			went by Order of Mr Phillips
			Infirm			12th April			Went to Mass Eloptt
	D			1st Sept 87					Shee haveing gon to the Salt Water
						1st Decr 86			Wint Out the Kitchen window
						9th Feb 87			Went Out the turf house Wind
			Infirm						
						1st Decr 86			Went Out the Kitcen Window
			Insane						
						23d April			
						10th Jany 87			Went Out the turf house window
						28th Decr 86			went Out the Street door
			Sickly	1st Jany 87					by Order of the Mayor
				1 Jany 87					by Order of the Mayor
			Insane	23d Decr 86					by Order of Hue brady Esqr
				[1]st Sept 1789					By Order of A Committee
					26th May				paid 1s 1d for A Coffin
				[1]st Sept 1789					By Order of A Committee
			Insane			14th July 87			Went Out to Walk
			Sickly		9th of May 87				
			Sickly						
			Infirm			29th Jany 87			Went Over the Garden wall
				7th June 87					by Order of the Mayor
						26th Jany 87			Went Out the Street door
						24th April			Went Out to Work Eloptd
			Infirm	28th June (erased)	28th June 87				
			Blind	9th June 88					
			Infirm			[1]st Decr 87			Went Over the Garden wall
				30th April					by Order of Capt Hill
			Infirm			31st Jany 88			went Over the backyard wall
			Infirm	2d April					By Capt Hill Esqr
			Infirm	6th April					by Order of the Mayor
				16th May 87					by Order of the Mayor
			Infirm	25th June 87					by Order of Capt Hill

Current No.	Names	Age	Religion Roman Catholic	Protestant	Occupation	Late residence	Admitted	Voluntary	Compulsory
1891	Nichs McMahon	15	*D*		Orphan	City Limk	12th April 87		
1892	Elinor Jackson	70		Pro	A poor H Keepr	City Limk	28th *D*		
1893	Dianna Connors	22	*D*		A bad Girl	City Limk	7th May 87		
1894	Joane Brown	60			Servant	City Limk	11th *D*		
1895	Willm Connell	60	*Do*		A Wevor	City Limk	15th *D* 87		
1896	Willm Bennit	18	*D*			County Limk	19th *D*		
1897	Margt Michell	26		P	A bad Woman	County Dublin	23d *D*		
1898	Cathr Ryen	60	*D*		A poor Woman	County Limk	24th *D*		
1899	John Ringrose	10			A Orphan	City Limk	25th *D*		
1900	Jams Brown	15	*D*		Servant	County Limk	28th *D*		
1901	Thoms Hastings	23			poor boy	County Kerry	14th *D*		
1902	Micl Neal	40	Rom		servant	County [Llar, altered to] Clar	15th June 1787		
1903	Laur Ryen	70	*D*		Maulster	City Limk	22d *D*		
1904	Jams Brown	17	*D*		Servant	County Limk	27th *D*		
1905	John Timmons	10		Pro	Orphan	City Limk	14th July 87		
1906	Micl McEnnerny	80	*D*		taylor	County Clar	9th *D*		
1907	Mary Powel	20				County Limk	21st *D*		
1908	Patt Terney	14			Orphan	County Limk	27th *D*		
1909	Elinor Jackson	80		Pro	A poor Woman	County Clar	3d Augt		
1910	Cathr Eyercourt	20	*D*		A poor Girl	City Limk	10th *D*		
1911	Patt Quane	20	*D*		Laborer	County Limk	15th		
1912	Cornels Buckley	50			wevor	City Cork	24th *D*		
1913	Reph Begly	60	*D*		wevor	County Cork	15th *D*		
1914	Richard Terry	70		Pro	Smyth	England	28th *D*		
1915	John Oakley	50		*D*	Bocklemaker	England	Sep [1]st		
1916	John Hogan	45	Rom		Pedler	County Clar	*Do*		
1917	John Sulivan	70	*D*		Wevor	City Limk	8th Sept		
1918	Norry Lynch	23	*D*		Harlot	City Limk	10th *D*		
1919	Danl Mahoney	17	*D*		A Orphan	City Limk	12th *D*		
1920	Elick McConnell	50		Pro	Wevor	City Limk	15th *D*		
1921	Cathr Grady	13	*D*		PoorGirl	City Limk	15th *D*		
1922	Joane Brown	50	*D*		Soldors Wife	City Limk	16th *D*		
1923	Bridgt Molowny	40	*D*		poor H Keeper	City Limk	17th *D*		
1924	Mary Bourk	20	*D*		Poor Girl	City Limk	17th *D*		
1925	Thoms Pottor	1			A Child	*D*	*D*		
1926	Jams Lynch	23		Pro	Laborer	County Limk	18th *D*		
1927	Margt McMahon	27	*D*		poor H Keeper	County Clar	24th *D*		
1928	Anstis McMahon	60	*D*		poor H Keeper	County Clar	24th		
1929	John Hallaran				A Child	*D*	*Do*		
1930	Nichs Whealon	50		Pro	A Servant	Clonmell	28th *Do*		
1931	Jams Lynch	[23, altered to] 33		Pro	Laborer	County Limk	3d Octor		
1932	Jaine Mellsup	27		*D*	A Servant	City Limk	1st *Do*		
1933	Mary May	50	*D*		A poor H Keeper	City Limk	18th *Do*		
1934	Patt Henery	50		Pro	A Comber	City Limk	25th Octr 87		
1935	Willm Bright	70		*Do*	Shoemaker	City Cork	30th *Do*		
1936	Danl O' Keeff	85	*Do*		Cleoather	City Limk	13th Novr 87		
1937	Elidgit Bloxham	39		*Do*	H Keeper	City Limk	16th *Do*		
1938	Elidgit Bloxham	10		*Do*	A poor Girl	*Do*	*Do*		
1939	Jaine Bloxham	8		*Do*	*Do*	*Do*	*Do*		
1940	Richd Bloxham	6		*Do*	*Do*	*Do*	*Do*		
1941	John Clark	70	Roman		Cleoather	*Do*	15th *Do*		
1942	Cathr McDonnold	60	*Do*		H Keeper	County Limk	17th *Do*		
1943	Judy Begly	50	*Do*		H Keeper	City Cork	17th *Do*		
1944	Elinor Scanlan	60	*Do*		H Keeper	City Limk	20th *Do*		
1945	Laur Ryen	68	*Do*		A mealman	City Limk	25th *Do*		
1946	Timethy McNemara	60	*Do*		A Stroler	County Limk	1st of Decr 87		
1947	John Kana	77	*Do*		Carpenter	City Limk	4th *Do* 87		
1948	Cathr Creagh	22	*Do*		A Harlot	County Dublin	18th *Do*		
1949	Margt Mitchell	50	*Do*		A poor Woman	City Limk	29th *Do* 87		
1950	Peter Johnston	17		Pro	A Laboror	City Limk	4th January 88		
1951	Thoms Cuningham	80		*Do*	Wevor	City Limk	5 *Do*		

No. of bed	Condition when received		Disease when received	How disposed of			Condition when discharged		Observations
	Healthy	Sickly		Discharged	Died	Eloped	Healthy	Sickly	
			Infirm	23d Augt 87					he haveing gon to servis
			Infirm	21st June 87					by Order of Capt Hill
						13th of May 87			Went Over the Wall
			blind 1 Eye	23d July 87					By Order of the Mayor
				13th Augt 87					by Order of the Mayor
			Start Mad	31st May 1787					he haveing Com to his senses
						1st June 87			Went Out the Necessary house
				31st May 87					by Alderman Widneham
				25th Sept 1789					he went to the Charter school
			Infirm	21st June 87					by Order of Capt Hill Esqr
			Infirm	20th July 87					by Lady Hartstonge
			Infirm						
				4th Sepr 87					By Order of the Mayor
				28th Octr 87					he haveing Listed
						30th Octr 87			Went Out the Street door
			Insane	22d July 87					by Order of the Mayor
			Insane						
			Infirm		13th Augt 87				the house bougt her Coffin
			19th Octr 1789						Shee haveing gon to servis
			Insane	18th Novr 87					By Capt Hill Esqr
			Sore Legs	29th Feby 88					he haveing found Mains to earn his bread
			Sore Legs			5th Decr 87			Went Out the Street door
			Infirm	4th Sept 87					By Order of Capt Hill
			Infirm	7th Sept 87					By Order of the Mayor
			Insane			30th Octr 87			broke the Cell door
			Infirm		7th Novr 87				his wife bought A Coffin
			in the bad disorder	15th March 1788					shee bound her self for Amerace
			Insane		22d Novr 1790				the house bougt his Coffin
			Infirm	14th Augt 1788					By Capt Hill
						22d Octr 87			Went Out the Street door
					21st March 1790				the house bougt her Coffin
			Insane	22d Sepr 87					By Order of the Mayor
				2d Octr 87					By Order of the Mayor
				2d Octr 87					By Order of the Mayor
			Insane	27th Sepr 87					By Alderman Widenham
				20th May 88					By Alderman Fitzgerald
				[1]st Sept 1789					By Order of A Committee
				25th sepr 1789					went to the Charter school
				22d July 88					By Order of Comittee
			Insane		13th Novr 87				Died start mad
				17th May 88					by Alderman Fitzgerald
			Infirm						
				2d June 88					By Order of Mr Ingram
			Infirm			23d Feby			Went Out the Street door
						14th Novr 87			Went Out the Street door
				2d May 88					by Alderman Fitzgerald
				2d May 88					by *Do*
				2d May 88					by *Do*
				2d May					by *Do*
			Infirm		23d Novr 87				His Frinds bougt A Coffin
				21st Augt 1788					By Alderman Fitzgerald
				10th Decr 87					by Capt Hill Esqr
			Infirm	14th April 1789					by Order of Mr Phillips
			Leam of One Leg			21st March 88			Went Out the Street door
						29th Decr 87			Went Over the Garden Wall
						16th Decr 87			Went Out to Mass Eloptd
				15th March 1788					bound her self for Ameraca
						31st Decr 87			Went Out the Street door
				11th March 88					he bound himself for Ameraca

Current No.	Names	Age	Religion Roman Catholic	Protestant	Occupation	Late residence	Admitted	Voluntary	Compulsory
1952	Richd Hall	50		*Do*	Clark	County Limk	5 January 88		
1953	John Molowney	60	*Do*		Whipmaker	City Limk	10th		
1954	Margt Hallanan	60		*Do*	H Keeper	City Limk	11th *Do*		
1955	Frans Barton	16	*Do*		A poor Girl	City Limk	15th *Do*		
1956	Brien Connor	60	*Do*		A Weavor	County Clar	18th *Do*		
1957	Eliza McNeal	52		*Do*	A Servant	North	28th *Do*		
1958	Mary Eagle	40	*Do*		H Keeper	County Waxford	28th *Do*		
1959	Mary Eagle	9	*Do*			*Do*			
1960	Sara Eagle	7	*Do*			*Do*			
1961	Ann Eagle	3	*Do*			*Do*			
1962	Elinor Carleton	40		*Do*	H Keeper	City Limk	3d Feby 88		
1963	Lusey Carleton	10		*Do*		*Do*	*Do*		
1964	Gye Carleton	8		*Do*		*Do*	*Do*		
1965	Mary Carleton	5		*Do*		*Do*	*Do*		
1966	Elinor Carleton	3		*Do*		*Do*	*Do*		
1967	Cathr Hogan	60	Rom		A Stroler	County Limk	5th Feby 88		
1968	Reph Begly	66	*Do*		A Weaver	City Cork	8th *Do*		
1969	Hana Gorman	80	*Do*		A Servant	County Clar	15th *Do*		
1970	Nichs McMahon	16	*Do*		A poor Boy	City Limk	*Do*		
1971	Dins Heanan	45	*Do*		School Master	County Clar	*Do*		
1972	Mary Devit	32	*Do*		A Beggar	City Limk	17th *Do*		
1973	Elinor Devit	3					*Do*		
1974	Jams Devit	1			Labourer (erased)		*Do*		
1975	Timethy Reagan	65			Labourer	*Do*	20th *Do*		
1976	Jams Lahiff	8			Orphan		21st *Do*		
1977	John Lahiff	5			*Do*		*Do*		
1978	Rebeca Veal	55		Pro	A Servant	City Limk	23d Feby 88		
1979	Cathr Dillon	40	*Do*		H Keeper	City Limk	25th *Do*		
1980	Pattr Dillon	1			A Child	*Do*	*Do*		
1981	Mary Blakeny	32	*Do*		A Stroler	County Clar	29th *Do*		
1982	Martin Blakeny	1			A Child	*Do*	*Do*		
1983	John Blakeny	7	*Do*		*Do*	*Do*	*Do*		
1984	Red Moll	30	*Do*		A tripe Woman	City Limk	1st March 88		
1985	Joane Sheehy	22	*Do*		A Beggar	County Limk	3d March		
1986	Betty Grady	1			Child	*Do*			
1987	John Cassedy	10				City Limk	9th *Do*		
1988	Peggy Shaughnessay	3			*Do*	*Do*	*Do*		
1989	Nell Cody	80	*Do*		A Beggar	City Limk	11th *Do*		
1990	Cathr Tierney	60	*Do*		A Beggar	City Limk	12th *Do*		
1991	Margt Mitchel	60			A Servant	City Limk	27th *Do*		
1992	Bridgt Mead	40			H Keeper	City Limk	3d April *Do*		
1993	Mary Devit	32			A Beggar	City Limk	9th *Do*		
1994	Peg Devit	12			*Do*	*Do*	*Do*		
1995	Elinor Devit	3			*Do*	*Do*	*Do*		
1996	Jam Devit	1					*Do*		
1997	George Camble	35		Pro	A Butchar	County Limk	18th April 1788		
1998	Ann Camble	30		*Do*		City Dublin	*Do*		
1999	Cathr Connors	50	Papt		Beggar	City Limk	12th *Do*		
2000	Anstis Brandon	80	*Do*		H Keeper	City Limk	12th *Do*		
2001	Cathr McDonnold	19	*Do*		A Servant	County Clar	12th *Do*		
2002	Thoms Bealy	60		Pro	Weaver	City Limk	19th *Do*		
2003	John Hickee	20	Papt		Baker	County Clar	19th *Do*		
2004	Ann Ferguson	22	*Do*			City Limk	20th *Do*		
2005	Mary Devit	32			H Keeper	City Limk	25th *Do*		
2006	Peg Devit	12				*Do*	*Do*		
2007	Elinor Devit	3				*Do*	*Do*		
2008	Jams Devit	1				*Do*	*Do*		
2009	Terry Scanlon	50			A Comber	City Limk	26th April		
2010	Winiford Dwyer	60	*Do*		A Servant	City Limk	4th May 88		
2011	John Collins	9	*Do*			*Do*	4th *Do*		
2012	Nell Collins	6	*Do*			*Do*	*Do*		
2013	Jams Collins	3	*Do*			*Do*	*Do*		

No. of bed	Condition when received Healthy	Sickly	Disease when received	How disposed of Discharged	Died	Eloped	Condition when discharged Healthy	Sickly	Observations
			Infirm			7th Januy 88			Went Out to the doctor
				7th April					By Alderman Fitzgerald
			Infirm						
				18th Feby 88					By Alderman Fitzgerald
			Infirm	19th June 88					By Order of Capt Hill
				27th March 88					By Order of Capt Hill
				7th April 88					By Alderman Fitzgerald
				7th *D*					by *Do*
				7th *D*					by *Do*
				7th *D*					by *Do*
			Infirm			6th June 88			Went Out the Street door
				[1]st Sept 1789					By Order of A Committee
				[1]st Sept 1789					By Order of A Committee
				[1]st Sept 1789					By Order of A Committee
				[1]st Sept 1789					By Order of A Committee
						11th March 88			Went Over the Garden Wall
						18th March 88			Went out the Street door
			Infirm						
			Do			6th Augt 1788			Went Over the Garden Wall
			Infirm	25th Feby 88					
				31st March 88					by Alderman Fitzgerald
				31st *Do*					By *Do*
				31st *Do*					By *Do*
				27th Augt 1789					By A Committee
				20th Augt 1788					By Alderman Fitzgerald
				16th June 88					By Capt Hill
				14th July 88					By Order of A Commitee
				14th *Do Do*					By Committee
			Infirm	4th March 88					by Order of the Mayor
				4th March 88					by Order of Do
				1st March 88					By Order of the Mayor
			Dead Drunk	3d June 88					By Order of the Mayor
				30th July 88					By Order of Capt Hill
				30th July 88					By Order of Capt Hill
				3d June 88					By Order of the Mayor
				3d June 88					By Order of *Do*
			Infirm	3d April 88					By Order of the Mayor
				14th March 88					by Order of the Mayor
				4th March 88					by Capt Hill
			Infirm		25th Octr 1788				Died Mad in the Cell
				11th April 88					by Capt Hill Esqr
				11th *Do*					by *Do*
				11th					by *Do*
				11th					by *Do*
			1 Leg	28th April 88					By Alderman Maunsell
				22d July 88					By Order of Committee
			Infirm		23d Decr 1788				the house bougt her Coffin
				17th June 88					by Capt Hill
				23d					By Capt Hill
				20th June 88					By Capt Hill
			Insane	2 May 88					by Alderman Fitzgerald he haveing come to his Senses
			Insane	9th Novr 1788					Shee having come to her Senses
				22d July 88					By Order of Committee
				28th April 88					Shee haveing gon to Servis
				22d July 88					By Order of Committee
				22d July 88					By Order of Committee
				25th May 88					by Alderman Fitzgerald
					4th Feby 1790				the House bougt her coffin
					9th Augt 1789				the House bougt A Coffin
				[1]st sept 1789					By Order of A Committee
				25 May 88					

Current No.	Names	Age	Religion Roman Catholic	Protestant	Occupation	Late residence	Admitted	Voluntary	Compulsory
2014	Corns Buckly	52	Papt		A Weaver	City Cork	8th May 88		
2015	Elinor Morris	50	*Do*		H Keeper	City Limk	8th *Do*		
2016	Dinnis O Donnold	83	*Do*		A Stroler	City Limk	17th		
2017	George Camble	40		Pro	A Butcher	County Limk	17th *Do*		
2018	Joane Shaughnessy	88	*Do*		A Begar	City Limk	17 *Do*		
2019	John Hickie	20	*Do*		A Baker	County Clar	20th		
2020	Malacky Mulcahy	60	*Do*		A Beggar	County Limk	25th		
2021	Matts Sulivan	60	*Do*		A Beggar	County Limk	25 *Do*		
2022	John Molony	60	*Do*		A Weavor	City Limk	28 *Do*		
2023	Peggy Molony	9	*Do*			*Do*	*Do*		
2024	Sarah McMahon	27	*Do*		A Bad Girl	County Limk	28 *Do*		
2025	Cathr Callaghan	78	*Do*		A Beggar	City Limk	31st		
2026	Eliza Lock	40	*Do*		A Bad Woman	City Limk	*Do*		
2027	Jams Lock	1					*Do*		
2028	John Mealy	30	*Do*		Tannor	City Limk	2d June		
2029	John Timmons	10				*Do*	4th		
2030	Dins Molony	11				*Do*	4th		
2031	Eliza Fitzgerald	50	Ro		A Beggar	Jersey	6th June 88		
2032	Margt Donovan	45	*Do*		H Keeper	County Limk	11th *Do*		
2033	Catrn Carleton	12		Pro		City Limk	24th June 88		
2034	Cathr Leddy	60	*Do*		H Keeper	City Limk	25th *Do*		
2035	Thoms Monagan	11	*Do*		Orphan	City Limk	27th		
2036	Mary Fool	20				County Limk	29th		
2037	Anstis Branwood	70	*Do*		A Beggar	City Limk	30th		
2038	Oliver Ryen	60			A Beggar	City Limk	3d July		
2039	Eliza McNeal	60		Pro	A Servant	City Limk	4th *Do*		
2040	Cathr Grady	12	*Do*			City Limk	14th *Do*		
2041	Hana Hartagan	33	*Do*		A Beggar	County Limk	15th *Do*		
2042	Micl Costola	12	*Do*		Orphan	City Limk	15th *Do*		
2043	Elinor Carleton	50		Pro	H Keeper	City Limk	17th *Do*		
2044	Danl Donovan	48	*Do*		A Beggar	County Cork	20th		
2045	Dins Kelly	92	Rom		Labouror	County Limk	22d *Do*		
2046	Willm Tracy	48	Rom		A briches Maker	City Limk	27th *Do*		
2047	Jams Harrold	47	Rom		A Shoe Maker	City Limk	27th		
2048	Elinor Kieth	50		Pro	A H Keeper	City Limk	5th Augt		
2049	Willm Kieth	12		*Do*		City Limk	5th		
2050	Mary Maley	70	Rom		A Beggar	County Limk	8th Augt 88		
2051	Danl Keeffe	89	*Do*		A Cleoathar	City Limk	18th Augt 88		
2052	Thoms Munavan	13	*Do*		Orphan	City Limk	22d *Do*		
2053	John Lahiff	12			*Do*	City Limk	*Do*		
2054	Thoms Keith	50		Pro	A Shoemaker	City Limk	23d *Do*		
2055	Christopher Bodly	64		*Do*	A Shoemaker	City Limk	26th *Do*		
2056	Madge Kelly	80	Rom		A Beggar	County Tipperary	27th		
2057	John Myors	60		Pro	A Barbor	County Limk	28th		
2058	Johana Myors	50		Pro		England	29th		
2060	Cathr Feheen	73	Rom		HKeeper	City Limk	30th Augt		
2061	Martin Austen	8		Pro	Orphan	City Limk	30th *Do*		
2062	Thoms Joice	48	Rom		Labouror	County Clar	10th Sept 88		
2063	Cathr McDonnold	60	Rom		poor H Keeper	County Clar	23d *Do*		
2064	Mary Shea	39		Pro	A Servant	County Limk	26th *Do*		
2065	Cathr Lee	18	Rom		A Beggar	City Limk	27th *Do*		
2066	Edmond Mulvehill	20	*Do*		A Beggar	County Limk	27th *Do*		
2067	Sophy Myors	12	*Do* [sic]	Pro		England	27th *Do*		
2068	Mary Purcel	53	*Do*		A Beggar	City Limk	1st Octr		
2069	Patrick Maynihane	32			A Shoemaker	City Limk	2d *Do*		
2070	Matts McMahon	40	*Do*		A Servant	City Limk	12th Octr 1788		
2071	Margt Hurley	56	*Do*		poor H Keeper	City Limk	19th *Do*		
2072	Elinr Kieth	50		Pro	poor H Keeper	City Limk	21st		
2073	Henery Gibson	20			Labourer	City Limk	22d		
2074	Ann O'Brien	60			poor H Keeper	County Limk	26th *Do*		

No. of bed	Condition when received: Healthy	Condition when received: Sickly	Disease when received	How disposed of: Discharged	How disposed of: Died	How disposed of: Eloped	Condition when discharged: Healthy	Condition when discharged: Sickly	Observations
				21st July 88					By Order of Committee
			Infirm			25th May 88			Went Out the Street door
			1 Leg	22d July 88					By Order of Committee
			Infirm	26th May					By Order of the Mayor
			Insane	25th Augt 1788					By Order of Mr Philips he haveing come to his senses
			Infirm	26th May 88					By Order of the Mayor
						25th May 88			Went Over the Garden Wall
				8th Feby 1790					By John Ferrar Esqr
						4th Augt 1789			went Out the street door
			Lost her toes	6th June 88					by Order of the Mayor
			Sickly						
				22d July 88					By Order of Committee
				22d *Do*					By Order of Committee
			Insane			17th July 1789			he went Out the door
				28th Augt 1789					By Order of A Committee
						19th Sepr 1788			went Out the Street door
				7th June 88					by Order of the Mayor
				26th July 88					by Order of Committee
					7th July 88				
			Infirm		31st Jany 1791				the house bougt her Coffin
				20th Augt 1788					by Order of Alderman Fitzgerald
			Insane		16th April 1790				Mad in the Cells
				14th July 88					By Order of A Commitee
			Blind	4th July 88					By Capt Hill
				21st June 1789					By Order of the Mayor
						15th July 88			Went Out the Street door
						21st July 88			Went Out the Street door
				[1]st sepr 1789					By Order of A Committee
						19th Octr 1788			Went Out the Street door
				22d July 88					By Order of A Committee
						11th Augt 88			Went Out the Street door
			Insane	29th Decr 88					by Order of the Mayor
			Insane	3d Augt 88					broke the Cell his frinds took him out
						10th Octr 1788			Went Out the Street door
						17th April 89			Went Out the Street door
			Infirm	11th Augt 88					By Order of the Mayor
						6th April 1789			Went Out the Street door
						21st July 1789			he went Over the Garden Wall
						21st Octr 1788			went Out the Street door
						13th April 1789			Went Out the Street door
				29th Augt 88					By Order of the Mayor
				4th Sept 88					By Order of the Mayor
						30th Augt 88			Went Out the Street door
			Insane		8th Novr 1788				Died Mad in the Cell
				15th Novr 1788					By Order of Mr Phillips and Mr Ferrar
				15th Novr 1788					By Order of *Do*
				28th Octr 1788					by Order of Mr Phillips
				21st April 1790					By Order of A Committee
						[1]st March 1789			Went out for water Elopd
				Dischargd 5th March (all erased)		7th Octr 1788			By order of the Mayor went Over the Garden Wall
			Insane			30th Octr 1788			went Over the Garden wall
						13th Decr 1788			went Over the Garden wall
				3d Octr 1788					By Order of the Mayor
			Infirm			17th Octr 1788			Went Out the Street door
			Infirm	26th Novr					By Order of Capt Hill
						20th Octr 1788			Went Out the Street door
						11th Decr 1788			Went Out the Street door
			Insane	2d Novr 1788					by Alderman Widenham
			Insane		7th Januy 1789				Died Mad in the Cells

Current No.	Names	Age	Religion Roman Catholic	Protestant	Occupation	Late residence	Admitted	Voluntary	Compulsory
2075	Timethy McNemara	70	*Do*		A Mason	County Limk	30th Octr 1788		
2076	George Parker	55		Pro		City Limk	31st		
2077	Allice Corbitt	44			A Beggar	County tipperry	31st *Do*		
2078	John Gurran	60		Pro	A Weaver	County Clar	Novr 1st		
2079	John Boyl	31		Pro	A Weaver	Kings County	5th		
2080	Gerald Fitzgibbons	14				County Limk	9th		
2081	Devid Flyn	70	R		A Comber	County Clar	10th		
2082	Brien Conners	60	R		A Weaver	County Clar	16th		
2083	Sarah O'Brien	40	R		H Keeper	City Limk	29th		
2084	Ann O'Brien	20	*Do*		Bad Girl	City Limk	29th		
2085	John O'Brien	12				City Limk	29th		
2086	Willm O'Brien	5				City Limk	29th		
2087	Micl Neal	40	Rom		Servant	County Clar	10th Decr 1788		
2088	Thoms Bealy	60		Pro	Comber	City Limk	11th *Do*		
2089	Mary Connors	60	R		Servant	City Limk	11th		
2090	Cathr Lee	19	R		A Beggar	City Limk	19th *Do*		
2091	Pattr Kelly	60	R		A weaver	City Limk	23d *Do*		
2092	Ricd Waller	20		Pro	A Grocer	City Limk	30th *Do*		
2093	Mary Carrol	40	Roman		A Beggar	County Limk	2d Januy 89		
2094	Margt Brien	90	*Do*		A Beggar	City Limk	15th *Do*		
2095	Margt McMahon	30	*Do*		A Servant	County Clar	17th *Do*		
2096	Rebeca Veal	50		Pro	A Servant	City Limk	24th *Do*		
2097	Laur Mahon	50	*Do*		A Grocer	City Limk	26th *Do*		
2098	John O'Brien	60	*Do*		A Servant	County Clear	30th *Do*		
2099	Cathr Grady	13	*Do*			City Limk	7th Feby		
2100	Matts Morony	14	*Do*		Orphan	City Limk	24th *Do*		
2101	Elinor Kieth	50		Pro	H Keeper	City Limk	25th *Do*		
2102	Margt Hogan	12	*Do*			City Limk	18th March 89		
2103	John Lahiff	12			Orphan	City Limk	23d March 89		
2104	Henery Edwords	26		Pro	Shoemaker	City Limk	6th April 89		
2105	Mary Kelly	27	Roman		A poor Girl	City Limk	10th *Do*		
2106	Thoms Nevil	12			*Do*	City Limk	14th *Do*		
2107	Mary Nevil	10			*Do*	*Do*	14th *Do*		
2108	Charlato Deane	25			A servant	County Limk	14th *Do*		
2109	Cathr Grady	13			*Do*	City Limk	14 *Do*		
2110	Robort Shepton	55	P [sic]	Pro	Shoemaker	City Limk	15th *Do*		
2111	Hon Horragen	30	Roman			County Limk	13th May 89		
2112	Chars Green	40		Pro	A Salor	England	18th *Do*		
2113	Mary Sulivan	25	Rom		H Keeper	City Limk	23d May		
2114	Danl Keeffe	85	Rom		Cloather	City Limk	28th May		
2115	Jams Flimmon	25	*Do*		Farmor	County Limk	11th June 1789		
2116	Margt Healy	30	Rom		Servant	County Limk	25th June 1789		
2117	George Parker	45		Pro	Farmor	City Limk	29th *Do*		
2118	John Frally	30	*Do*			County Limk	29th *Do*		
2119	John Nealon	28	*Do*		A Carpentor	County Limk	7th July		
2120	John Hogan	40	*Do*		A Pedler	County Clar	18th *Do*		
2121	Jams Flimmon	26	*Do*		A Farmor	County Limk	22d *Do*		
2122	Garret Gibbons	70	*Do*		A Portor	City Limk	[1]st August		
2123	Cathr Kennedy	35	*Do*		H Keeper	City Limk	3d *Do*		
2124	Francis McDonnold	17		Pro	A Stocken Maker	City Limk	13th *Do*		
2125	Johana Landers	70	*Do*		A poor H Keeper	City Limk	17th *Do*		
2126	Devid Cudmore	70	*Do*		Labouror	County Clar	23d *Do*		
2127	Danl Ferris	70	*Do*		A Farmor	County Kerry	26th *Do*		

No. of bed	Condition when received		Disease when received	How disposed of			Condition when discharged		Observations
	Healthy	Sickly		Discharged	Died	Eloped	Healthy	Sickly	
			Infirm		2d April 1789				Died Sodently, his friend bought A Coffin
			Insane			17th Novr 1788			broke the Cell & Carred Away his boults & Bed Cloaths
			A Sore Brest	11th Novr 1788					by Order of the Mayor
			Insane	6th Januy 1789					by Order of the Recorder
			Infirm		23d June 1789				he Died with the lax
			Insane			16th Novr 1788			Went Over the Garden wall
			Infirm						
				31st April 1790					by Order of two Governers
			Infirm	10th April 1790					By Order of A Committee
				21st April 1789					By Order of Mr Phillips
				[1]st Sept 1789					By Order of A Committee
				[1]st sept 1789					By Order of A Committee
				20th March 1789					By Order of Committee
					6th July 1789				Shee Died in the 61 year of her Age
			One Hand	6th March 1789					by Order of the Mayor
				20th Jany 1789					By Order of the Mayor
			Insane	2d Januy 1789					his Father brougt him Away
			Insane						
			Infirm		26th Jany 1789				
				22d March 1789					by Mr Phillips Shee haveing gon to servis
					Died 10th May 1791				the house bougt her Coffin
			Insane	8th Feby 1789					by Order of Capt Hill Esqr
				25th July 1789					By Order of Capt Hill Esqr
			Insane			10th March 1789			went Out the street door
				26th Febry 1789		26th Feby			Went Over the Garden Wall
						3d March 1789			Shee went Out the street door
				[1]st sept 1789					By Order of A Committee
				27th Augt 1789					By Order of A Committee
			Insane	11th May 1789					By Order of Mr Phillips
				3d June 1790					By Order of A Committee
						22d May 1789			Went Out the Street door
						12 June 1789			Went Over the Garden Wall
			Insane			23d July 1789			Shee went Over the Wall & Came to her senses
			Insane			24th June 1789			Went Over the Garden Wall
			Wants the Use of his hand			Died 28th June 1793			the house bougt his Coffin
			Insane	23d Novr 1789					by John Ferrar Esqr
			Insane						
			Insane	25th May 1789					By Order of the Mayor, Shee having Come to her senses
			Infirm		Died 28th Decr 1790				the house bougt his Coffin
			Insane			19th June 1789			his frinds & the Doctor brought him to walk
			Insane	[1]st of Octr 1789					Shee haveing Come to her senses
			Insane			22d July 1789			he went Out the Street door
			Insane			3d July 1789			he Went Over the Garden Wall
			Insane & blind			26th May 1790			he Went Out of the door of the Garden
			Insane			31st July 1789			he went Over the Garden Wall, he haveing come to his senses
			Insane			26th July 1789			he got Out of Bed Innent [sic] to the keeper he went over the wall & carred Away his Jacket & Boults
					Died 17th March 1791				the house bougt his Coffin
			Insane						
						16th Augt 89			he went Over the Garden Wall
			Infirm						
			Insane		7th Octr 1789				Died Mad in One of the Cells
			Infirm	27th Augt 1789					By Order of A Committee

Current No.	Names	Age	Religion Roman Catholic	Protestant	Occupation	Late residence	Admitted	Voluntary	Compulsory
2128	Margt Hogan	13				City Limk	3d Sepr 1789		
2129	Honr Fitzgerald	45	*Do*		A Beggar	City Limk	11th *Do*		
2130	Willm Connell	56	*Do*		A weaver	City Limk	20th *Do*		
2131	Cathr Colebret	37		Pro	A H Keeper	A servant [sic]	25th *Do*		
2132	Micl Neal	44	*D*		A Servant	County Clar	3d Octr		
2133	Willm Fitzgerald	79	*D*		A Labour	County Limk	15th *Do*		
2134	Thoms Stack	70	*D*		A Weavor	City Limk	15th		
2135	John Johnson	70	*D*		A Dealor	County Limk	15th		
2136	Elize Fitzgerald	52	*D*		A Beggar	Jersey	15th		
2137	Bridgt Bouland	30	*D*		A Beggar	City Limk	15th		
2138	Jams Mead	75	*D*		A Beggar	County Clar	17th		
2139	Pattr Culhane	70	*D*		A Beggar	City Limk	21st		
2140	Hugh Shaughnessy	85	*D*		A Beggar	County Clar	23d		
2141	Dins Donnolan	80	*D*		A Beggar	County Limk	23d		
2142	Own Sulivan	35	*D*		A Beggar	County Cork	24th		
2143	Mary Kennedy	35	*D*		A Butonmaker	from Clonmell	23d		
2144	George Parker	40		Pro	A Farmor	City Limk	27th *Do*		
2145	Timethy McNemara	19	Rom		A Fool	County Limk	27th Octr 1789		C
2146	John Heffernan	70	*Do*		A Beggar	County Limk	29th *Do*		C
2147	Dens Hallanan	13	*Do*		Idle Boy	City Limk	29th *Do*		C
2148	Micl Brown	44	*Do*		A Farmer	County Limk	29th *Do*		
2149	Mary Kennedy	25	*Do*		A Beggar	City Limk	30th *Do*		C
2150	Jams Rourke	40	*Do*		A Beggar	County Clar	31st Octr 89	V	
2151	Nell Toomy	50	*Do*		A Beggar	City Limk	31st *Do*	V	
2152	Mary Kennedy	21	*Do*		A Beggar	City Limk	30th *Do*		C
2153	Mary Connelly	60	*Do*		A Beggar	City Limk	Novr 1st		C
2154	Cathr Hogan	60	*Do*		A Beggar	City Limk	*Do*		C
2155	Mary Ryan	70	*Do*		A poor H Keeper	County Limk	3 *Do*	V	
2156	Bridgt Butler	50	*Do*		A Beggar	City Limk	3 *Do*		C
2157	timethy Sulliven	70	*Do*		A taylor	County Cork	4th *Do*	V	
2158	Bridgt Dwyer	50	*Do*		A Beggar	County Limk	4th	V	
2159	Devid Reedy	70	*Do*		A weaver	City Limk	5th *Do*	V	
2160	Micl Conoway	30	*Do*		A Cobler	City Limk	5th *Do*		C
2161	Timethy McNemara	60	*Do*		A Beggar	County Limk	7th *Do*		C
2162	Redmond Hayes	65	*Do*		A Beggar	City Limk	7th *Do*		
2163	Fans Donovan	55	*Do*		A Beggar	City Limk	11th *Do*		
2164	John Mealy	30	*Do*		A tanner	City Limk	11th *Do*		
2165	Willm Duggan	60	*Do*		A weaver	Connought	12th *Do*		
2166	Honr Donnovan	30	*Do*		A poor Girl	City Limk	13th *Do*		
2167	Bridgt Dwyer	50	*Do*		A Beggar	County Limk	14th *Do*		
2168	Margt Redden	70	*Do*		A Beggar	County Limk	16th *Do*		
2169	Elinor Carleton	40			A poor H Keeper	City Limk	18th *Do*		
2170	Elinor Carleton	4			A Child	*Do*	*Do*		
2171	Elinor Kennedy	20	*Do*		A poor woman	City Limk	19th *Do*		
2172	Allas Brown	35	*Do*		A Beggar	City Limk	20th *Do*		
2173	Honr Horragan	30	*Do*			County Limk	26th *Do*		
2174	Ann Hogan	27	*Do*		A Beggar	County Clar	28th *Do*		
2175	Pattr Lascy	69	*Do*		A weaver	City Limk	28th *Do*		
2176	Margt Ledwill	35		Pro	A Beggar	City Limk	30th Decr 1789		
2177	Mary Prasson	65	*Do*		A poor H Keeper	County Limk	2d Decr		
2178	John Thompson	70		P	A stocking Maker	City Lork [sic]	4th Decr 1789		
2179	Walter Spring	70	*Do*		A Sletor	City Limk	4th *Do*		
2180	Mary Redden	70	Rom		A poor H Keeper	City Limk	6th Decr 1789		
2181	Pattr Sheehy	79	*Do*		A Farmor	County Limk	6th *Do*		
2182	Jeremiah Connors	60	*Do*		A servant	County Limk	9th *Do*		
2183	Matha Keily	20	*Do*		A Servant	County Clar	11th *Do*		
2184	Micl Flanery	70	*Do*		A Weavor	City Limk	12th *Do*		

No. of bed	Condition when received Healthy	Sickly	Disease when received	How disposed of Discharged	Died	Eloped	Condition when discharged Healthy	Sickly	Observations
			Insane			22d Sepr 1789			Went Out for the Cloaths, Elopt
			Infirm	25th Feby 1792					by Order of Mr Andw Watson
				24th Novr 1789					By Order of Mr Phillips
					Died 21st May 1791				the house bougt his Coffin
				26th Feby 1790					By Order of John Ferrar Esqr
					30th Decr 1789				the House bougt his Coffin
				19th Octr 1789					By Order of John Ferrar Esqr
			wants the Use of her hand	5th Decr 1789					Shee Got Security she will not beg
				18th Octr 1789					By Order of John Ferrar Esqr
				3d June 1790					by Order of A Committee
						27th Novr 1789			he Went Over the wall
				4th Novr 1789					By John Ferrar Esqr
			A Cripple	26th Octr 1789					By Order of John Ferrar Esqr
			Insane			28th Octr			he broke the Cell door & carred Away his hand Cuffs
			Insane						
			Sick & Infirm	3d Novr 1789					by John Ferrar Esqr
				5th Novr 1789					by Order of the Mayor
			Insane	6th Novr 1789					by Order of John Ferrar Esqr
			Insane						
			A Cripple	6th April 1790					By A Committee
			A Cripple						
				3d Novr 1789					by John Ferrar Esqr
				11th Novr 1789					by John Ferrar Esqr
					26th March 1790				the hous bought her Coffin
			7th Novr 1789 [sic]						by Order of John Ferrar Esqr
				12th Novr 1789					by Order of John Ferrar Esq
				10th Novr 1789					by Order of John Ferrar Esq
			Infirm		5th Decr 1789				AGed 70
			he Came in Drunk			7th Novr 1789			he went over the Wall of the Nessecary
			he Wants the Use of his Limbs	2d Januy 1790					By J Ferrar Esqr
					Died 9th June 1791				the house bougt his Coffin
			Insane			27th Novr 1789			he went Over the Garden wall
						19th Novr 1789			he went Over the Garden wall
						15th May 1790			Shee went Over the Kitchen yard wall
				27th Novr 1789					By John Ferrar Esqr
						6th Decr 1789			Shee went Out to Mass, Elopt
				4th May 1790					By A Committee
				4th May 1790					By A Committee
			Blind	6th April 1790					By Order of A Committee
			Infirm			Eloptd [1]st Decr 1789			Shee went went [sic] Over the Wall
			Insane						
			Infirm	3d Feby 1790					By J Ferrar Esqr shee went home to the County Clar
				30th March 1790					By John Ferrar Esqr
			Blind	2d Decr 1789					Shee haveing pd Fees 1s 1d
			Blind			22d May 1791			Shee went Out to Mass, Eloptd
			Infirm		Died 2d June 1791				the house bougt his Coffin
			Infirm	16th Augt 1790					By Order of J Ferrar Esqr
				30th Decr 1789					By Order of J Ferrar Esqr
				24th April 1790					By Order of A Committee
				7th Augt 1791					By Order of Mr Andw Watson
			broke his Leg		26th Decr 1789				the House bougt his Coffin
				9th June 1790					By Order of A Committee

Current No.	Names	Age	Religion Roman Catholic	Protestant	Occupation	Late residence	Admitted	Voluntary	Compulsory
2185	John Shanahan	80	*Do*		A Weavor	City Limk	17th Decr 1789		
2186	Denis Reerdon	58	*Do*		A Salour	County Limk	17th *Do*		
2187	John Mathous	30	*Do*		A Servant	the west Indous	17th *Do*		
2188	Jams Dwyer	14	*Do*		A Idle Boy	City Limk	18th *Do*		
2189	John Shea	14	*Do*		A Idle Boy	City Limk	19th *Do*		
2190	Honr McMahon	72	*Do*		A Beggar	City Limk	18th *Do*		
2191	Ann Marshel	60	*Do*		A Beggar	City Limk	18th *Do*		
2192	Mary Molony	90	*Do*		A Beggar	County Clar	19th *Do*		
2193	Mary Hopkins	80	*Do*		A Beggar	County Golloway	19 *Do*		
2194	Pattr Reedy	59	*Do*		A Servant	County Limk	21st *Do*		
2195	Mary Connelly	45	*Do*		A poor Woman	County Clar	23d *Do*		
2196	John Hogan	40	*Do*		A Pedler	County Clar	30th		
2197	Joane Heffernan	60	*Do*		A Beggar	County Limk	1st Jany 1790		
2198	Jams Sheehan	60	*Do*		A Sailor	City Limk	3d *Do*		
2199	Margt Flyn	60	*Do*		A H Keeper	City Limk	4th *Do*		
2200	Jams Dwyer	14	*Do*		A bad Idle Boy	City Limk	6th *Do*		
2201	Elinor Sullivan	14	*Do*		A Idle Girl	City Limk	8th *Do*		
2202	Jams Welsh	70	*Do*		A Labouror	County Limk	9th *Do*		
2203	Micl Quinlevan	70	*Do*		A Charman	County Limk	12th *Do*		
2204	Margt Therry	70	*Do*		A Beggar	County Limk	14th *Do*		
2205	Cathr Dillon	40	*Do*		A H Keeper	City Limk	15th *Do*		
2206	Eliza Hall	36		Pro	A poor Girl	Kings County	18th *Do*		
2207	Mary Warnock	40		Pro	A Solders Wife	North	20th *Do*		
2208	Willm OBrien	40		Pro	A stocking wevor	City Limk	23d Jany 1790		
2209	Bridgt Butler	50	Rom		A Stroler	City Limk	25th *Do*		
2210	Ann Kennane	20	*Do*		A Servant	County Limk	26th *Do*		
2211	Pattr Fahy	26	*Do*		A Weavor	County Clar	26th *Do*		
2212	Edward Bourk	50			A Sealor	County Limk	29th *Do*		
2213	Ann McNemara	30	*Do*		A Simstress	County Limk	1st Feby 1790		
2214	Mary McLean	73	*Do*		A Beggar	County Limk	1st *Do*		
2215	John Murry	75	*Do*		A weavor	County Clar	1st *Do*		
2216	Laur Mulcaky	18	*Do*		A poor Boy	County Limk	1st *Do*		
2217	John Daly	50	*Do*		A stroler	County Limk	3 *Do*		
2218	Bridgt Smyth	17		Pro	A Servant	City Limk	3 *Do*		
2219	Henery Conners	60	*Do*		A Weavor	County Kerry	4th *Do*		
2220	John Lynch	60	*Do*		A Molster	City Limk	4th *Do*		
2221	Moses Fox	60		Pro	A Weavor	City Limk	4th *Do*		
2222	Ann Hogan	30	*Do*		A poor woman	County Clar	5th *Do*		
2223	Willm McGrath	60	*Do*		A Labouror	County Clar	8th *Do*		
2224	Ann Miller	60	*Do*		A poor H Keeper	County Limk	8th *Do*		
2225	Alice Costelloe	90	*Do*		A poor H Keeper	City Limk	12th *Do*		
2226	Bridgt Bolond	25	*Do*		A Beggar	City Limk	25th *Do*		
2227	Elinor Hartney	70	*Do*		A Beggar	County Limk	26th *Do*		
2228	Ann Dunn	50	*Do*		A Beggar	County Limk	28th *Do*		
2229	Dens McInerny	70	*Do*		A Charman	County Clar	28th *Do*		
2230	Hana Hartigan	30	*Do*		A Beggar	County Limk	28th *Do*		
2231	Cathr Eyrecourt	25		Pro	A Servant	City Limk	[1]st March		
2232	Denis Doherthy	60	*Do*		A Weaver	City Limk	2d *Do*		
2233	John Kelly	63	*Do*		A smith	Carreg	1st *Do*		
2234	Danl OBrien	60	*Do*		A Charman	County Limk	3d *Do*		
2235	John Mealy	25	Rom		A tanner	City Limk	4th March 1790		C
2236	Mary Kean	34	*Do*		A Poor H Keeper	City Limk	5th *Do*		
2237	Micl Dineen	18	*Do*		A Weavor	City Limk	6th *Do*		
2238	Jams Wilson	21	*Do*		A Weavor	North	7th *Do*		
2239	Bridgt Butler	50	*Do*		A stroler	City Limk	10th *Do*		C
2240	Willm Duggan	60	*Do*		A troler	Connought	16th *Do*		

No. of bed	Condition when received Healthy	Sickly	Disease when received	How disposed of Discharged	Died	Eloped	Condition when discharged Healthy	Sickly	Observations
						17th Decr 1789			he went Out for his Cloaths
				26th April 1790					By Order of A Committee
						28th Decr 1789			he went Over the Garden wall
						28th Decr 1789			he went Over the Garden wall
				17th Jany 1790					By John Ferrar Esqr Shee haveing pd her fees
				20th Decr 1789					By John Ferrar Esqr
					Died 5th sepr 1792				the house bout her Coffin
				24th Decr 1789					By J Ferrar Esqr as shee gave security she will not beg
				11th April 1790					By Order of A Committee
			Insane			26th May 1790			he went Out the Garden door
			Insane	3d Feby 1790					By Order of J Ferrar he having come to his senses
				2d Jany 1790					by JFerrar Esqr
			he wants the use of his hand						
						2d April 1790			he Went Out the street door
						9th Jany 1790			Shee went Out the street door
				dischargd 30th Augt 91					by Order of Mr Andw Watson
					Died 15th June 1791				the house bougt his Coffin
						19th March 1790			Shee went Out with the House, Cloaths
				8th Feby 1790					By John Ferrar Esqr
						16th Jany 1790			Shee went Out the street door
						5th April 1790			he went Out the street door
						28th 1790			Shee went Over the Garden wall
			Insane						
			Infirm	28th Jany 1790					By John Ferrar Esqr
				9th Feby 1790					By John Ferrar Esqr
			Infirm						
			Infirm						
			Infirm	19th Feby 1790					By Order of J Ferrar Esqr
			Ded A One side			2d July 1790			he Went Out the turf house Window
						11th Feby 1790			he broke the Cell & Carred, Away A sheet he went over the wall
					Died 6th March 1790				
			Infirm	9th Feby 1790					By John Ferrar
			Infirm	8th Feby 1790					By John Ferrar Esq
			Insane						
			A Cripple	31st March 1790					Shee haveing Givin Security Shee will not Beg
			Infirm	28th Feby 1790					By Order of J Ferrar Esqr
			Infirm	24th April 1790					By Order of A Committee
				26th April 1790					By Order of A Committee
				16th March 1790					Shee haveing gone to Servis
				5th March 1790					by J Ferrar Esqr
			Insane						
			Insane	10th March 1790					he haveing Come his senses
			Infirm	31st March 1790					By Order of J Ferrar Esqr
			Infirm			6th June 1791			Shee went Over the Garden wall
						Eloptd 29th March 1790			he broke the lock of the Cell door & Carred Away A sheet

Current No.	Names	Age	Religion Roman Catholic	Protestant	Occupation	Late residence	Admitted	Voluntary	Compulsory
2241	Honr OBrien	25	*Do*		A servant	County Clar	15th March 1790		
2242	Doro OBrien	28	*Do*		A servant	County Clar	16th *Do*		
2243	John Molony	60	*Do*		A Weavor	City Limk	23d *Do*		
2244	John Ferris	70	*Do*		A Beggar	County Kerry	26th *Do*		
2245	Micl Dineen	18	*Do*		A Weavor	City Limk	27th *Do*		
2246	John Barton	72	*Do*		A Labouror	County Clar	27th *Do*		
2247	Bridgt Brien	60	*Do*		A Beggar	City Limk	[1]st April		
2248	Mary Hackett	70	*Do*		A Beggar	City Limk	2d *Do*		
2249	George Parker	40		Pro	A Farmor	City Limk	5th *Do*		
2250	Ann Ryen	30	*Do*		A sarvant	County Clar	6th *Do*		
2251	Elinor Gardner	19	*Do*		A servant	County Clar	6th *Do*		
2252	Bridgt Boulond	25	*Do*		A Beggar	City Limk	7th *Do*		C
2253	Luke Hartewell	33		Pro	A weavor	City Limk	8th		
2254	Danl Ferris	70	*Do*		A Beggar	County Kerry	9th		C
2255	Jams Mead	74	*Do*		A Beggar	County Clar	11th		C
2256	Pattr Donovan	40	*Do*		A Beggar	County Cork	11th		C
2257	Micl Clark	75		Pro	A Beggar	County Waterford	11th		C
2258	James Nellson	77		Pro	A Beggar	Scotland	12th		C
2259	Brien O Loghlin	83	Rom		A wrighting Master	City Limk	13th		
2260	Bridgt Hopkins	80	*Do*		A Beggar	Connought	12th		C
2261	Johanah Russell	73	*Do*		A Beggar	City Limk	12th		C
2262	Eliza McNeal	60		Pro	A servant	City Limk	12th		
2263	Mary Murphy	76	Rom		A Beggar	City Limk	13th April 1790		C
2264	Pattr Desmond	31	*Do*		A Beggar	City Limk	16th *Do*		C
2265	Edword Bourk	36	*Do*		A Beggar	County Limk	14th *Do*		C
2266	Micl Moran	70	*Do*		A Labouror	City Limk	17th *Do*	V	
2267	John Carmody	70	*Do*		A Labouror	City Limk	20th *Do*	V	
2268	Petor Lillis	16	*Do*		A Rouge	City Limk	21st *Do*		C
2269	Danl Healy	13	*Do*		A Rouge	City Limk	21st *Do*		C
2270	Eliza Llyod	98	*Do*		A Beggar	County Cork	21st *Do*		C
2271	Danl Murphy	77	*Do*		A ShopKeeper	City Corke	24th *Do*	V	
2272	John Duffey	76	*Do*		A Nealor	Linstir	24th *Do*		C
2273	Hestor Lyndon	40		Pro	A H Keeper	City Dublin	24th *Do*	V	
2274	Johanah Gavin	55	*Do*		A H Keeper	City Limk	27th *Do*	V	
2275	Jams Flimming	25	*Do*		A Farmer	County Limk	30th *Do*	V	
2276	Edword Moor	60	*Do*		A Beggar	City Limk	3d May		C
2277	Jams Williams	23	*Do*		A Beggar	County Waxford	3d *Do*		C
2278	Jaine Hunter	67	*Do*		A servant	North	3d *Do*	V	
2279	George Parker	40		Pro	A Farmor	City Limk	4th *Do*		C
2280	Margt Hurly	45	*Do*		A Beggar	City Cork	4th *Do*		C
2281	Micl Dineen	18	*Do*		A Weavor	City Limk	5th *Do*	V	
2282	Eliza Llyod	98	*Do*		A Beggar	County Cork	5th *Do*		C
2283	Mary Connors	80	*Do*		A Beggar	County Limk	6th *Do*		C
2284	Devid Dwyer	15	*Do*		A Idle Bad boy	City Limk	7th *Do*		C
2285	Willm Duggan	60	*Do*		A Beggar	Connaught	15th *Do*		C
2286	Micl Sculley	30	*Do*		A Beggar	County limk	15th		C
2287	Hestor Lyndon	43		Pro	A H Keeper	City Dublin	17th	V	
2288	Thoms Collins	42	*Do*		A Beggar	County Clar	19th		C
2289	Simon Newlan	70	*Do*		A wigmaker	County Clar	24th	V	
2290	Christopher Bodly	65		Pro	A shoemaker	City Limk	25th		C
2291	Edmond Fitzgerald	18		Pro	A Poor boy	County Limk	26th	V	
2292	Robort Sadler	60	*Do*		A Beggar	Scotland	3d June	V	
2293	Mary Sadler	56	*Do*		A Beggar	Dublin	3d *Do*	V	
2294	John Kana	75	Rom		Carpenter	City Limk	8th June 1790		
2295	Cathr Sulivan	56	Rom		A H Keeper	City Limk	9th *Do*	V	
2296	George Parker	45		Pro	A Farmor	City Limk	10th *Do*		C

No. of bed	Condition when received Healthy	Sickly	Disease when received	How disposed of Discharged	Died	Eloped	Condition when discharged Healthy	Sickly	Observations
			Insane			24th May 1790			See broak the hasp of the Cell door & went Over, the the Wall
						19th April 1790			the doorkeeper let her Out
			Infirm		6th March 1790				the House bougt his Coffin
			he come in Dead drunk	29th March 1790					he haveing giving Security he will not beg
			Insane	7th April 1790		7th April 1790			he went out of the Cells
			Infirm	14th July 79	14th July 1790				his frinds bougt his Coffin
			Infirm	2d April					Shee haveing giving Security shee will not Beg
			Infirm						
			Insane			7th April 1790			he went Out of the Cells
			Insane	5th June 1790					By Order of A Committee
			Insane	5th June 1790					By Order of A Committee
			A Cripple	14th July 1790					By Order of A Committee
				Dischargd 27th April 179					by Mr Andw Watson
			Infirm	1st June 1790					By Order of A Committee
			Infirm						
			Infirm			26th May			he went out the Garden door
			Infirm	13th April 1790					By A Commitee pd fees 1s 1d
				17th April 1790					By A Committee fees 1s 1d
			Infirm		24th April 1790				the Hous bougt his Coffin
			Infirm						
			Infirm	12th Novr 1790					By A Committee
			Infirm	14th April 1790					By Order A Committee
						17th April 1790			he went Out the street door
						26th May 1790			he went Out the Garden door
						24th April			he broke the lock of the Cell & went Over the Garden wall
						24th April			he broke the lock of the Cell door & Went over the Wall
				22d April 1790					By A Committee
			Infirm	3d May 1790					By A Committee
			Infirm	26th April 1790					By A Committee
			A Dropsey	11th May 1790					By A Committee
			Infirm	3d May 1790					By A Committee
			Insane						
				5th May 1790					By A Committee
						31st July 1790			he went Out the Shore of the Necessary
			Insane	3d May 1790					By Order of A Committee
				5th May 1790					By A Committee
			Insane	15th May 1790					By A Committee
			Infirm		Died 14th June 1790				the house bougt her Coffin
			Infirm	8th May 1790					By A Committee
						10th May			he went Over the garden wall
				[1]st June 1790					By Order of A Committee
			Insane	[1]st June 1790					By Order of A Committee
			A Dropsey			8th July 1790			the doorKeeper let her Out
						the 21st May 1790			he went Out the turf house window
					Died 12th May 1791				the house bougt his Coffin
			Infirm			[1]st Augt 1790			he went Out the shore of the Necessary house
			Blind	9th June 1790					By Order of A Committee
			Infirm	9th June 1790					By Order of A Committee
			Infirm		28 Novr 1790				the house bougt his Coffin
			Insane			15th June 1790			the hasp of the Cell door was broake & he went over the wall

Current No.	Names	Age	Religion Roman Catholic	Protestant	Occupation	Late residence	Admitted	Voluntary	Compulsory
2297	Mary Sulivan	21	Rom		A poor Girl	City Limk D [sic]	15th June 1790	V	
2298	Micl Conners	12		Pro	A sealor	England	16th		C
2299	Joane Flyn	20	Rom		A servant	City Limk	17th	V	
2300	Rebeca Carthy	40	Rom		A stroler	County Dublin	18	V	
2301	Cathr Eyrecourt	24		Pro	A servant	City Limk	19th	V	
2302	Timothy Clifford	78	Rom		A Beggar	County Clar	20th	V	
2303	Ann Ferguson	22	Rom		A Servant	City Limk	23d	Vo	
2304	Miles Bourke	47		Pro	A Redust Gentleman	County Limk	26th	V	
2305	Pattr Sheehy	75	Rom		A Farmor	County Limk	28th	Vo	
2306	Mary Rock	46		Pro	A servant	County Limk	29th	Vo	
2307	Pattr Reedy	70	Rom		A servant	County Limk	30th	Vo	
2308	Own Gilbreth	84	Rom		A Beggar	County Limk	3th July	Vo	
2309	Pattr Kelly	76		Pro	A Mat Maker	City Limk	8th	V	
2310	Cathr Eyrecourt	24		Pro	A servant	City Limk	10th	V	
2311	Ricd Williams	77		Pro	A tanner	City Limk	12th	V	
2312	Honr Child	60	Rom		A servant	City Limk	19th	V	
2313	Elinor Carleton	50		Pro	A H Keeper	City Limk	19th	V	
2314	Elinor Carleton	3			A Child	*Do Do*	*Do*		
2315	James Russell	60	Rom		Weavor	City Limk	19th	V	
2316	Thoms Clune	50	Rom		A Shipcarpenter	City Limk	23d		Compeld
2317	Honr OBrien	26	Rom		A Servent	County Clar	23d		
2318	Micl Sullivan	30	Rom		A Porter	City Limk	23d		Compeld
2319	Bridgt Munchane	57	Rom		A H Keeper	County Clare	25th	V	
2320	Cathr Ryan	60	Rom		A Beggar	City Limk	27th		Compeld
2321	John Willson	30		Pro	A scholer	County Dublin	29		Compeld
2322	Pattr Bourk	33	Rom		A Beggar	County Cork	31st		Compeld
2323	James Pursal	48	Rom		A Labourer	County Clar	4th	V	
2324	John Bowdy	70		Pro	A ShopKeeper	City Limk	6th Augt 1790		
2325	Richard Cahill	70	Rom		A Weavor	City Limk	8th *Do*		
2326	Ann Hallaran	30	Rom		A servant	City Limk	17th *Do*		
2327	Andw Meade	60	Rom		A Comber	City Limk	21st *Do*		
2328	John Brown	60	Rom		A shoemaker	County Limk	24th *Do*		
2329	Mary Daly	24	Rom		A servant	City Limk	29th *Do*		
2330	Margt Harty	23	Rom		A servant	City Limk	31st *Do*		
2331	Isaac Clampett	67	Rom		A weavor	City Limk	4th Sept 1790		
2332	Danl Foowler	58		Pro	A weavor	City Limk	4th *Do*		
2333	Cathr Neal	30	Rom		A servant	City Dublin	4th *Do*		
2334	Mary Redden	70	Rom		A Beggar	City Limk	10th *Do*		
2335	Mary Reagen	40	Rom		A Beggar	County Limk	21st *Do*		Com
2336	John McNemara	50	Rom		A Charman	City Limk	28th *Do*		
2337	Margt Bourke	30	Rom		A poor H Keeper	City Limk	28th *Do*		
2338	Margt Ryan	60	Rom		A poor H Keeper	County Limk	29th *D*		
2339	John King	60		Pro	A Solder	England	2d Octr		
2340	Jams Mead	63	Rom		A Beggar	County Clar	2d *Do*		
2341	Barneby Mason	80		Pro	A Fidler	England	5th *Do*		
2342	Sarah Julian	56	Rom		A poor H Keeper	County Clar	6th *Do*		
2343	George Roche	70	Rom		A Farmor	County Limk	11th *Do*		
2344	Cathr Hogan	70	Rom		A Beggar	City Limk	13th *Do*		
2345	Sarah Dohorthy	50	Rom		A servant	North	13th *Do*		
2346	Sarah Madden	80	Rom		A H Keeper	County Limk	19th *Do*		
2347	Mary Lahiff	17	Rom		A servant	City Limk	19th *Do*		
2348	Cathr Keough	47	Rom		A H Keeper	City Limk	20th *Do*		
2349	Willm Kennedy	65	Rom		A Weavor	City Limk	27th *Do*		
2350	Margt Jordon	28	Rom		A Beggar	City Limk	3d Novr		
2351	Mary Sulivan	70	Rom		A Beggar	County Kerry	5th *Do*		Com
2352	Bridgt Butler	60	Rom		A Beggar	City Limk	6th *Do*		Com
2353	Margt Tierny	44	Rom		A H Keeper	County Limk	7th Novr		
2354	Jams Bourke	40	Rom		A Beggar	City Limk	8th Novr 1790		
2355	Edward Martin	70		Pro	A Nealor	City Limk	10th *Do*		

No. of bed	Condition when received Healthy	Sickly	Disease when received	How disposed of Discharged	Died	Eloped	Condition when discharged Healthy	Sickly	Observations
			Sick in the bad Disorder	15th March 1791					By Order of John Ferrar Esqr
				14th July 1790					By Order of the Mayor
				2d July 1790					By Order of J Ferrar Esqr
						21st June 1790			Shee went Out the street door
				21st June 1790					by John Ferrar Esqr
			Infirm		9th July 1790				the house bougt his Coffin
			Insane			7th June 1791			Shee went Over the Garden Wall
				6th sept 1790					By Order of John Ferrar Esqr
				14th July 1790					
			Infirm	13th July 1790					By A Committee
			blind of One Eye		Died 5th 11th July Jany 1791				the doorkeeper let him out By Order of A Committee
				26th Decr 1790					By Order of J Ferrar Esqr
			Infirm	17th Augt 1790					By Order of A Committee
					Died				the [sic] bougt her Coffin
				13th June 1792					by Mr Andw Watson
				13th June 1792					by Mr Andw Watson
			Infirm	16th Sepr 1790					By Order of John Ferrar Esqr
				31st July 1790					By Order of A Committee
			Insane	24th Augt 1790					By Order of the Doctor Shee haveing Come to her senses
			he Came in drunk	11th Augt 1790					By Order of A Committee
						29th July 1790			Shee went out the shore of the necessary
				31st July 1790					By Order of A Committee
			Insane	16th 1790					By Order of A Committee
				16th Augt 1790					By Order of A Committee
				17th Feby 1792					By Mr Andw Watson
			sore Legs						
				24th Augt 1790					By Order of John Ferrar Esqr
					Died 15th May 1791				the house bougt his Coffin
			Infirm		6th Decr 1790				the house bougt his Coffin
			Insane			7th June 1791			Shee went Over the Garden wall
			A sore Leg	7th Octr 1790					By Order of John Ferrar Esqr
			Infirm			30th Decr 1790			he went Out the street door
				29th sepr 1790		With Out fees [sic]			By Order of John Ferrar Esqr
			Insane						
			Infirm						
			Lunatic		Died 13th Jany 1792				the house bougt her Coffin
				12th Novr 1790					By Order of Mr Ferrar
					9th Octr 1790				the house bougt his Coffin
				3d Novr 1790					By Order of John Ferrar Esqr
				the 9th Octr, by A Committee [sic]					by Order of A Committee
			A sore Leg						
				21st Octr 1790					By Order of A Committee
			Blind						
			Infirm	16th Novr 1790					By Order of J Ferrar Esqr
			Sick	24th Novr 1790					By Order of John Ferrar Esq
			Infirm	10th Decr 1790					By Order of John Ferrar Esq
			Blind		31st Octr 1790				the house bougt his Coffin
				16th March 1792					by Mr Andw watson
			Infirm		Died 22d March 1791				the house bougt her Coffin
						13th Novr 1790			Shee went Out the shore of the necessary
			Insane	21st Novr 1790					by Order of John Ferrar Es
			A Cripple						
			Sickly		16th Novr 1790				the house bougt his Coffin

Current No.	Names	Age	Religion Roman Catholic	Protestant	Occupation	Late residence	Admitted	Voluntary	Compulsory
2356	Thoms Croneen	17	Rom		A poor boy	County Limk	12th Novr 1790		
2357	Thoms Gorman	53	Rom		A Labourer	County Limk	17th *Do*		
2358	Thoms Farrell	37	Rom		A Labouror	County Limk	17th *Do*		
2359	Micl Rowles	48	Rom		A Servant	County Limk	19th *Do*		
2360	Bridgt Boulond	27	Rom		A Beggar	City Limk	13th *Do*		
2361	Bridgt Sulivan	20	Rom		A Quilter	City Limk	20th *Do*		
2362	Sarra Julian	60	Rom		A poor H Keeper	County Limk	20th *Do*		
2363	James Pursall	54	Rom		A poor Seaman	County Clar	22d *Do*		
2364	Denis Rightson	60		Pro	A Labouor	County Limk	26th *Do*		
2365	Pattr Henery	55		Pro	A Comber	City Limk	27th *Do*		
2366	Mary Lahiffe	17	Rom		A Servant	City Limk	1st Decr		
2367	Willm Tinsly	63	Rom		A Flaxdreser	City Limk	4th *Do*		
2368	Sara Madden	80	Rom		A poor H Keeper	County Limk	6th *Do*		
2369	Mary McMahon	17	Rom		A Idle Girl	City Limk	6th *Do*		
2370	John Daly	46	Rom		A Stroler	County Limk	11th		
2371	Pattr Sarsfeeld	40	Rom		A poor seaman	County Limk	11th *Do*		
2372	Mary Jones	60		Pro	A servant	County Limk	12th		
2373	Danl Ferris	76	Rom		A Beggar	County Kerry	14th		
2374	John Hogan	45	Rom		A Pedler	County Clar	16th		
2375	John Fitzgerald	75		Pro	A servant	County Limk	22d		
2376	Mary Kennedy	49	Rom		A spinner	City Limk	18th		
2377	Margt Tierney	44	Rom		House Keeper	County Limk	29th		
2378	Cathr Keogh	47	Rom		A poor H Keeper	City Limk	30th		
2379	John Clanchy	17	Rom		A poor boy	County Limk	8th Jany 1791		
2380	Walter Spring	72	Rom		A Sletor	City Limk	8th		
2381	Christian Duhig	18	Rom		A servant	City Limk	8th		
2382	Charles Tennent	40		Pro	A sealor	England	11th Jany		
2383	Micl Fitzgerald	36	Rom		A seaman	County Golloway	14th *Do*		
2384	Edmond Howly	36			A schoolmaster	County Sligo	15th *Do*		
2385	Micl Madden	33	Rom		A Butcher	City Limk	19th Jany 1791		
2386	Jams Green	66	Rom		A Servant	County Clar	19th	V	
2387	John Hogan	45	Rom		A Pedler	County Clar	the 21st		C
2388	John Halanan	70	Rom		A Pedler	City Limk	the 22d	V	
2389	Bridgt Sulivan	20	Rom		A Quiltor	City Limk	the 20th		C
2390	Micl Costola	15	Rom		A poor boy	City Limk	the 22d	V	
2391	Richard Williams	70		Pro	A tanner	City Limk	the 24th	V	
2392	Mary Hogan	36	Rom		A H Keeper	County Cork	the 24th		C
2393	Margt Parker	29		Pro	A poor Gerril	England	the 27th		C
2394	Margt Connelly	50	Rom		A poor H Keeper	County Clar	the 29th		C
2395	Dens Guerin	66	Rom		A weaver	County Clar	the 29th	V	
2396	Dens Hartney	80	Rom		A Beggar	County Limk	the 31st	V	
2397	Bridgt Butler	60	Rom		A Beggar	City Limk	the 31st	V	
2398	Margt Harty	30	Rom		A Lace Maker	City Limk	the 1st Feby		C
2399	Redmond Maguire	61	Rom		A servant	North	the 2d	V	
2400	Willm Ryan	70	Rom		A Labouror	County Limk	the 2d	V	
2401	Micl Hogan	60	Rom		A Labouror	County Limk	3d	V	
2402	Henery Conners	60	Rom		weavor	County Kerry	7		
2403	Mary Foresight	27		Pro	A servant	County Limk	8th	V	
2404	Mary Enright	40	Rom		A poor H Keeper	City Limk	9th	V	
2405	Thoms Scanlan	70	Rom		A Boat Man	City Limk	9th	V	
2406	John Veel	70	Rom		A Weavor	City Limk	12th	V	
2407	Ann Veel	80	Rom		A poor H Keeper	City Limk	12th	V	
2408	Margt Miller	75	Rom		A poor H Keeper	County Limk	16th	V	
2409	Cathr Keough	48	Rom		A poor H Keeper	City Limk	16th	V	
2410	Luscy Cuhoon	70	Rom		A poor H Keeper	City Limk	18th	V	
2411	Mary Murphey	30	Rom		A Harlot	County Dublin	22d	V	
2412	Margt Duffy	60	Rom		A poor H Keeper	City Limk	24th	V	
2413	Eliza Boldwin	27	Rom		A Beggar	County Limk	25th Feby 1791		C
2414	Mary Shea	70	Rom		A H Keeper	City Limk	28th *Do*	V	
2415	Mary Shea	17	Rom		A Mantamaker	City Limk	28th *Do*	V	
2416	Mary Doogan	70	Rom		A Beggar	City Limk	28th *Do*	V	

No. of bed	Condition when received Healthy	Sickly	Disease when received	How disposed of: Discharged	Died	Eloped	Condition when discharged Healthy	Sickly	Observations
			Insane						
			A Cripple						
			Insane		Died 5th Jany 1791				the house bougt his Coffin
			Sickly		Died 7th Febuary 179				the house bougt his Coffin
			Insane						
			Insane	17th May 1791					by Order of Mr Andw Watson
				15th March 1791					by Order of J Ferrar Esqr
			Insane						
					Died 24th May 1791				the house bougt his Coffin
				13th Jany 1791					By Order of J Ferrar Esqr
			Infirm		Died 15th Jany 1791				the house bougt his Coffin
				19th sepr 1791					by Order of Mr Willm Jackson
						31st Decr 1790			he broake the hasp of the Cell door & went over the wall
				11th March 1791					by Order of John Ferrar Esqr
			Infirm						
			Infirm						
			Insane			22d Decr 1790			he went out the turf house window
			Infirm						
				28th March 1791					by Order of John Ferrar Esqr
			Insane	13th Feby 1791					by Order of John Ferrar Esqr
				9th Feby 1791					by Order of A Committee
			Infirm			5th March 1791			he went Out the street door
				28th March 1791					by Order of John Ferrar Esqr
			Insane	10th May 1791					by Order of Mr Andw Watson
			Insane	16th Jany 1791					by Order of J Ferrar Esqr
			One Arm		Died				the house bougt his Coffin
				23d April 1791					by Order of Mr Andw Watson
			Infirm		Died 5th March 1792				his frinds bougt his Coffin
			Insane	10th Febuary 1791					by Order of A Committee
			Infirm			13th Feby 1791			he Went out to Mass
			Insane						
			Infirm						
			Insane	the 30th Jany 1791					by Mr Stuart Shee haveing Come to her senses
			Blind	the 3d March 1791					by Order of John Ferrar Esqr
			Insane						
			Sick & Infirm	9th Feby 1791					by Order of A Committee
			Infirm			5th June 1791			Shee went Over the Garden wall
				12th Feby 1791		5th Feby 1791			Shee Went Out the street door
			Infirm		Died 18th Feby 1791				the house bougt his Coffin
					Died 31st March 1791				the house bougt his Coffin
			Infirm	9th March 1791					by Order of J Ferrar Esqr
				28th Feby 1791					by Order of John Ferrar Esqr
				23d April 1791					by Order of Mr Andw Watson
					Died 12th March 1791				the house bougt his Coffin
					Died 15th May 1791				the house bougt his Coffin
				25th May 1791					by Order of Mr Andw Watson
				15th April 1791					by Order of Mr Andw Watson
				16th sepr 1791					by Order of Mr Andw Watson
			In the bad disorder		Died 31st July 1791				the house bougt her Coffin
			Sick & Infirm	15th Novr 1792					by Mr Andw Watson
				25th Feby 1791					by Order of the sherriff McMahon
					Died 6th Novr 1791				the house bougt her Coffin
				28th March 1791					by Order of John Ferrar Esqr
						1st March 1791			shee went Out the street door

Current No.	Names	Age	Religion Roman Catholic	Protestant	Occupation	Late residence	Admitted	Voluntary	Compulsory
2417	Mary Fool	40	Rom		Insane	County Limk	28th Feby 1791		C
2418	John Hallanan	50	Rom		A Labouror	County Limk	28th *Do*	V	
2419	Darby Doolan	68	Rom		A servant	City Limk	28th *Do*	V	
2420	Thoms Hayse	60	Rom		A Basketmaker	County Limk	28th *Do*	V	
2421	John Hogan	45	Rom		A Pedler	County Clar	6th March		C
2422	Holmes Williams	60		Pro	A Weavor	City Limk	6th *Do*		
2423	Pattr Bourk	40	Rom		A Balatsinger	City Limk	7th *Do*		C
2424	Timothy Delany	75	Rom	Pro	A weavor	City Limk	8th *Do*		
2425	John Hinchey	70	Rom		A Shoemake	City Limk	10th *Do*	V	
2426	Danl Godfrey	55	Rom		A Beggar	County Limk	17th *Do*	V	
2427	Mary Sullivan	28	Rom		A Harlot	County Limk	18th	V	
2428	William Smithis	66		Pro	A Farmor	County Tipparry	22d *Do*	V	
2429	Elinor Suliven	14	Rom		A knitter	City Limk	24th *Do*	V	
2430	Eliza Guilmer	9			A Child	City Limk	26th *Do*	V	
2431	Margt Mealy	55	Rom		A poor H Keeper	County Limk	29th *Do*	V	
2432	Christopher Brien	60		Pro	A Gardner	County Limk	29th *Do*	V	
2433	Margt Dillon	60	Rom		A poor H Keeper	City Limk	5th April	V	
2434	John Daly	47	Rom		A stroler	County Limk	12th April		C
2435	Margt Preston	23	Rom		A servent	City Limk	13 *Do*		
2436	Dins Nash	22	Rom		A Stroler	City Cork	15th *Do*		C
2437	Honor Murphey	60	Rom		A Beggar	County Limk	15th *Do*		C
2438	Cathr Eyrecourt	24		Pro	A Servant	City Limk	15th *Do*	V	
2439	Edward Fitzgerald	15	Rom		A poor boy	City limk	16th *Do*	V	
2440	John Ferrell	85	Rom		A penter	County Clare	25th *Do*	V	
2441	Richard Ancher	30		Pro	A sailor	England	27th *Do*	V	
2442	Henery Conners	49	Rom		A weavor	County Limk	2d May	V	
2443	Brien Sweeny	63	Rom		A Shoemaker	County Clar	2d *Do*	V	
2444	Nichlos McMahon	17	Rom		A Beggar	City Limk	9th May 1791		
2445	Ann Lynch	26	Rom		A Servan	Ros Crea	11th *Do*	V	
2446	Mary Ryan	33		Pro	A Beggar	County tipperary	18th May		C
2447	Mary Shouldice	30		Pro	A servant	County tippary	18th *Do*		C
2448	Mary Grady	40	Rom		A servant	County Limk	20th May	V	
2449	Edmond Sheihy	66	Rom		A shoemaker	County LimK	22d *Do*	V	
2450	Cathr Harris	31		Pro	A poor H Keeper	Queens County	24th *Do*	V	
2451	Margt Mitchell	55	Rom		A Servant	City Limk	27th *Do*	V	
2452	John Leary	21	Rom		A Labourer	City Limk	28th *Do*	V	
2453	Mary Casey	18	Rom		A servant	County Limk	30th *Do*		
2454	Dennis Carthy	35	Rom		A Carpenter	City Limk	9th June	V	
2455	Mary Dwyer	45		Pro	A HKeeper	City Limk	14th *Do*		Com
2456	Mary Leary	19		Pro	A Lawmaker	City Limk	15th *Do*	V	
2457	Bridgt Daly	13	Rom		A bad Girl	County Limk	17th *Do*		C
2458	Mary Hurly	17	Rom		A Harlot	City Limk	20th *Do*		C
2459	Pattr Healy	60	Rom		A Beggar	County Clar	21st *Do*		C
2460	Martin Austin	12			A poor boy	City Limk	21st *Do*		
2461	Mary Boucher	25		Pro	A poor HKeeper	City Limk	21st *Do*	V	
2462	Elinor McNamara	40		Pro	A poor HKeeper	City Limk	23d *Do*	V	
2463	James Hinchy	10	Rom		A poor boy	City Limk	24th *Do*	V	
2464	John Blake	74	Rom		A Farmer	County Limk	27th *Do*	V	
2465	Mary Sulivan	22	Rom		A Harlot	County Limk	27th *Do*	V	
2466	Richard Ancher	30		Pro	A Sailor	England	28th *Do*	V	
2467	Margt Loughlin	20	Rom		A spinner	City Limk	28th *Do*	V	
2468	Margt Ryan	40	Rom		A H Keeper	County Limk	30th *Do*	V	
2469	Margt Healy	30	Rom		A Servant	County Limk	the 4th July		
2470	Mary Lynch	45	Rom		A Thief	County Limk	4th		C
2471	Mary Coleman	65	Rom		A H Keeper	City Dublin	7th	V	
2472	Margt Coleman	29		Pro	A Semstress	City Dublin	7th	V	
2473	Ann Welsh	40		Pro	A poor H Keeper	City Dublin	14th		C
2474	Margt Lynch	25	Rom		A Harlot	City Limk	18 July 1791		C
2475	William Quin	60		Pro	A Nealor	City Limk	20th *Do*	V	
2476	Margt Hurly	60	Rom		A Beggar	City Cork	23d	V	

No. of bed	Condition when received Healthy	Sickly	Disease when received	How disposed of Discharged	Died	Eloped	Condition when discharged Healthy	Sickly	Observations
			Insane						
			Sick & Infirm		Died 25th March 1791				the house bougt his Coffin
						2d March 1791			he went Out the street door
			Insane			23d March 1791			he went Over the wall
				9th March 1791					By Order of J Ferrar Esqr
				4th July 1791					By Order of Mr Andw Watson
			Infirm						
			In the bad disorder	23d April 1791					by Order of Mr Andw Watson
						the 11th April 1791			Shee went Out the turf house window
				5th April 1791					by Order of John Ferrar Es
					Died 25th Augt 1791				her frinds bougt her Coffin
			Infirm	17th Octr 1791					By Order of Mr Andw Watson
			Infirm	11th Octr 1791					By Order of Mr Andw Watson
						6th June 1791			Shee Robd the poor & went out the Kitchen window
				17th April 1791		they pd fees 1s 7d [sic]			by Mr Andw Watson
				15th April 1791					by Order of Mr Andw Watson
				19th April 1791					By Order of Doctor Lear
			Infirm		Died				the house bougt her Coffin
			Soer Ledgs	7th June 1791					by Mr Andw Watson
				17th July 1792					by Mr J Hill Phillips
			Sick & Infirm	dischargd 2d Augt 1792					by Mr Andw Watson
						22d Augt 1791			shee went Out for water Eloptd
				22d 1791					By Order of Mr Andw Watson
			Insane	30th June 1791					By George Evans Bruce Esqr
			Sick		Died 16th Augt 1792				the house bougt her Coffin
				13th sepr 1791					by Order of Mr Andw Watson
				30th May 1791					by Order of Mr Andw Watson
				19th sepr 1791					by Order of Mr Andw Watson
			Infirm	15th June 1791					by Order of Mr Andw Watson
			Insane						
			Insane	10th Sepr 1791					by Order of Mr Andw Watson
				19th Feby 1792					Marred discharg by Mr Andw Watson
				1st July 1792					by Order of Mr Andw Watson
				the 22d Jany 1792					by Order of A Committee
						the 25th Jany 1792			he went Over the Garden wall
			Sick & Infirm		Died 25th June 1791				the house bougt her Coffin
			Lost the Use of his Arm						
						17th July 1791			he went Out to Mass Eloptd
			in the bad disorder			15th July 1791			shee went Out the Garden wall
				4th July 1791					By Order of Mr Andw Watson
				2d March 1792					By Order of Mr Andw Watson
			Insane	17th Feby 1792					By Mr Andw Watson
			Sick & Infirm	3d Augt 1791					by Order of Mr Andw watson
				3d *Do*					by Order of Mr Andw watson
			Sick	5th sepr 1791					by Order of Mr Andw watson
				26th sepr 1791					by Order of Mr Andw watson
			Sick & Infirm			7th Augt 1791			shee went Out to Mass Eloptd

Current No.	Names	Age	Religion Roman Catholic	Protestant	Occupation	Late residence	Admitted	Voluntary	Compulsory
2477	Mary Doyl	48	Rom		A balladsinger	Queens County	27th July 1791		C
2478	Bridgt Doyl	18	Rom		a balladsinger	London	27th *Do*		C
2479	John Ryan	13	Rom		A poor boy	City Limk	29th *Do*		
2480	Mary Considine	42	Rom		A Beggar	City Cashall	31t *Do*		C
2481	Bridt Lynch	60	Rom		A Beggar	City Limk	1st Augt		C
2482	Pattr Kelly	20	Rom		A Carpenter	County Clar	8th *Do*	V	
2483	Thomas Reagan	70	Rom		A Cooper	City Limk	8th *Do*	V	
2484	Mary Clanchey	36	Rom		A poor H Keeper	County Limk	9th *Do*	V	
2485	Ann Clanchey	6	*Do*			City Limk	9th *Do*	V	
2486	Margt Dwyer	18	Rom		A Thief	City Limk	11th *Do*	V	
2487	Mary Daly	26	Rom		A Mantamaker	City Limk	12th *Do*	V	
2488	Danl Lusey	58	Rom		A Labourer	County Corke	23d *Do*	V	
2489	John Webb	30		Pro	A weavor	City Limk	24th *Do*	V	
2490	John Markhan	71	Rom		A Beggar	City Limk	28th *Do*		C
2491	Cornelos McInnerny	75	Rom		A Beggar	County Clar	28th *Do*		C
2492	Elinor Conners	70	Rom		A Beggar	County Limk	28th *Do*		C
2493	Mary McDonnold	50	Rom		A Beggar	North	28th *Do*		C
2494	Eliza Thompson	40	Rom		A Beggar	City Limk	28 *Do*		C
2495	Margt Collins	36	Rom		A Beggar	City Limk	28th *Do*		C
2496	Mary Colophey	11	Rom		A Beggar	City Limk	28th *Do*		C
2497	Peggy Colophey	6	*Do*		*Do*	*Do Do*	28th *Do*		C
2498	James Collins	10	*Do*		*Do*	*Do Do*	28th *Do*		C
2499	Denis Collins	5	*Do*		*Do*	*Do Do*	28th *Do*		C
2500	Ann Egan	40	Rom		A Beggar	City Dublin	29th Augt 1791		C
2501	James Crowly	30	Rom		A Beggar	County Limk	29th *Do*		C
2502	Devid Dwyer	15	Rom		A thief	City Limk	30th *Do*		C
2503	Own Gilbreth	70	Rom		A Labourer	City Limk	3d Sepr 1791	V	
2504	Mary Kennedy	25	Rom		A Beggar	City Limk	5th *Do*		C
2505	Mary Windon	6	*Do*		*Do*	City Limk	10th *Do*		
2506	Thomas Brick	6	*Do*		*Do*	*Do Do*	10th *Do*		
2507	Cathr Delany	29	Rom		A Beggar	Queens County	12th *Do*		C
2508	Bridgt Brien	4	*Do*			City Limk	13th *Do*		
2509	Mary Fitzgerald	38	*Do*		A Beggar	County Clar	22d *Do*	V	
2510	Cathr Sulivan	60	*Do*		A poor H Keeper	County Limk	2d Octr		C
2511	Judy Collins	34	*Do*		A Servant	City Limk	3d *Do*	V	
2512	Mary Hunter	65		Pro	A poor H Keeper	City Limk	4th *Do*	V	
2513	Honr Commins	33	*Do*		A Harlot	County Tipperry	15th		C
2514	Thoms Hayse	67	*Do*		A servant	City Limk	18th	V	
2515	John Hinchy	72		Pro	A shoemaker	City Limk	19th	V	
2516	Mary Murphey	26	*Do*		A Beggar	City Limk	19th	V	
2517	Jams Daly	3	*Do*		*D*	*D*	19th	V	
2518	Margt Holmes	56	*Do*		A Beggar	County Limk	19th	V	
2519	John Lucas	60	*Do*		A servant	County Clar	24th	V	
2520	John Brien	65	*Do*		A Farmer	County Limk	25th	V	
2521	Peter Wators	25	*Do*		A Farmer	from Gort	26th	V	
2522	Honr Ryan	60	*Do*		A Beggar	County Limk	27th		C
2523	Christopher O Brien	65		Pro	A Gardiner	County Limk	30th	V	
2524	Mary Enright	44	*Do*		A servant	City Limk	6th Novr	V	
2525	Mary Kennedy	38	*Do*		A Buttenmaker	County Tipperry	8th	V	
2526	Mary Daly	20	*Do*		A Mantamaker	City Limk	8th	V	
2527	Mary Jent	30		Pro	A servant	County Tipperry	9th	V	
2528	Joane Daly	30	*Do*		A Beggar	City Limk	9th	pd the constable 1 1	
2529	Matty Jameson	18	*Do*		A servant	County Limk	14th		
2530	Frans Farrol	40	*Do*		A servant	County Limk	15th		
2531	Peggy Hogan	13	*Do*		A poor Girl	City Limk	15th Novr 1791		
2532	John Daly	45	*Do*		A stroler	County Limk	16th *Do*		C
2533	Thomas Daly	10	*Do*		*Do*	City Limk	16th *Do*		C
2534	Mary Brennan	3	*Do*			City Limk	21st *Do*	V	
2535	James Meehon	30	*Do*		A talor	City Limk	22d *Do*	V	
2536	Darby Shaughnessey	70	*Do*		A Labourer	County Limk	24th *Do*	V	
2537	Darby Purtil	58	*Do*		A wigmaker	City Limk	24th *Do*	V	

No. of bed	Condition when received Healthy	Sickly	Disease when received	How disposed of Discharged	Died	Eloped	Condition when discharged Healthy	Sickly	Observations
				1st Auagust 1791					by Order of Mr Andw watson
				1st Augt 1791					by Order of Mr Andw watson
						15th Jany 1792			he went Out to Mass
						6th Augt 1791			shee went Out the nessecry house Elopt
			Sick & Infirm	8th sepr 1791					by Order of Mr Andw Watson
			Infirm	19th sepr 1791					by Order of Mr Andw watson
			Sick & Infirm						
						19th sepr 1791			shee went Out the Nessecary house
				14th Sepr 1791					by Order of Mr Andw watson
			Sickly	24th sepr 1791					by Order of Mr Andw watson
				7th sepr 1791					by Order of the Mayor
			Infirm	6th sepr 1791					by Mr Andw watson
				9th sepr 1791					by Order of Mr Andw watson
				9th sepr 1791					by Order of the Mayor
				9th sepr 1791					by Order of the Mayor
				5th Sepr 1791					By Order of the Mayor
				9th sepr 1791					by Order of the Mayor
				9th sepr 1791					by Order of the Mayor
				5th sepr 1791					By Order of the Mayor
				5th sepr 91					By Order of the Mayor
				8th sepr 1791					By Order of the Mayor
			Insane						
			Sick & Infirm		Died 27th Octr 1791				the house bougt his Coffin
			A Cripple	4th Augt 1792					by Mr Andw watson
				16th March 1792					by Order of Mr Andw Watson
			Sick & Infirm	26th June 1792					by Mr Andw Watson
				19th Sepr 1791					by Order of Mr Andw watson
				26th June 1792					by Mr Andw Watson
			Insane	22d April 1792					by Mr Andw Watson
				19th April 1792					by A Committee
			Infirm	28th Decr 1791					by Order of Mr Andw watson
				7th Novr 1791					by Order of Mr Andw Watson
						30th Octr 1791			he went Out to Mass Eloptd
			Infirm	18th June 1792					by Mr Andw watson
				27th Octr 1791					he went Out on furlow by Order of Mr Aw Watson
				30th Octr 1791					by Order of Mr And Watson
			Insane		Died 13th March 1792				the house bougt his Coffin
				24th Decr 1791					by Order of the sherriff
					Died 3d Octr 1792				the house bougt his Coffin
				13th Decr 1791					by Order of Mr Andw Watson
				4th Jany 1792					by Order of Mr Andw watson
			Sickly		Died 1st Jany 1792				her frinds bougt her Coffin
				28th Jany 1792					by Order of A Committee
				20th Jany 1792					shee haveing gon to the Infermery
				28th Jany 1792					by Order of A Committee
				28th *Do*					by Order of A Committee
					7th Decr 1791				the house bougt her Coffin
			Sick & Infirm						
			Infirm						
				14th May 1792					by Order of Mr Andw watson

Current No.	Names	Age	Religion Roman Catholic	Protestant	Occupation	Late residence	Admitted	Voluntary	Compulsory
2538	John Mountgomery	17	*Do*		A Beggar	Golloway	1st Decr 1791	V	
2539	Honr Nelson	70	*Do*		A H Keeper	City Limk	8th *Do*	V	
2540	Elinor Hewit	70	*Do*		A Beggar	County Limk	9th *Do*	Compd [sic]	
2541	Thoms Hewit	6	*Do*		*Do*	*Do*	9th *Do*	C [sic]	
2542	Bridgt Brien	27	*Do*		A poor H Keeper	City Limk	10th *Do*	V	
2543	John Brien	5	*Do*			City Dublin	10th *Do*	V	
2544	Mary Brien	4 Months	*Do*			City Limk	10th *Do*	V	
2545	John Butler	30	*Do*		A weaver	City Limk	12th *Do*	V	
2546	Cathr Brien	70	*Do*		A buttonmaker	City Limk	21st *Do*	V	
2547	Danl Ward	50	*Do*		A Broaugmaker	City Limk	26th *Do*	V	
2548	Micl Ward	3	*Do*			City Limk	26th *Do*	V	
2549	Bridgt Ward	40	*Do*		A poor H Keeper	City Limk	26th *Do*	V	
2550	Danl Brien	53	*Do*		A weavor	County Clar	26th *Do*	V	
2551	Thoms Butler	20		Pro	A sealor	Carreginsure	28th *Do*	V	
2552	Bridgt Dwyer	40	*Do*		A poor H Keeper	County tipperry	4th Jany 1792		
2553	Mary Neal	7	*Do*			City Limk	4th *Do*		
2554	Will Dancher	50	*Do*		A Smith	County Limk	5th *Do*	V	
2555	Judith Hynds	50	*Do*		A poor H Keeper	County Limk	5th *Do*	V	
2556	John Ryan	13	*Do*		A bad Boy	City Limk	14th *Do*		
2557	Jams Moron	30	*Do*		A Labourer	City Limk	18th *Do*	V	
2558	Danl Robearts	30	*Do*		A Old solder	City Limk	19th *Do*	V	
2559	Richard Anchor	35		Pro	A sealor	England	21st Jany 1792	V	
2560	Willm Conners	44	Rom		A poor H Keeper	City Limk	23d *Do*	V	
2561	Cathr Eagan	50	Rom		A poor H Keeper	City Limk	25th *Do*	V	
2562	John Hillard	80	Rom		A poor Farmer	County Limk	26th *D*	V	
2563	Richard Man	80	Rom		A poor Farmer	County Limk	27th *D*	V	
2564	Malakey Keough	65	Rom		A weavor	County Limk	27th *D*	V	
2565	Peter McNamara	70	Rom		A Labourer	County Limk	27th *D*	V	
2566	Edword Sheahy	30	Rom		A sealor	County Limk	28th *D*		C
2567	Willm Wallace	60		Pro	A weavor	City Limk	1st Feby	V	
2568	John Hogan	40	Rom		A Pedler	County Clar	3d *Do*		C
2569	Barth Scilly	60	Rom		A Weavor	County Clar	8th *Do*	V	
2570	Edmond Buckly	63	Rom		A Hattor	City Limk	11th *Do*	V	
2571	Dens McInnerny	70	Rom		A Labourer	City Limk	14th *Do*	V	
2572	Micl Kelaher	60	Rom		A Labourer	County tippary	14th *Do*		C
2573	Cathr Ryan	70	Rom		A Beggar	County Limk	14th *Do*		C
2574	John Grant	65		Pro	A weavor	City Limk	15th *Do*	V	
2575	Cathr Creighton	65			A poor H Keeper	City Limk	16th *Do*	V	
2576	Willm Smithis	70		Pro	A Farmer	County tippery	22d *Do*	V	
2577	John Bowdy	70		Pro	A poor Merchant	County Clar	22 *Do*	V	
2578	Ferguson Crowly	20	Rom		A poor boy	City Limk	22d *Do*	V	
2579	Bridgt Duhig	70	Rom		A poor H Keeper	County Limk	22d *Do*	V	
2580	Cathr Eagan	50	Rom		A poor H Keeper	City Limk	23d	V	
2581	John Heale	60		Pro	A Nealer	City Limk	24th		
2582	Cathr Fitzgerald	30	Rom		A bad Girl	County Limk	25th		Com
2583	John Heale	10		Pro		City Limk	27th	V	
2584	Micl Maddin	35	Rom		A Butcher	City Limk	27th	V	
2585	Mary Redden	30	Rom		A poor H Keeper	County Limk	9th March 92	V	
2586	Cathr Keough	46	Rom		A Lacemaker	City Limk	21st	V	
2587	Ann Keough	10	Rom			City Limk	21st	V	
2588	Micl Lawlor	70	Rom		A Labourer	County Limk	24th	V	
2589	Margt Jurdon	33	Rom		A Harlot	City Limk	25th	V	
2590	Mary Windon	7	*Do*			*Do Do*	25th		
2600	John Prestwidge	56		Pro	A servant	County Limk	28th March 92	V	
2601	Tady Sulivan	38	Rom		A Beggar	County Kerry	1st April		Compeld pd 1 1
2602	Mary Rickson	50		Pro	A Beggar	City Limk	1st *Do*		Compeld pd 1s 1d
2603	Cathr Jurdon	14		Pro	A Beggar	City Limk	1st *Do*		Compeld
2604	John McNaly	52		Pro	A servant	City Dublin	2d *Do*	V	
2605	Jeremiah Lahy	39	Rom		A stroler	County kerry	2d *Do*		Compeld pd 1s 1d
2606	Mary Devit	38	Rom		A Begger	City Limk	2d *Do*	V	
2607	Mary Devit	5 Months	*Do*			*Do*	2d *Do*	V	
2608	Timothy McNamara	60	Rom		A Beggar	County Clar	7th *Do*		Compeld pd 1 1

No. of bed	Condition when received Healthy	Sickly	Disease when received	How disposed of Discharged	Died	Eloped	Condition when discharged Healthy	Sickly	Observations
				21st May 1792					by Order of Mr Andw watson
				19th Feby 1792					by Order of Mr Andw Watson
				19th *Do Do*					by Mr Andw Watson
				19th *Do Do*					by Mr Andw Watson
						12th Feby 1792			he went to Mass Eloptd
			Sick & Infirm		Died 6th Jany 1791				the house bougt his Coffin
									he went Out to Mass
			Insane						
				16th Jany 1792					by Mr Andw watson
				19th Feby 1792					by Mr Andw watson
			Infirm						
			Infirm						
			Sick & Infirm			10th April 92			he went to doctor Eloptd
			Sick	22d Feby 1792					by Order of Mr Andw watson
			Insane						
			Infirm	9th May 1792					by Mr Andw Watson
				19th March 1792					by Order of Mr Andw Watson
			Insane	10th Feby 1792					by Mr Andw watson he haveing come to his sensis
						14th May 1792			he went Out to Mass Eloptd
			Sick		17th Feby 1792				the house bougt his Coffin
			Sick & Infirm						
				17th April 1792					by A Committee
				16th Augt 92					by Mr Andw watson
						21st Feby 1792			Shee went Out the street door
						3d Augt 1792			he went Out the street door
			Infirm	3d July 1792					by Mr Andw watson
				27th Feby 1792					by sir, Chrisr Knight
				1st March 1792					by Order of Mr Andw watson
				16th Augt 1792					by Mr Andw watson
						10th May 92			went Out the back window
						22 April 1792			Eloptd shee went Out the street door
				20th April 1792					by Mr Andw Watson
				20th *Do*					by Mr Andw Watson
			Infirm	16th April 1792					by A Committee
				19th *Do* 92					by A Committee
				19 *Do Do*					by A Committee
					Died 16th Octr 1792				his frinds bougt his Coffin
			Lame of One Leg	6th April 92					by Alderman Fitzgerald
				10th April 92					by Alderman Fitzgerald
				11th *Do*					by Alderman Fitzgerald
						4th April 92			he went to the doctor
				10th April 92					by Mr Andw Watson
						20th April 1792			Went Out the street door
									Went Out the Street door
			Lame of boath his Legs						

Current No.	Names	Age	Religion Roman Catholic	Protestant	Occupation	Late residence	Admitted	Voluntary	Compulsory
2609	Honr Welsh	70	Rom		A Beggar	County Limk	11th April 92		Compeld pd 1s 1d
2610	Margt Mitchil	60	Rom		A Servant	City Limk	11th *Do*	V	
2612	Margt Sulivan	70	Rom		HouseKeeper	City Limk	13th	V	
2613	Mary Carrol	18	Rom		A poor Girl	County Limk	18th	V	
2614	Edmond Danoland	17	Rom		A Labourer	County Clar	21st	V	
2615	Johana Dunn	33	Rom		A poor H Keeper	City Limk	24th	V	
2616	Willm Dunn	13	Rom			City Limk	24th	V	
2617	Mary Fitzgerald	17	Rom		A servant	County Kerry	25th		Compeld
2618	Margt Winter	50		Pro	A poor H Keeper	County Clar	25th		
2619	Cathr Kennedy	30	Rom		A Harlot	City Limk	27th	V	
2629	Bridgt Butler	56	Rom		A Beggar	City Limk	27		C
2630	Mary Daly	25	Rom		A Mantamaker	City Limk	27th	V	
2631	Micl Moran	13	Rom			City Limk	29th	V	
2632	Nell Collins	8	Rom		A Lacemaker	City Limk	2d May	V	
2633	Mary Fitzgerald	12	Rom		A Lacemaker	City Limk	2d *Do*	V	
2634	Margt Miller	70	Rom		A poor H Keeper	County Limk	3d	V	
2635	Bridgt Spellman	60	Rom		A Beggar	County Dublin	2d	V	
2636	Peter finn	60	Rom		A weaver	City Cork	8th	V	
2637	Eliza Swift	60	Rom		poor H Keeper	City Cork	8th	V	
2638	Cathr Keough	55	Rom		A Lacemaker	City Limk	10th	V	
2639	Ann Keough	13	Rom		A Lacemaker	City Limk	10th	V	
2640	Mary Ryan	60	Rom		A Beggar	County Limk	10th May 1792		pd the Constapel 1s 1d [sic]
2641	Mary Wild	40	Rom		A Beggar	County Clar	10th *Do*		pd *Do* 1s 1d [sic]
2642	Edmond Sheehy	70	Rom		A Cobler	County Limk	10th *Do*	V	
2643	Mary Daly	25	Rom		A Mantamaker	City Limk	17th	V	
2644	Susannah Butler	33	Rom		A Weaver	City Dublin	18th	V	
2645	Margt Dwyer	18	Rom		A Harlot	County Clar	19th		pd *Do* 1s 1d [sic]
2646	Mary Ryan	20	Rom		A servant	County Clar	20th		
2647	Maryann Butler	27	Rom		A Idle Girl	England	22d		pd *Do* 1s 1d [sic]
2648	Ann Hamelton	26	Rom		A servt	City Limk	24th	V	
2649	William Quin	70		Pro	A Nealor	City Limk	26th	V	
2650	Darby Purtil	26	Rom		A Barbor	City Limk	28th	V	
2651	Edmond Houlihan	60	Rom		A Butcher	City Limk	29th	V	
2652	James Williams	20	Rom		A Beggar	County Dublin	29th		C pd 1s 1d [sic]
2653	Jaine Brown	50		Pro	A Beggar	North	31st		
2654	Mary Clanchey	40	Rom		A poor H Keeper	City Limk	1st June	V	
2655	Patt Clanchey	13	Rom		A Quilwinder	City Limk	1st *Do*	V	
2656	John Leary	15		Pro	A Weaver	City Limk	1st *Do*	V	
2657	John Bourk	78	Rom		A fencining Master	County Kerry	1st *Do*		C pd 1s 1d [sic]
2658	Mary Kennedy	20	Rom		A Servent	City Limk	6th		
2659	Eliza Beauchamp	26		Pro	A poor H Keeper	City Limk	7th	V	
2660	Johana Cullin	six Months							
2661	Allas Hogan	50	Rom		A servant	County Limk	12th *Do*	V	
2662	John Kelly	70	Rom		A servant	County Clar	14th	V	
2663	Mary Ann Stray	50		Pro	A beggar	County Kerry	14th		C pd *Do* 1s 1d [sic]
2664	Mary Markhane	28	Rom		A servant	County Clar	18th	V	
2665	David Kennedy	5	Rom			County Limk	18th		
2666	Mary Kennedy	2	*Do*			*Do*	18th		
2667	Margt Healy	30	Rom		A servt	County Clar	18th		
2668	Mary Devit	38	Rom		A Beggar	City Limk	22d	V	
2669	Mary Devit	seven Months							
2670	Thoms Ramsey	26		Pro	A sealor	Kilkeny	22	V	
20671	Gillon Arkins	11	Rom			City Cork	4th July 1792		
20672	Honor Ryan	41	Rom		A beggar	County Limk	4th *Do*	V	
20673	Ann Neal	5	Rom			City Limk	4th *Do*	V	
20674	Mary Corbit	10	Rom			County Clar	9th *Do*	V	
20675	Mary Neal	24	Rom	A Lace maker [sic]	A LaceMaker	City Limk	12th *Do*	V	
20676	Danl Eagan	80	Rom		weavor	City Limk	17th *Do*		

No. of bed	Condition when received Healthy	Sickly	Disease when received	How disposed of Discharged	Died	Eloped	Condition when discharged Healthy	Sickly	Observations
				16th April 1792					by Order of A Committee
				30th July 1792					by Mr Andw watson
			Infirm						
			Sick & Infirm						
				8th May 1792					by Order of Lady Hartstonge
						Eloptd 27 April 1792			he went Over the Garden wall
				12th Augt 1792					by Order of Mr Andw watson
			in the bad disorder	20th July 1792					by Order of Doctor Hassett
			Insane						
			Insane						
						15th July 1792			Shee went Out the Nesseary
				14th May 1792		14th May 1792			Shee went Out the street door
				16th Octr 1792					By Mr Andw Watson
				25th May 1792					by Order of the Mayor
			Infirm						
			Insane						
				31st May 1792					by Mr Andw watson
				24th May 1792					by Doctor Hassett
			Insane						
			Insane	31st May 1792					by Mr Andw watson
			Insane	17th Sepr 1792					by Mr Willm Jackson
				17th July 1792					by Mrr J Hill Phillips
			Insane			Eloptd 29th June 1792			he went Out the shore of the Necessary
				18th July 1792					by Mr J Hill Phillips
				6th June 1792					by Mr Andw watson
			in a bad disorder						
				7th Octr 1792					by Mr Andw watson
				7th Octr 1792					by Mr Andw watson
			Infirm						
				24th sepr 1792					by Mr Andw watson
				18th June 1792					by Mr Andw watson
				21st June 1792					by Mr Andw watson
				3d July 1792					by Mr Andw watson
						27th March 1793			Shee went Out the street door
				28th March 1793					by A Committee
				17th Octr 1792					by Mr Andw watson
				28th March 1793					by A Committee
					Died 11th April 1793				the house bougt his Coffin

Current No.	Names	Age	Religion Roman Catholic	Protestant	Occupation	Late residence	Admitted	Voluntary	Compulsory
20677	Margt Kelly	19	Rom		A Harlot	City Limk	21st July 1792		
20678	Edmond Moor	56	Rom		weavor	City Limk	23d *Do*		
20679	John Brien	1	*Do*			*Do Do*	23d *Do*		
20680	Mary Bourk	16	Rom		A Harlot	City Limk	29th *Do*		Compd pd 1s 1d [sic]
20681	Elinor Bourk	40	Rom		H Keeper	City Limk	1st Augt		
20682	Bridgt Bourk	20	Rom		A spinner	City Limk	2 *Do*		
20683	Edmond McGan	75	Rom		weavor	City Limk	3d *Do*		
20684	James McGan	14	Rom		winder	City Dublin	3d *Do*		
20685	James Carrol	40	Rom		Labourer	County Limk	3d *Do*		
20686	Mary Carrol	20	Rom			County Limk	3d *Do*		
20687	Edmond Moor	56	Rom		weavor	City Limk	3d *Do*		
20688	Danl Donovan	50	Rom		Labourer	City Cork	7th *Do*		
20689	Mary Daly	22	Rom		Mantamaker	City Limk	7th *Do*		
20690	Margt Inright	40	Rom		servent	City Limk	7th *Do*		
20691	Danl Lusey	40	Rom		Labouror	County Cork	10th *Do*		Compeld pd 1s 1d [sic]
20692	Jaine Fox	57	Rom		H Keeper	City Limk	12th		
20693	Cathr Sweeny	13	Rom			City Limk	20th		
20694	Cathr Hewse	33	Rom		Servent	City Cashell	23d		
20695	Pattr Keane	27	Rom		Pedler	County Clar	24th		
20696	Mary Herragan	80	Rom		H Keeper	County Limk	27th		
20697	Elinor Leo	46	Rom		H Keeper	County Limk	28th		
20698	Mary Murphy	27	Rom		Beggar	City Limk	1st Sepr		Compeld
20699	James Daly	4	*Do*			City Limk	1st *Do*		Compeld
20700	Mary Lynch	50	Rom		Beggar	City Limk	1st *Do*		Compeld
20701	Thomas Lynch	9	*Do*			City Limk	1st *Do*		Compeld
20702	Marg Brien	65	Rom		Beggar	City Limk	1st *Do*		Compeld
20703	Elinor Irwin	70	Rom		Beggar	County Limk	1st *Do*		Compeld
20704	John Ellot	27	Rom		Beggar	County Cork			Compeld
20705	Pattr Clanchey	13	Rom		Quilwinder	City Lim	7th		
2706	Honr Bourk	50	Rom		A ervant	County Limk	20th sepr 1792		
2707	John Fitzgerald	67	Rom		A Labouror	City Limk	24th *Do*		
2708	Danl Brien	50	Rom		A Weaver	County Clar	24th *Do*		
2709	Willm Smithes	70		Pro	A Farmer	County tippery	29th		
2710	Willm Black	59		Pro	A weaver	Scotland	29th		
2711	John Black	10		Pro		County Kerry	29th		
2712	John Dunn	12	Rom			City Limk	13th		
2713	John Keys	64		Pro	A soyor	County Clar	14th		
2714	Darby Toohy	65	Rom		A Labouror	City Limk	3d		
2715	Willm Brasell	78	Rom		A Beggar	County Limk	3	pd 1s 1d [sic]	Com
2716	Bridgt Quigly	20	Roman		A Harlot	City Limk	6th	pd 1 1 [sic]	Com
2717	Willm Hallanan	9	Rom			County Cork	7th		
2718	Pattr McNamara	30	Rom		A balladsinger	County Cork	8th	pd 1s 7d [sic]	Com
2719	John McNamara	50	Rom		Charman	County Limk	9th		
2720	Mary Leary	60	Rom		H Keeper	County Limk	15th		
2721	Mary Hall	8	Rom			City Limk	17th		
2722	Margt Honan	70	Rom		H Keeper	County Clar	18th		
2723	Margt Sulivan	25	Rom		A servt	County Limk	20th		
2724	Danl Brien	50	Rom		Weavor	County Clar	20th		
2725	John Kerwig	70	Rom		weavor	County Limk	22d		
2726	John Carrol	40	Rom		A Farmer	County Limk	23d		
2727	Poll Murphy	25	Rom		A Beggar	City Limk	23d		
2728	Margt Holmes	60	Rom		A Beggar	County Limk	24th		
2729	John Hall	7	Rom			City Limk	24th		
2730	Eliza Barry	57	Rom		A Beggar	City Dublin	25th		
2731	Elinor Carleton	50		Pro	A H Keeper	City Limk	28th		
2732	Elinor Carleton	7		*Do*		City Limk	28th		
2733	Elinor Foolue	25	Rom		A Harlot	County Limk	29th		
2734	Margt Halloran	60		Pro	A servant	County Carlow	29th		

No. of bed	Condition when received Healthy	Sickly	Disease when received	How disposed of Discharged	Died	Eloped	Condition when discharged Healthy	Sickly	Observations
						5th Nov 1792			Shee went Out the street door
			Insane	discharged 29th July 1792					by Mr Andw watson
						5th Novr 1792			Shee Went Out the street door
				dischargd 1st Augt 1792					by Mr Andw watson
				dischargd 1st *Do*					by Mr Andw watson
				Dischargd 25th Novr 1792					by Mr Andw watson
									by Mr Andw watson
			Insane			19th sepr 1792			Went Over the Garden wall
			Sick & Infirm	dischargd 7th sepr 92					by Mr Andw watson
			Insane						
			Insane	9th Augt 92					by Mr Andw watson
				28th Augt 1792					by Mr Andw watson
				10th sepr 1792					by Mr Andw watson
			Dropsey		Died 14th Octr 1792				the house bougt her Coffin
			Sick						
			Infirm	28th Augt 1792					by Mr Andw Watson
			Insane						
						2d Sepr 92			Went Out the street door
						2d sepr 92			Went Out the street door
				2d sepr 1792					by Order of the sherriff
				6th sepr 92					by the Revd John Hoare
				9th sepr 1792					by Mr Andw watson
				17th sepr 1792					by Mr Andw watson
				3d Octr 1792					by Mr Andw Watson
				7th Novr 1792					by Mr Andw watson
				4th Octr 1792					by Mr Andw watson
			A soar Mought	10th Octr 1792					by Mr Andw Watson
				10th Novr 1792					by Mr Andw watson
						10th Octr 1792			he went Over the Garden wall
						11th Novr 1792			Shee went Out to Mass
						31st Novr 1792			the door Keeper let her Out
				dischargd 20th May 1793					by Mr Andw watson
			Sick						
			Insane						
				9th Novr 1792					by Mr And watson
			A Cripple						
			big with Child			5th Novr 1792			Shee went Out the street door

Current No.	Names	Age	Religion Roman Catholic	Protestant	Occupation	Late residence	Admitted	Voluntary	Compulsory
2735	Mary Shea	40	Rom		A Beggar	City Cork	31st [Oct.] 1792		
2736	John McDonnold	86		Pro	wheelright	City Limk	[1]st Novr 1792		
2737	Mary McDonnold	82	Rom		H Keeper	City Limk	[1]st *Do*		
2738	Elinor Mealy	60	Rom		A servant	City Limk	2d *Do*		
2739	Elinor Callanane	60	Rom		H Keeper	Clonmell	12th *Do*		
2740	Margt Dwyer	18	Rom		A Harlot	County Clar	12th		Com
2741	Cathr Bratchaw	19	Rom		Harlot	City Limk	12th		Com
2742	Charles Roche	34		Pro	sealor	City Limk	18th		
2743	John Timmons	12		Pro		City Limk	19th		
2744	Mary Hall	9	Rom			City Limk	22d		
2745	Micl O' Donnold	30	Rom		A Roag	County Cork	25th		Com
2746	Elinor Shea	53	*Do*		poor H Keeper	City Limk	26th		
2747	James Fitzgerald	70		Pro	A servant	City Limk	30th		
2748	Pattr Quin	60	Rom		Schoolmaster	County Limk	1st Decr 1792		Com
2749	Margt Coony	44	Rom		poor H Keeper	County Clar	1 *Do*		
2750	John Coony	13	Rom			County Clar	1 *Do*		
2751	Timethy Coony	11	Rom			County Clar	1 *Do*		
2752	Mark Coony	7	Rom			County Clar	1 *Do*		
2753	Eliza Barry	50	Rom		A Beggar	City Dublin	5th *Do*		
2754	Hana Murphey	35	Rom		A waterwoman	City Limk	8th *Do*		
2755	Bridt Fitzgerald	30	Rom		poor H Keeper	City Dublin	8th *Do*		
2756	Ambros Hopkins	20		Pro	Plummer	City Limk	10th *Do*		
2757	Thoms Desmond	36	Rom		Stroler	County Cork	11th *Do*		
2758	Edmond Sweeny	63	Rom		P Baker	City Limk	11th *Do*		
2759	Cathr Fitzgerald	44		Pro	poor H Keeper	City Limk	13th		
2760	Micl Fitzgerald	3		*Do*		City Limk	13th		
2760	Mary Butler	8	Rom			City Dublin	15th		
2761	John Dunn	13	Rom			City Limk	15th		
2762	John Madden	66	Rom		weavor	City Limk	17th		
2763	John Madden	12	Rom			City Limk	18th		
2764	John Mountgomery	17	Rom						
2765	Micl Lauler	70	Rom		Begger	County Limk	23d		
2766	Judy Molony	30	Rom		A LaceMaker	City Limk	29th Decr 1792		
2767	Danl Cannan	50	Rom		Miller	City Limk	30th	V	
2768	Ned Cannan	5	*Do*			*Do Do*	30th *Do*		
2769	Mary Cannan	44	*Do*		poor H Keeper	City Limk	30th *Do*	V	
2770	Mary Molony	25	*Do*		poor H Keeper	City Limk	30th *Do*		
2771	Mary Brien	40	*Do*		A Idlewoman	County Limk	31st *Do*		C
2772	John Mahony	23	*Do*		A weavor	City Cork	1st Jany 1793		
2773	Elinor McNamara	40	*Do*		poor H Keeper	City Limk	4th *Do*		
2774	Mary Mitchel	22	*Do*		A LaceMaker	City Limk	5th *Do*		
2775	John Madden	13	*Do*			City Limk	5th *Do*		
2776	Matt Hogan	15	*Do*		A Rober	City Limk	7th		C
2777	Darby Purtil	60	*Do*		A Barbor	City Limk	7th *Do*		
2778	Mary Corbit	12	*Do*			City Limk	7th *Do*		
2779	Eliza Hopkins	55		Pro	poor H Keeper	City Limk	7th *Do*		
2780	Judy Keane	75	*Do*		poor H Keeper	City Limk	7th *Do*		
2781	Jane Dea	10	*Do*			City Limk	7th *Do*		
2782	Willm Ferguson	18	*Do*		A weavor	City Limk	8th *Do*		
2783	John Fitzgerald	60	*Do*		A Labouror	County Limk	14th *Do*		
2784	Bridgt Connor	63	*Do*		A Knitter	City Limk	14th *Do*		
2785	Mary Condon	19	*Do*		A servant	City Limk	14th *Do*		
2786	Hana Hartagan	35	*Do*		A Beggar	County Limk	14th *Do*		
2787	Joane Reily	30	*Do*			County Limk	14th *Do*		
2788	Frans Hernan	60		Pro	poor H Keeper	City Limk	14th *Do*		
2789	Margt Hernan	18		*Do*	A servant	City Limk	14th		
2790	Mary Dunn	24	*Do*			County Clar	22d		
2791	John Dilehan	30	*Do*		A Seaman	County Limk	23d		
2792	James Moran	45	*Do*		A Porter	City Limk	31st		
2793	Pattr Clanchey	13	*Do*			City Limk	1st Feby		
2794	James Reedy	4	*Do*			City Limk	2d *Do*		
2795	Garret Reedy	6	*Do*			*Do Do*	2d		
2796	Mary Reedy	36	*Do*		poor H Keeper	City Limk	2d		

No. of bed	Condition when received		Disease when received	How disposed of			Condition when discharged		Observations
	Healthy	Sickly		Discharged	Died	Eloped	Healthy	Sickly	
			Sick & Infirm		Died 3d Jany 1793				the house bougt her Coffin
			Infirm						
						19th Novr 1792			went Over the Garden wall
						5th Decr 1792			went Over the Garden wall
			Sick & Infirm						
			Sick & Infirm						
						28th Novr 1792			he broake the Cell went Over the wall
			Sick		Died 3d May 1793				the house the [sic] bougt her Coffin
			Sick & Infirm		Died 28th March 93				the house bougt his Coffin
			Sick & Infirm		Died 7th Decr 1792				the house bougt his Coffin
				Dischargd 20th May 1793					by Mr Andw watson
				Dischargd 20th *D*					by Mr Andw watson
				Dischargd 20th *D*					by Mr Andw Watson
				Dischargd 20th *Do*					by Mr Andw Watson
				28th March 1793					by A Committee
			Sick						
						15th Decr 1792			Went Over the Garden wall
			Sick & Infirm		Died 10th Jany 1793				the house bougt his Coffin
			Infirm		Died 19th March 1793				the house bougt his Coffin
				20th March 1793					by Mr Andw watson
				20th March 1793					by Mr Andw watson
			Sick & Infirm			6th Jany 1793			he went to Mass
						8th Jany 1793			broke the Cell went Over the wall
			Sick						
			Insane (erased)						
			Insane	14th Jany 1793					he haveing Come to his senses
			Sore hand	4th April 1793					by Mr Andw watson
				28th March 1793					by A Committee
			Insane						
			Sick						
			Insane						
			Sick		Died 3d May 1793				the house bougt his Coffin
				17th April 93					by Mr Andw Watson
				17th April 93					by Mr Andw watson
				17th April 1793					by Mr Andw watson

Current No.	Names	Age	Religion Roman Catholic	Protestant	Occupation	Late residence	Admitted	Voluntary	Compulsory
2796	Elinor Molony	4	Rom			City Limk	2d Feby 1793		
2797	Cathr Dunn	40	*Do*			County Limk	2d Feby 1793		
2798	Mary Fitzgerald	17	*Do*		A bad Girel	County Limk	6th *Do*		
2799	Cathr Dillon	55	*Do*		poor H Keeper	City Limk	14th		
2800	Thoms Leane	35	*Do*		A horsRider	County Limk	15th Feby		
2801	Thoms Healy	55	*Do*		Old solder	County Clar	20th *Do*		
2802	John Grant	65		Pro	A weaver	City Limk	28th *Do*		
2803	Danl Brien	40	*Do*		A weaver	County Clar	28th *Do*		
2804	Nichs McMahon	16	*Do*		A Quilwinder	City Limk	5th March		
2805	John Sheals	25	*Do*		A turfporter	City Limk	21st *Do*		
2806	Bridgt Duhig	75	*Do*		poor H Keeper	County Limk	23 *Do*		
2807	Mary Horrogan	80	*Do*		poor H Keeper	County Limk	24th *Do*		
2808	Pattr Toohy	70	*Do*		A tanner	County Limk	28 *Do*		
2899	Edword McMahon	60	*Do*		A Labouror	County Clar	28th *Do*		
2890	Willm Dunn	14	*Do*			City Limk	1st April		
2891	Tobby Bourk	54	*Do*		A Brewer	City Limk	8th		
2892	Pattr Welsh	18	*Do*			County Limk	10th *Do*		
2893	Mary Howly	12	*Do*			County Limk	13th *Do*		
2894	Ann Howly	8	*Do*			County Limk	13th *Do*		
2895	Bridgt Quigly	25	*Do*		A Harlot	City Limk	20th		C
2896	Diana Guppy	30	*Do*		A Harlot	City Limk	20th		C
2897	Eliza Miller	33	*Do*		A poor H Keeper	City Cork	22d	V	
2898	Devid Barry	70	*Do*		A Shoemaker	City Limk	25th	V	
2899	Edmond McGan	70	*Do*		A weavor	City Limk	3d May		
2900	Willm McClaskey	70	*Do*		A Weaver	County Clar	4th		
2901	Ann Ferguson	22	*Do*		A servant	City Limk	5th		
2902	Willm Dunn	14	*Do*		A Quilwinder	City Limk	6th		
2903	Margt Kelly	26	*Do*		A Harlot	City Limk	6th		C
2904	Mary ONeal	70	*Do*		A poor H Keeper	City Limk	8th		
2905	Mary Balman	24th		Pro	A solders wife	Jersey	8th		
2906	Thoms Balman	six Months				*Do*	8th		
2907	Thoms Brandon	60	*Do*		A Gardner	City Limk	9th		
2908	John Boulond	60	*Do*		A Servant	City Limk	9th		

No. of bed	Condition when received		Disease when received	How disposed of			Condition when discharged		Observations
	Healthy	Sickly		Discharged	Died	Eloped	Healthy	Sickly	
			Insane						
				2d April 1793					by Mr And Watson
				8th March 1793					by Mr Andw Watson
				12th March 1793					by Mr Andw Watson
			Sick & Infirm		Died 19th April 1793				the house bougt her Coffin
			Sick						
			Insane	17th April 93					by Mr Andw Watson
			Infirm						
			Insane		Died 11th May				the house bougt his Coffin
			in the bad disorder						
			Infirm						
			Insane						
			in the bad disorder			Eloptd 8th May 93			the door Keeper let her Out
			Sick & Infirm						
			Infirm						

INDEX OF PERSONS

References are to entry number in the register.
Names are shown here in their modern form; variations which appear in the register are included in parentheses.
Occupation and age have been used to distinguish persons with identical names.